20414

The Providence of God

The Providence of God

Benjamin Wirt Farley

BAKER BOOK HOUSE
Grand Rapids, Michigan 49516

Scripture quotations are from the Revised Standard
Version Bible, copyright 1946, 1952, 1971 by the
Division of Christian Education of the National
Council of Churches of Christ in the USA, and are
used by permission.

Library of Congress Cataloging-in-Publication Data

Farley, Benjamin W.
    The providence of God.

    Bibliography: p.
    Includes index.
    1. Providence and government of God—History of
doctrines.   2. Reformed Church—Doctrines.   I. Title.
BT135.F37   1988   231'.5   88-6251
ISBN 0-8010-3540-6

To

George Lawrence Abernethy

Whenever I am drawn to Plato's forms,
Those perfect patterns of truth and good,
My thoughts return to you.

Contents

Preface

THE IDEA FOR THIS BOOK WAS FIRST CONCEIVED IN THE WINTER OF 1980 while I was translating Calvin's *Treatise Against the Libertines*. As I was working through chapters 13–16, I was struck by the clarity and simplicity of Calvin's argument against the Libertines' pantheistic and deterministic interpretation of nature and history. Here was a clear, convincing, and powerful analysis of the providence of God that proved Calvin's theology to be far less deterministic than I had previously thought it to be. As I pondered this, it occurred to me that no one, to my knowledge,[1] had ever traced the history of the idea of the providence of God, as we have come to inherit it in the West, and that it would be challenging to do so, keeping in view Calvin's own approach as a sort of guiding norm.

This volume is hardly the complete history of so complex a story, but I have sought to do three things: (1) to reflect on and explore the boundaries of a Reformed understanding of the providence of God (meaning by "Reformed" anyone who appreciates Calvin's general system and the legacy it has inspired); (2) to review the positions of major philosophers and theologians who have contributed to our understanding of God's interaction with the world; and (3) to offer occasional commentary and criticism of the same from a Reformed perspective.

In general, what I offer here is a handbook, written from a sympathetic perspective, as well as a kind of essay on the subject. I am aware that for specialists this volume will be entirely too brief, and represents at best a

---

1. Complementary studies do exist; see, for example, Leo Scheffczyk, *Creation and Providence*, trans. by Richard Strachan (New York: Herder & Herder, 1970); and Francis Oakley, *Omnipotence, Covenant, & Order: An Excursion in the History of Ideas from Abelard to Leibniz* (Ithaca: Cornell University Press, 1984).

cursory study that they will need to supplement with their own explorations. For others, my theological views may impose limitations that they might wish to set aside. Nonetheless, I have attempted to provide objective summaries and analyses of the positions I review, and then I have reflected on them in the light of a Reformed perspective.

I am also aware that, from a conceptual point of view, I could have limited this volume to either a history of, or a discussion of, *Reformed* reflection on the providence of God. Certainly, one cannot technically speak of a "Reformed perspective" until the time of the Reformation. Why, therefore, begin the analysis earlier?

There are many reasons I could cite, but there is one in particular which, I believe, best captures my goal. Calvin was never a theologian of the Scriptures alone. He was also a theologian of the church and a scholar whose humanist studies influenced his theology in the light of the best classical, patristic, and medieval nuances he deemed compatible with revelation. Therefore, it seemed appropriate that a volume exploring a Reformed understanding of the providence of God had to do more than summarize Reformed thought per se. Thus, I sought to review those classical, patristic, and medieval (as well as modern and contemporary) views that provide a historical framework for appreciating what the Reformers and their successors achieved, as well as material for a provocative commentary, vis-à-vis a contemporary Reformed position.

There are some personal notes I should also like to add. First, the reader will sense several transitions in this work. They were unavoidable, and it might be helpful to know what they are. Since the volume was written over a five-year period, the following chapters were written as units: 1–2, 3–5, 6–8, and 9–11. In the final revision, however, every effort was made to keep the threefold purpose (outlined above) central at all times.

Second, for an entire year, the project was buried in my files and would have remained there were it not for Allan Fisher of Baker Book House who rescued it from the "dogmatic slumber" of a college professor's ruminations. I cannot express adequately enough my gratitude to him and to Baker Book House for their encouragement and willingness to risk the publication of this volume.

Third, if by chance this book should prove to be helpful, I owe one man above all others lasting gratitude for that possibility. George L. Abernethy taught philosophy at Davidson College and sought to instill in his students a love for sound ideas and a willingness to honor those who offer them to us as stepping-stones toward the truth and the good. So to him I dedicate this book.

Finally, there are important acknowledgments to honor. I am grateful to the Erskine College Library staff, whose efficiency made my own research easier; to Professor John H. Wilde, Librarian; and to staff members Jack Pitzer, Edith Brawley, Helen Hall, and Alice Haddon.

Appreciation is also due to Mrs. B. C. Aycock, Reference Librarian, Union Theological Seminary in Virginia, for acquiring copies of many critical texts, and, above all, to Professor Richard A. Muller, Fuller Theological Seminary, who patiently and meticulously reviewed the first draft of the manuscript, making numerous valuable suggestions for its improvement, both in scope and content.

Chapter One

Introduction, Definition, and Theological Context

THE DOCTRINE OF THE PROVIDENCE OF GOD IS WIDELY ATTESTED TO throughout Scripture. This attestation characterizes the doctrine as one belonging to the biblical message itself—not as one merely derived from that message.

To paraphrase Emil Brunner, the providence of God is a biblical kerygma, not simply a kerygma of the church.[1] It belongs to the central faith of the Bible; it is not a theological doctrine that merely complements the church's faith and message. Consequently, it belongs to the sphere of the church's message, not simply to the sphere of theology.

This is not to say that Reformed theology, past and present, has not, from time to time, been guilty of presenting the doctrine as though it were little more than an abstract dogma belonging to the sphere of formal theology. Nor is it to deny that the biblical message containing this doctrine requires extraction, reflection, analysis, clarification, and defense. Rather, this note is sounded to emphasize that the providence of God is truly a scriptural kerygma, a message proclaimed throughout the Bible, and therefore a message deserving of a central place in Christian faith and practice.

The Bible is quite clear about this, even though aspects of the doctrine elude perspicacious attempts to clarify them. In the Bible, the providence of God is a reality to which poets, historians, prophets, and evangelists witness. It is a confessional theme that narrators, prophets, wisdom writ-

1. Emil Brunner, *The Christian Doctrine of God,* vol. 1 of *Dogmatics,* trans. by Olive Wyon (Philadelphia: Westminster, 1950), 206.

15

ers, and apostles alike assert. It is an undeserved, holy, and redemptive mystery that haunts them all. This is its splendor, urgency, and appeal.

The providence of God in the Reformed tradition, specifically, may be defined as the conviction that God, in his goodness and power, preserves, accompanies, and directs the entire universe. This divine preservation, accompaniment, and direction pertains to all of God's creation: the physical universe, the biological world of organisms, plants, and sentient creatures, and, above all, the realm of history—human beings and nations.

As Calvin explains:

> To make God a momentary Creator . . . would be cold and barren. . . . [We] see the presence of divine power shining as much in the continuing state of the universe as in its inception. . . . [Therefore] faith ought to . . . conclude [that] he is also everlasting Governor and Preserver—not only in that he drives the celestial frame as well as its several parts by a universal motion, but also in that he sustains, nourishes, and cares for, everything he has made. . . .[2]

The word *providence* is traceable to Genesis 22:14 (*Yahweh jireh,* 'Yahweh will provide'). In the Vulgate the Hebrew *Yahweh jireh* was translated *Deus providebit.* Hence, the English word *providence* is based on the Latin verb *provideo,* which means "to provide for, to foresee."

Karl Barth believes that in exegeting Genesis 22:14, *jireh* is best translated as "to see about."[3] Barth prefers this interpretation because it better captures the biblical sense of God's care for Abraham and transcends the notion of foreknowledge alone: "For the world, for men and for the Church God sees to that which in their earthly lot is necessary and good and therefore planned and designed for them according to His wisdom and resolve."[4]

The closest corresponding Greek terms are the noun *pronoia* and the verb *pronoeō.* The noun can be translated as "forethought, providence, provident care, or provision" (see Acts 24:2; Rom. 13:14). The verb means "to perceive beforehand, foresee; to provide for" (see 1 Tim. 5:8).[5] None of these terms, however, as they appear in the New Testament, pertains to God.

Nevertheless, the concept of providence is taught throughout Scripture.

2. John Calvin, *Institutes of the Christian Religion,* ed. by John T. McNeill, trans. by Ford Lewis Battles (Philadelphia: Westminster, 1960), 1.16.1.

3. See Karl Barth's discussion of providence in *Church Dogmatics,* trans. by G. W. Bromiley and R. J. Ehrlich (Edinburgh: T & T Clark, 1976), 3.3:3.

4. Ibid., 4.

5. See *The Analytical Greek Lexicon* (New York: Harper & Bros., n.d.), 345.

Everywhere the Bible speaks of God as one who creates, preserves, upholds, wills, acts, governs, foreordains, elects, calls, predestines, judges, redeems, forgives, reconciles, provides for, protects, heals, and loves. That God is directly in command of his universe—past, present, and future—is not merely a supposition of biblical faith, it is a central motif of the Bible.

As Paul explains in his Letter to the Romans, "for from him and through him and to him are all things" (Rom. 11:36). Note how in this single passage the creation (*ex autou*), preservation (*di autou*), and eschatological orientation (*eis auton*) of the entire cosmos (*ta panta*) are all proclaimed.

That the Reformed tradition has acknowledged and defended the providence of God with the fervor it has rightly attests to this tradition's biblical roots. But even more so, it attests to the central place that this doctrine occupies in the Bible.

Before exploring the Reformed understanding of the providence of God and its biblical foundations, the theological context in which the doctrine generally appears requires exploration and some comment. To facilitate this discussion, the following themes will be examined: providence, faith, and revelation; providence, predestination, the divine decrees, and election; and providence and creation.

Providence, Faith, and Revelation

The doctrine of the providence of God is, above all, a doctrine of faith, based on revelation. It is not a postulate of reason. It is necessary to assert this for two reasons.

First, the Bible alone is the primary source for all Christian reflection about God and knowledge of God and his activity. No other source may compete with the Bible, replace it, or subject it to principles of interpretation that would result in theologies which might actually repudiate, contradict, or compromise the central motifs of the Bible. This has always been the danger of mediating theologies, both past and present. Certainly, in the Reformed tradition, *sola scriptura* has been the standard intended by its adherents to ensure that the Bible serves as the foundation for all theological reflection about Christian faith and practice as well as the means by which such theologies are tested.

The tools of exegesis, the principles of hermeneutics, knowledge of the forms and functions of language, the historical debates, creeds, and formulations of the fathers, the wisdom of the Reformers, the insights of philosophy, psychology, and related disciplines, as well as the particular crises and struggles of one's own time all influence and shape theology. None, however, may usurp the role of the Bible.

In the Reformed tradition, the Bible is the authoritative source for hearing and understanding God's will and activity. It is revelation, the epistemological center for knowing God.

Second, the providence of God is a doctrine of faith. It is neither a postulate of reason or science nor a philosophical position. It is a conviction of faith, based on revelation. It is confessional and practical. Its purposes are to challenge, comfort, and edify the believer in all that he thinks and does. In the Bible, these aspects always take precedence over the more formal, propositional, impersonal, and deductive nuances of the doctrine.

For example, consider the way in which the writer of the Book of Judges presents the providential activity and reality of God to Gideon. Gideon, that "mighty man of valor," was reluctant to commit himself to God. He doubted whether Yahweh was still active in the world or Israel's life. "Pray sir, if the LORD is with us, . . . where are all his wonderful deeds which our fathers recounted to us? . . ." God replies, "Go in this might of yours and deliver Israel from the hand of Midian; do not I send you?" (Judg. 6:13, 14).

The doctrine of the providence of God is a doctrine of faith. It has to do with trust, confidence, and hope. It has to do with action, not passivity; it has to do with mighty deeds, valor, and deliverance, not speculation about causal series per se.

Faith is a matter of no small consequence. In the Reformed tradition, there has always been a reluctance to place primary emphasis on faith (as a human work) at the expense of God's grace, will, decrees, wisdom, power, and goodness. The majesty and will of God come first. But where faith is understood as trust in God's presence in the universe, obedience to him, and commitment to his purposes, then faith is integral to any biblical understanding of providence.

One might concede that, although the doctrine of the providence of God is not a postulate of reason or science, it is a postulate of a reasoned faith. Because faith is a response to what God is doing in the universe, this provides an intellectually defensible principle for interpreting human experience that is compatible with what is known about the "laws" of the universe as scientists are able to theorize and express them in propositional form.

Faith, in the biblical sense, involves many facets. There are at least three interconnecting motifs that surface in Scripture: faith as a subjective encounter with and acceptance of the one, true living God of the universe;

faith as a historical witness to and commitment to God's objective activity in the world; and faith as the work and gift of God.

Faith as Subjective Encounter and Acceptance

Faith is an act for which no other human act, or the act of any other human, may substitute. It is a profoundly individual act. As such, it is a solitary, subjective, and personal act, an act that is unavoidable and inevitable for all human beings. As the writer of the Letter to the Hebrews explains: "For whoever would draw near to God must believe that he exists and that he rewards those who seek him" (Heb. 11:6). It is recognized especially as a principal virtue of that paradigm of all believers, Abraham: " 'Go from your country and your kindred and your father's house to the land that I will show you. . . .' So Abram went, as the LORD had told him" (Gen. 12:1, 4). " 'Look toward heaven, and number the stars. . . . So shall your descendants be.' And he believed the LORD" (Gen. 15:5–6). Faith's relevance to providence is even seen in the fool's remark, "There is no God" (Ps. 14:1). For the absence of faith has staggering repercussions for those who choose the way of unbelief. "And he could do no mighty work there. . . . And he marveled because of their unbelief" (Mark 6:5–6).

There is simply no substitute for this searching, subjective act of faith in God. God clearly seeks it. And its relevance to his providential activity is clear. God's providential presence and purposes not only seek faith but build on faith. And though in the Reformed tradition God's will cannot be limited by the absence of faith, it is certainly clear that wherever God's presence and purposes are not embraced, many potential "mighty works" that might have been done remain unactualized (Matt. 11:21, 23). God's freely offered "possibilities" are simply missed by those who prefer their self-autonomy to God's presence.

It is Jesus who sums up the stakes and brings out the relationship between faith and the providence of God: "For whoever would save his life will lose it, and whoever loses his life for my sake and the gospel's will save it" (Mark 8:35).

The subjectivity of faith is certainly a reality that Calvin understood. He was aware of the "anxiety" of faith and of the fact that even believers struggle constantly with their unbelief (*Institutes*, 3.2.1f.). Luther's bouts with the devil are a hallmark of his personal spiritual struggles and development. Nonetheless, the understanding of faith as a dynamic tension of one's ultimate concern probably best belongs to the modern period. The subjectivity of faith has been brought to contemporary awareness most convincingly through Soren Kierkegaard's *Fear and Trembling*, Martin Buber's *I-Thou,* Emil Brunner's *Truth as Encounter,* and Paul Tillich's *Dynamics of Faith.*

Faith, as Reformed dogmatics developed it, was seen as a work of spiritual regeneration, following (in order) God's eternal decrees, election, effectual calling, regeneration, and conversion of the elect. Later orthodox theologies also made a careful distinction between common faith (*fides communis*) and strict faith (*fides propria*), the latter alone pertaining to the elect. They also divided *fides propria* into three types: *notitia,* the intellect's grasping of those things necessary for salvation; *assensus,* the affirmation and acknowledgment of those things that Scripture transmits as true; and *fiducia,* the personal trust one exercises in applying the gospel to oneself.[6]

Faith as Historical Witness and Commitment

Biblical faith, however, is never merely subjective. It is also a response to signs and wonders that require a decision. The events of history require a principle of interpretation that illumines and makes sense of one's personal life as well as one's participation in humankind. This is precisely what God's presence and mighty acts in history accomplish.

This is articulated in many places in the Old Testament. No passage expresses it as clearly or eloquently as the locus classicus, Deuteronomy 6:20–24:

> When your son asks you in time to come, "What is the meaning of the testimonies and the statutes and the ordinances which the LORD our God has commanded you?" then you shall say to your son, "We were Pharaoh's slaves in Egypt; and the LORD brought us out of Egypt with a mighty hand; and the LORD showed us signs and wonders, great and grievous, against Egypt and against Pharaoh and all his household, before our eyes; and he brought us out from there, that he might bring us in and give us the land which he swore to give to our fathers. And the LORD commanded us to do all these statutes, to fear the LORD our God, for our good always, that he might preserve us alive, as at this day."

In the New Testament, God's presence and mighty acts are above all manifest in the life, death, and resurrection of Christ. Faith in Jesus as the Son of God, whose own message and miracles witness to the "inbreaking" of God's kingdom, is what gives life its highest sense of purpose, its ethical direction, and its power.

---

6. See Heinrich Heppe's discussion of faith in *Reformed Dogmatics,* ed. by E. Bizer, trans. by G. T. Thomson (Grand Rapids: Baker Book House, 1978), 530.

Jesus' deeds, parables, and message underscore this theme, in his teaching "with authority" (Mark 1:22), in his casting out of the unclean spirit (Mark 1:23–26), in his parable of the grain of mustard seed (Matt. 13:31–32), and in his call to seek first God's kingdom and his righteousness, in the assurance that what one eats, drinks, or wears will be provided (Matt. 6:30–33).

The kerygmatic sermons of Peter, the letters of Paul, and the general and Johannine epistles also proclaim God's presence and providential activity in Jesus Christ, who is "the hidden wisdom of God" and who alone points to the center. He is "the one ordained by God to be judge of the living and the dead" (Acts 10:42); "he is before all things, and in him all things hold together" (Col. 1:17); "he reflects the glory of God . . . , upholding the universe by his word of power" (Heb. 1:3); "that which we have seen and heard we proclaim also to you, so that you may have fellowship with us; and . . . that our joy may be complete" (1 John 1:3–4).

These confessions underscore the relationship between faith and the providential activity of God. God's activity, as an objective event that reaches its climax in the revelation of Jesus Christ, both invites faith in him and provides the principle of interpretation that gives meaning to one's individual and collective destiny.

The believer, who in his subjective loneliness risks a "Yes" before God, is lifted, through the historical Christ, out of that solitude and made a participant, by God's grace, in the universal and eternal. The believer is now able to see how extensively God is at work "for his good," preserving him, healing him, and redeeming him, not only from meaninglessness, but from his own miscalculations and deeds of ignorance and pride.

Thus, biblical faith is the conviction that the God to whom the Israelites and apostles witness is alone God. Aside from him there is no other god, no other principle, no other cause or causes worthy of life's highest commitment. God's Word and Spirit are as mightily at work today as in any previous era. Now as then, his activity invites belief in what he is doing. Now as then, he seeks a decision and commitment that will issue in service and that offers a fellowship and peace of the profoundest possible satisfaction.

Faith as the Work and Gift of God

In the final analysis, biblical faith transcends the categories of subjectivity and objectivity. True, God's activity in history causes the human heart the most anguished self-searching a person can undergo ("Thou hast said, 'Seek ye my face.' My heart says to thee, 'Thy face, LORD, do I seek.' Hide not thy face from me" [Ps. 27:8–9]). Moreover, God's mighty acts (in both the Old and New Testaments) provide a historical framework that makes the faith decision a reasonable and intellectually responsible one. As such, it lifts the act of faith out of the coils of an insidious infinite regress that would reduce it to the level of solipsism and emotivism.

The Bible proclaims infinitely more. For biblical faith is not only a dynamic phenomenon of a faith/trust tension between the human spirit and what the people of God have understood as the Divine, but it is equally a phenomenon directly influenced by and under the merciful control of God himself. In fact, it is this dimension that the Reformed tradition has grasped so clearly and has been so reluctant to relinquish or compromise.

Biblical faith is first and foremost a gift. It is the work and will of the gracious Creator, who is the God and Father of Jesus Christ, and of his Holy Spirit. The New Testament kerygma proclaims this with clarity and power: "For by grace you have been saved through faith; and this is not your own doing, it is the gift of God" (Eph. 2:8); "Now there are varieties of gifts. . . . To one is given . . . wisdom, . . . to another faith" (1 Cor. 12:4, 8, 9); "When we cry, 'Abba! Father!' it is the Spirit himself bearing witness with our spirit that we are children of God" (Rom. 8:15); "This is why I told you that no one can come to me unless it is granted him by the Father" (John 6:65); "Therefore, . . . work out your own salvation with fear and trembling; for God is at work in you, both to will and to work for his good pleasure" (Phil. 2:12, 13); "Blessed are you, Simon Bar-Jona! For flesh and blood has not revealed this to you, but my Father who is in heaven. And I tell you, you are Peter, and on this rock I will build my church, and the powers of death shall not prevail against it" (Matt. 16:17–18).

The faith that finally comes to fruition in the believer, though it is his own, is nevertheless the work and gift of God. And it is this faith that becomes an instrument of God's providential presence, by means of which he achieves his "good pleasure" and prevails against the very gates of hell.

The believer's faith and his achievements of faith must never be confused with God's providential presence or activity. Even the absence of faith does not and cannot limit God. But the absence of faith definitely limits human possibilities, which (like the coin that the frightened servant buried) yield no interest, no reward, and no joy.

Providence, Predestination, the Divine Decrees, and Election

One of the central tenets of Reformed theology is the normative role predestination and the decrees of God play in the hermeneutical process.

The Reformation did not merely give rise to the broad principle of *sola scriptura*. More concretely, it produced several hermeneutical principles for interpreting *sola scriptura*. Theologians refer to this development under the rubric of *norms*.

As Tillich explains, the emergence of these norms was unintentional; each was subject to a historical process.[7] In the early church, the material norm was the "rule of faith," or the creed. The formal norm was the church proper and its hierarchy of ecclesiastical authorities. In Tillich's view, the rise of the papacy lent such importance to the formal norm that "the need for a material norm disappeared."[8]

With the Reformation, the question of norms reappeared. In Lutheranism, the problem of norms was solved by making justification through faith the material norm and the authority of Scripture the formal norm. In Calvinism, the problem was solved somewhat differently. Tillich claims that in Calvinism, "justification was more and more replaced by predestination, and the mutuality of the material and the formal norms was weakened by a more literalistic understanding of biblical authority."[9] From our perspective, however, this does not mean that either the Reformers or the orthodox thereby diminished the importance of justification by faith.

In a manner similar to Tillich's, Brunner argues that the broad Lutheran principle of the authority of Scripture was replaced in orthodoxy by the tendency to equate the "Word of God" (as revelation) with the literal words of the Bible.[10] This "fact," as Brunner calls it, caused a drastic shift in the focus and content of orthodox theology. As a result, its doctrines became increasingly authoritarian and impersonal, and its content emphasized more and more the message about Christ and less and less the person of Christ. Consequently, Christ was no longer the "sole content of the Scriptural faith"; "all the content of Scripture" was "given the same value."[11]

Brunner prefers to replace predestination and the divine decrees with their true biblical context, election. Brunner warns that with the question of divine decrees, one enters "the danger-zone," in which "theological thinking may easily stray into disastrous error."[12] Yet, he acknowledges that theology has to deal with the decrees, "because the witness of rev-

---

7. Paul Tillich, *Systematic Theology* (Chicago: University of Chicago Press, 1951), 1:47.
8. Ibid.
9. Ibid.
10. Brunner, *Dogmatics,* 1:28.
11. Ibid., 112.
12. Ibid., 303.

elation . . . forces this subject upon" the church.[13] This is so, because "election constitutes the centre of the Old and the New Testament," behind which lies the mystery of God's will.[14]

Pursuing this point, Brunner maintains that election occurs before the creation of the world (Matt. 25:34; Eph. 1:4; 1 Peter 1:20), and that creation cannot be understood apart from Jesus Christ, through whom, in whom, and unto whom it was created. Election, therefore, means that before creation, from all eternity, God chose to draw believers to himself through Jesus Christ. This call to faith was addressed in the Old Testament to the nation of Israel, but it is now addressed to "the sinful individual person." Hence, to encounter the Christ in the Word is to encounter the eternal will of God, and to know that one is "beloved" and has "been loved from all eternity."[15]

Thus, for Brunner, the question about divine decrees and predestination is better understood as a question about election, which means that the divine decrees and predestination are functions of divine election and not separate hermeneutical principles.

The relevance of Brunner's position to the doctrine of the providence of God is immediately obvious. The providence of God is itself a function of election; it becomes a temporal and contemporary means by which God fulfills his eternal purposes in Jesus Christ. Election is the formal and final cause of God's presence and providential activity in history. It is the *telos,* the goal. To allow other matters to obscure this sine qua non is to drive theological reflection into "the danger-zone."

Brunner is confident that as long as the believer gazes on the historical Christ, "the foreground," then the believer will know that he belongs to Jesus Christ and not to himself. But once the believer concentrates on "the background" (God's mysterious will and election), then faith becomes perverted by speculations that are "too high for it."[16] This is why, in Brunner's estimation, the older orthodoxy cannot be followed today, in spite of the fact that it was right to grapple with the question of the divine decrees.

Barth adopts a similar position and draws parallel conclusions. He opens his discussion of providence by distinguishing between predestination and providence. In Barth's scheme, predestination is the presupposition upon which providence rests.

Barth defines predestination as "a matter primarily and properly of the

13. Ibid.
14. Ibid.
15. Ibid., 311.
16. Ibid., 342.

eternal election of the Son of God to be Head of His community and of all creatures."[17] It is a matter "of the eternal decree without which God would not be God. . . . He is either the gracious God of this eternal choice, or He is not this God . . . at all."[18]

The difference between "predestination, election, the covenant and its history on the one hand and providence, i.e., the preservation and over-ruling of the creatures" on the other hand must not be "obliterated." The decree of God's election comes first; "providence belongs to the execution of this decree."[19]

Barth does not hesitate to use the term *decree*, because God's "eternal decree" is rooted in grace. Consequently, predestination, election, and the divine decrees are all functions of grace, which explains why predestination can become the presupposition of "God's overruling, and the basis and goal of its realisation."[20] When this acknowledgment is ignored or misunderstood, then the doctrine of the providence of God loses its Christian content (which, in Barth's view, is precisely what happened in the older Reformed theologies).

A study of the pertinent scriptural motifs and texts tends to support Barth and Brunner. There are formidable biblical foundations for inter-preting the divine decrees and predestination as components of a gracious divine plan in which "election" (as Brunner defines it) and "predestina-tion" (as Barth defines it) are the basis and goal of God's providential activity.

This would not require that all of God's activity be limited solely to fulfilling his purposes of election, but it would give his activity that chris-tological accent which both Barth and Brunner find missing in the older Reformed dogmatics. It would also redirect the doctrine of the providence of God away from "the danger-zone" and toward less authoritarian, spec-ulative, and deductive motifs.

For example, the *Heilsgeschichte* motif certainly supports this position. Beginning with the historical call of Abraham and ending with John's apocalyptic visions, Scripture portrays God as acting redemptively in his-tory for both Israel's sake and all humankind's. From the "wandering Aramean credo" of the ancient Israelite to the kerygmatic sermons of the apostles, this salvation-history motif is reiterated time and again. This is the central story and drama of human history. And it culminates in the person of Jesus Christ, through whom and in whom and for whom all

17. Barth, *Church Dogmatics*, 3.3:4.
18. Ibid., 5.
19. Ibid.
20. Ibid., 4.

things were created. It is a story in which both the ancient Israelite and the New Testament saint not merely witness to God's redemptive activity and overruling but become "chosen" ambassadors and agents of God's reconciling and providential activity.

Heilsgeschichte may logically flow from "predestination" and "the divine decree," but it witnesses principally to a gracious and faithful God, whose "elect" know him to be precisely this God of unfathomable election. "Go from your country and your kindred . . . and I will bless you . . . ; and by you all the families of the earth will bless themselves" (Gen. 12:1, 2, 4); "the LORD your God has chosen you to be a people for his own possession, . . . not because you were more in number . . . , but it is because the LORD loves you, and is keeping the oath which he swore to your fathers" (Deut. 7:6, 7, 8); "Lord, now lettest thou thy servant depart in peace, . . . for mine eyes have seen thy salvation which thou hast prepared in the presence of all peoples" (Luke 2:29–31).

In addition to the general *Heilsgeschichte* motif, the specific subjects of divine decrees, predestination, and election also support the Barthian and Brunnerian thesis (i.e., that the decrees and predestination are functions of divine grace and ought not stand as isolated hermeneutical principles). The major references are the following:

On the divine decrees

I will tell of the decree of the LORD: He said to me, "You are my son, today I have begotten you. Ask of me, and I will make the nations your heritage, and the ends of the earth your possession" (Ps. 2:7–8).

But we impart a secret and hidden wisdom of God, which God decreed before the ages for our glorification (1 Cor. 2:7).

On predestination

We know that in everything God works for good with those who love him, who are called according to his purpose. For those whom he foreknew he also predestined to be conformed to the image of his Son. . . . And those whom he predestined he also called. . . .

What then shall we say to this? If God is for us, who is against us? He who did not spare his own Son but gave him up for us all, will he not also give us all things with him? Who shall bring any charge against God's elect? . . .

For I am sure that [nothing] . . . will be able to separate us from the love of God in Christ Jesus our Lord (Rom. 8:28, 29, 30, 31–33, 38, 39).

He chose us in him before the foundation of the world. . . .

He destined us in love to be his sons through Jesus Christ, according to the purpose of his will. . . . For he has made known to us in all wisdom and insight the mystery of his will, according to his purpose which he set forth in Christ as a plan for the fulness of time, to unite all things in him, things in heaven and things on earth (Eph. 1:4, 5, 9, 10).

For God has not destined us for wrath, but to obtain salvation (1 Thess. 5:9).

He was destined before the foundation of the world but was made manifest at the end of the times for your sake (1 Peter 1:20).

On election

Though they were not yet born and had done nothing either good or bad, in order that God's purpose of election might continue, not because of works but because of his call. . . . (Rom. 9:11).

Lest you be wise in your own conceits, I want you to understand this mystery, . . . all Israel will be saved. . . . As regards the gospel they are enemies [momentarily] . . . ; but as regards election they are beloved for the sake of their forefathers (Rom. 11:25, 26, 27, 28).

These major references place the decrees and predestination within the larger context of God's gracious election and redemptive purposes. It is this larger context of grace and election that stands as the presupposition of God's providential activity in history.

Providence and Creation

Reformed theology has maintained that the providence of God is a doctrine closely related to the doctrine of creation. The great confessional statements of the Reformed tradition follow this order. For example, the *Gallic Confession* (1559), the *Belgic Confession* (1562), and the *Westminster Confession* (1647) all present the doctrine of creation first and immediately follow it with a statement about providence. So does the nineteenth-century Reformed theologian Charles Hodge in his *Systematic Theology*. Berkhof, Barth, and Brunner follow a similar pattern: creation first, then providence.

Barth explains that medieval scholasticism treated providence as part of the doctrine of God. This was a mistake. Barth charges that, in so doing, medieval theology made election subordinate to rival motifs. Barth prefers to think of creation and providence as "outer works" of God rather than as "inner works."[21]

21. Ibid., 6.

Reformed dogmatics during the seventeenth century identified creation with providence as a single act of God. Heppe explains:

> The Reformed conception of the doctrine of Providence is characterized . . . by the fact, that in it the conception of Providence is validated as an element in the conception of creation or as the reverse side of it. The creation and government of the world constitute a single activity of God, which is shown first of all creatively and then as sustaining and governing.[22]

Johannes Braunius outlines this course: "In respect of God the same action is creation and providence; God works all things by a single, most unifold will, that they exist, remain in existence and work."[23] Heidegger, Alsted, and others maintain a similar position.[24]

In fact, Reformed dogmatics identifies preservation (*conservatio*) with continuous creation (*continuata creatio*). Cocceius asserts that "preservation is a kind of creation continued."[25] So also Amesius: "Preservation is nothing else than a sort of *creatio continuata*."[26] These seventeenth-century views, however, have been rejected in modern times. Charles Hodge, Louis Berkhof, and Karl Barth have all objected to such an identification.

Hodge argues that creation, preservation, and government are clearly different and must not be confused with a doctrine of continuous creation: "Creation . . . is the calling into existence what before did not exist," while preservation is "continuing, or causing to continue what already has a being." Moreover, "in creation there is and can be no cooperation, but in preservation there is a *concursus* of the first, with second causes." Hodge warns that if the two are confused and replaced with a theory of continuous creation, then "God becomes the sole agent and the sole cause in the universe." Such a position leads inevitably to pantheism and makes God the cause of human sin. Hodge appeals to the "plain doctrine of the Scriptures" to refute such a view.[27] Berkhof also rejects continuous creation for reasons similar to Hodge's.[28]

---

22. Heppe, *Reformed Dogmatics*, 251.
23. Johannes Braunius, *Doctrina Foederum sive Systema Theologiae didacticae et elenc-ticae* (Amsterdam, 1668), 1.2.12.1. [Cited in Heppe, *Reformed Dogmatics*, 251.]
24. See Charles Hodge, *Systematic Theology* (New York: Charles Scribner's Sons, 1899), 1:577.
25. Johannes Cocceius, *Summa Theologiae ex Scriptura repetita* (Amsterdam, 1665), 28.9. [Cited by Heppe, *Reformed Dogmatics*, 257.]
26. Gulielmus Amesius, *Medulla Theologica* (Amsterdam, 1634), 1.9.18. [Ibid.]
27. Hodge, *Systematic Theology*, 1:581.
28. See Louis Berkhof, *Systematic Theology* (Grand Rapids: Wm B. Eerdmans, 1959), 171.

Barth, too, objects to the identification of creation with providence. For Barth, "the work of creation . . . is a once-for-all act, not repeated or repeatable, beginning in and with time and ending in it." On the other hand, the work of providence "guarantees and confirms the work of creation." What now follows is "the history of the covenant" (which is the meaning, basis, and goal of creation) and "the rule of divine providence which accompanies, surrounds and sustains the history of the covenant."[29]

Barth finds justification for this distinction in the conclusion to the first creation saga (Gen. 2:1–3): "Thus the heavens and the earth were finished. . . . And on the seventh day God finished his work which he had done." Hence the seventh day represents a "break between the work of creation and all the divine work which follows." Therefore, "creation and providence are not identical."[30]

Barth does acknowledge, however, that the older Reformed theologies were correct in recognizing "that creation and providence, like all the works of God, are one in their divine origin." But they are not a single activity of God: "We must not interpret providence as *continuata creatio*, but as *continuatio creationis*."[31] That is, providence is not a continuous creation but a continuation of the creation.

Once Barth has clarified the difference between creation and providence, he draws attention to their relationship. If creation is a "first action" of the Creator toward the creature, then the concept of providence is the "second action of the Creator." Providence means that it is "impossible for the Creator to leave His work to itself."[32] Hence, he "accompanies, surrounds and sustains" the creature and the work of creation.

Barth cites the following biblical passages in support of this Reformed concept in which the providence of God is related closely to the doctrine of creation while not being confused with it: "Thou hast granted me life and steadfast love; and thy care has preserved my spirit" (Job 10:12); "My Father is working still, and I am working" (John 5:17); "The God who made the world and everything in it, . . . himself gives to all men life and breath and everything" (Acts 17:24, 25); "My help comes from the LORD who made heaven and earth" (Ps. 121:2); "upholding the universe by his word of power" (Heb. 1:3); "all things were created through him and for him" (Col. 1:16).

In the light of the above discussion, a biblical doctrine of the providence of God in the Reformed tradition would seem well advised to follow

29. Barth, *Church Dogmatics*, 3.3:6.
30. Ibid., 8.
31. Ibid., 7f.
32. Ibid., 9.

Chapter Two

The Reformed Position
and Its Biblical Foundations

THE REFORMED TRADITION CHARACTERIZES GOD'S PROVIDENTIAL activity as a threefold work encompassing his preservation of creation, his cooperation with all created things, and his direction and guidance of all things toward his ultimate purposes and their highest fulfillment in Christ Jesus.

This concept has been maintained and defended by many Reformed writers. Braunius notes: "The acts of providence are three: (1) He preserves all things in their being and duration; (2) He moves all things to their action by concurrence, in fact by precurrence; (3) He steers and guides all things to the desired end to which they were appointed from eternity."[1] Berkhof observes that "providence may be defined as that continued exercise of the divine energy whereby the Creator preserves all His creatures, is operative in all that comes to pass in the world, and directs all things to their appointed end."[2] Barth writes: "By 'providence' is meant the superior dealings of the Creator with His creation, the wisdom, omnipotence and goodness with which He maintains and governs in time this distinct reality according to the counsel of His own will."[3]

This chapter will examine each of these three aspects of divine providence and will explore their biblical foundations.

1. Braunius, *Doctrina Foederum*, 1.12.2. [Cited by Heppe, *Reformed Dogmatics*, 256.]
2. Berkhof, *Systematic Theology*, 166.
3. Barth, *Church Dogmatics*, 3.3:3.

Providence and Preservation

The Reformed tradition has, first of all, understood the providential activity of God as a preserving, sustaining, and upholding of what he has created. God continues to see that the creation is maintained, that order prevails, and that life is sustained through, over, and above the species' divinely given power to propagate themselves. It is God's divine work of *conservatio* or *sustentatio*.

This divine preservation of all things is explicitly taught in many passages of Scripture. Berkhof cites the following principal references: "Deut. 33:12, 25–28; I Sam. 2:9; Neh. 9:6; Ps. 107:9; 127:1; 145:14, 15; Matt. 10:29; Acts 17:28; Col. 1:17; Heb. 1:3."[4] To this list he adds others that speak of God's preservation of his people: "Gen. 28:15; 49:24; Exod. 14:29, 30; Deut. 1:30, 31; 2 Chron. 20:15, 17; Job 1:10; 36:7; Ps. 31:20; 32:6, 7; 34:15, 17, 19; 37:15, 17, 19, 20; 91:1, 3, 4, 7, 9, 10, 14; 121:3, 4, 7, 8; 125:1, 2; Isa. 40:11; 43:2; 63:9; Jer. 30:7, 8, 11; Ezek. 34:11, 12, 15, 16; Dan. 12:1; Zech. 2:5; Luke 21:18; 1 Cor. 10:13; 1 Pet. 3:12; Rev. 3:10."[5] (There are other passages, however, that are equally important. These include Gen. 45:5, 7; Deut. 6:24; 33:27; 1 Chron. 29:11–12; Ps. 36:7–8; 73:23; Isa. 40:26; Rom. 11:36; 1 Cor. 8:6; and esp. Ps. 104:27–30.)

To uncover the biblical sense of God's preserving activity, a closer study of select passages is instructive. In the Bible, God's preserving work is threefold.[6] God preserves the physical universe, the earth, and all of its species; humankind in general; and his covenant people in particular. Preservation is a divine work, the express purpose of which is the uniting of all things in Christ Jesus.

Preservation of the Physical Universe, the Earth, and Its Species

The Bible teaches that God directly upholds, maintains, and preserves his entire universe. From the starry sky, to the planet Earth, to all life teeming upon it, God is at work sustaining his creation.

> Lift up your eyes on high and see: who created these? He who brings out their host by number, calling them all by name; by the greatness of his might, and because he is strong in power not one is missing (Isa. 40:26).

> Thou art the LORD, thou alone; thou hast made the heaven . . . with all

---

4. Berkhof, *Systematic Theology,* 169.
5. Ibid.
6. Cf. Charles Hodge's fourfold scheme (*Systematic Theology,* 1:575).

their host, the earth and all that is on it, the seas and all that is in them; and thou preservest all of them (Neh. 9:6).

And God saw that it was good. And God blessed them, saying, "Be fruitful and multiply and fill the waters in the seas, and let birds multiply on the earth" (Gen. 1:21, 22).

O LORD, how manifold are thy works! . . . the earth is full of thy creatures. . . . These all look to thee, to give them their food in due season (Ps. 104:24, 27).

Moreover, God's preserving activity is a divine work in which the Son of God participates and that exists for his glory: "For from him and through him and to him are all things" (Rom. 11:36); "he is before all things, and in him all things hold together" (Col. 1:17); "he reflects the glory of God . . . , upholding the universe by his word of power" (Heb. 1:3).

Scripture teaches that God does not simply create the universe and leave it on its own; "faith ought to penetrate more deeply [than that]."[7] Rather, in addition to the power of self-propagation that God has granted to the species, God the Father through Christ the Son directly continues to maintain his universe.

The very stars and the distant galaxies owe their present order and continued existence to God. Indeed, so intimate is his relationship to the heavens, that God names the individual stars and fills the night with their scintillating wonder. In his commentary on Colossians 1:17, J. B. Lightfoot explains: "He is the principle of cohesion in the universe. He impresses upon creation that unity and solidarity which makes it a cosmos instead of a chaos."[8] This is a contemporary work; and it extends to plants and animals, which are wholly dependent upon God for their existence.

Hodge concludes from such passages "(1) that the universe as a whole does not continue in being of itself. It would cease to exist if unsupported by his power. (2) That all creatures, whether plants or animals, in their several genera, species, and individuals, are continued in existence not by any inherent principle of life, but by the will of God."[9]

An uncritical endorsement of the idea of preservation, however, raises questions that Reformed theology has been careful to address. Berkhof notes that not only does the idea of preservation emphasize that all created

7. Calvin, *Institutes*, 1.16.1.

8. J. B. Lightfoot, *Saint Paul's Epistles to the Colossians and to Philemon* (Grand Rapids: Zondervan, 1957), 156.

9. Hodge, *Systematic Theology*, 1:575.

substances have "only such active and passive properties as they have derived from God," but all such substances through their active powers [inferred from Gen. 1:22] have "a real . . . efficiency as second causes, so that they are able to produce the effects proper to them."[10] God's work of preservation, therefore, does not substitute for or eradicate a creature's uniqueness or capacity to fulfill its God-endowed beingness. Nevertheless, created substances are not self-existent. All creatures still have "the ground of their continued existence in Him and not in themselves."[11] Hence, Berkhof defines preservation as "that continuous work of God by which He maintains the things which He created, together with the properties and powers with which He endowed them."[12]

Brunner's position is similar to Berkhof's, though far less abstract. Brunner places a greater emphasis on the order and constancy of nature: "God has given the world its 'orders,' and it is precisely in these orders that He *constantly* reveals His Creator-Spirit, and His Power as Creator." Moreover, "God reveals Himself and His Presence in this constancy which He grants to things. It is thus that God acts—not nature, independent of God."[13] Hence, God's preserving work is to be seen in the constancy of the orders and forms of nature, which are expressions both of the divine will and of God's faithfulness to his creation.

Preservation of Humankind

Not only does God maintain the cosmos at large, but God the Father through Christ the Son also preserves and upholds human life. He does this both through the commandment to the original couple to be fruitful and multiply and to have dominion over the earth, as well as through the ineffable working of his Spirit and his steadfast loyalty to his servants.

"And God blessed them, and God said to them, 'Be fruitful and multiply, and fill the earth and subdue it' " (Gen. 1:28); "in thy hand are power and might; and in thy hand it is . . . to give strength to all" (1 Chron. 29:12); "thy care has preserved my spirit" (Job 10:12); "The LORD is your keeper; . . . he will keep your life. The LORD will keep your going out and your coming in" (Ps. 121:5, 7, 8); "the eternal God is your dwelling place, and underneath are the everlasting arms" (Deut. 33:27); "he himself gives to all men life and breath and everything. . . . Yet he is not

10. Berkhof, *Systematic Theology,* 170.
11. Ibid.
12. Ibid.
13. Emil Brunner, *The Christian Doctrine of Creation and Redemption,* vol. 2 of *Dogmatics,* trans. by Olive Wyon (Philadelphia: Westminster, 1952), 152; emphasis added.

far from each one of us, for 'In him we live' and move and have our being' " (Acts 17:25, 27–28); "yet for us there is one God, the Father, from whom are all things and for whom we exist, and one Lord, Jesus Christ, through whom are all things and through whom we exist" (1 Cor. 8:6).

Old and New Testament alike ascribe the preservation of human life to the personal activity of God. It is God who upholds the species ("gives to all men life"). Yet God does not simply sustain the species. The Bible proclaims that God sustains each human life. It is God whose edict of care "preserves" and "keeps" the individual. The Hebrew word *shāmar* means "to keep, to preserve, to protect." It is the central theological verb used to describe Yahweh's faithfulness to his servants and is employed in many passages (Gen. 28:15; Exod. 23:20; Num. 6:24; Josh. 24:17; Job 29:2; Ps. 16:1; 91:11). It heralds the good news that Yahweh is the supreme Keeper and Preserver of his servants—*Yahweh sho-m^e-rē-kah,* "the LORD is your keeper" (Ps. 121:5).

Barth entails a number of equivalent terms in the Greek New Testament that also proclaim God's preserving work in human life. He anchors the Latin verb *conservo* to *servo,* implying that God's gracious election precedes preservation. Barth observes that there are five New Testament verbs that convey the concept of *conservo: tēreō, phroureō, phulassō, bebaioō,* and *stēizō:*[14] "I kept (*etēroun*) them in thy name; . . . I have guarded (*ephulaxa*) them, and none of them is lost (John 17:12); "who by God's power are guarded (*phrouroumenous*) through faith" (1 Peter 1:5); "established (*bebaioumenoi*) in the faith" (Col. 2:7); "but the LORD is faithful; he will strengthen you and guard you (*stērixei kai phulaxei*) from evil" (2 Thess. 3:3).

It should be noted that Barth deliberately links the preservation of human life with salvation: "Because the creature is saved by Him, because it partakes of this salvation by Him, the creature is sustained and preserved by Him."[15] Moreover, Barth accepts the finite limitations that God has given to creation and to human life. No creature exists without limitations, and man is no exception. Each human being exists in a particular time and in a particular place. As such, human beings are free "to experience and accomplish that which is proper to [them], to do that which [they] can do, and to be satisfied. It is in this freedom that [they are] preserved by God."[16]

Such existence is an "opportunity" that can lead toward participation

14. Barth, *Church Dogmatics,* 3.3:82.
15. Ibid., 85.
16. Ibid., 84.

in the kingdom of God and, therefore, an opportunity that reflects the very "goodness of God." Yet Barth warns:

> As life itself shows, neither in prosperity nor in adversity is there any comfort or security either for the people or the individual except in the election, in the covenant, in the history of the covenant with its concrete experiences, and finally and decisively in Yahweh Himself as He who acts as Lord of the covenant.[17]

One may not care to subsume, as completely as Barth does, the pres-ervation of human life under the rubric of salvation or election. Never-theless, the Scriptures clearly teach that it is *God* who keeps and guards mankind, who preserves human life and its possibilities. It is he whose power gives strength to all, whose presence is never far from anyone, whose everlasting arms offer suport, whose Son is the very principle of one's profoundest cohesion, through whom God has acted redemptively for all, and in whom he continues to guard and to strengthen and to establish human beings in faith.

This divine preservation of human life is not merely a passive work of God, in which he sits back and watches both world events and human searching unfold, but it is an active work of the Godhead. It is an active work because God takes the initiative and achieves these things for man-kind's sake.

It is this conviction of faith, based on revelation, that makes the doctrine of the providence of God an edifying and pragmatic one. Neither the universe nor human life is an independent or self-contained phenomenon. Both may be reduced to that by modern science and humanistic philos-ophy, but that is not the message of the Scriptures.

It is the active work of God that maintains, keeps, guards, upholds, and strengthens life. This is what ultimately "preserves" human life. This is what gives it its power and joy.

Preservation of the People of God

God's work of preservation is above all a preservation of his servant Israel and of his church. God's divine upholding is inseparable from the covenant and his purposes of election in Christ Jesus. Neither the universe nor human life possesses absolute value in itself. The cosmos and human life exist for a higher purpose than self-continuance or the propagation of the species. Both exist for the glory of God, who, in Christ Jesus, resolved

17. Ibid.

from eternity "to unite all things in him, things in heaven and things on earth" (Eph. 1:10).

Hence, God elects, maintains, and preserves a community of believers, with whom he makes his everlasting covenant, and through whom he guides humanity to Christ Jesus. Thus, God in Jesus Christ becomes the guarantor, the steadfast promise-keeper, who preserves his servant Israel and the Christian community from dissolution and from ultimate bondage, death, and the gates of hell (Gen. 45:5, 7; Deut. 6:24; Matt. 16:18; Rom. 8:38–39).

Preservation is an active work of God, pragmatic and edifying, that issues in and nourishes Christian courage and faith:

> Beside us to guide us, our God with us joining,
> Ordaining, maintaining His Kingdom divine;
> So from the beginning the fight we were winning;
> Thou, Lord, wast at our side; all glory be Thine!

Providence and God's Cooperation with All Things

Reformed theology has also understood God's providential activity as a divine cooperation with all creatures, or as a divine operation that accompanies the activity of all creatures. This doctrine is known as the idea of divine concurrence, following the older dogmatics' use of the term *concursus*. Berkhof defines it as "the co-operation of the divine power with all subordinate powers, according to the preestablished laws of their operation, causing them to act and to act precisely as they do."[18] Its intention, as G. C. Berkouwer understands it, is to underscore "God's invincibility" and "sovereign reign" both "over and in the creaturely activity of man," while not blotting out human activity or mitigating the role human freedom plays.[19]

Berkhof notes that this doctrine implies two things:

(1) That the powers of nature do not work by themselves, . . . but that God is immediately operative in every act of the creature [a qualification against deism]. (2) That second causes are real, and not to be regarded simply as the operative power of God. It is only on condition that second causes are

18. Berkhof, *Systematic Theology,* 171.
19. G. C. Berkouwer, *Studies in Dogmatics: The Providence of God,* trans. by Lewis Smedes (Grand Rapids: Wm. B. Eerdmans, 1952), 140f.

real, that we can properly speak of a concurrence or co-operation of the
First Cause with secondary causes [a qualification against pantheism].[20]

The seventeenth-century Reformed theologian Johann Heidegger defines the doctrine in a succinct but broader statement: "Concurrence or
co-operation is the operation of God by which He co-operates directly
with the second causes as depending upon Him alike in their essence as
in their operation, so as to rule or move them to action and to operate
along with them in a manner suitable to a first cause and adjusted to the
nature of second causes."[21]

Heidegger spells out the philosophical meaning of this position. First,
God is a universal cause, while all second causes are particular and subordinate to him. Second, God's cooperation with second causes is direct,
so much so that the activity of second causes is actually God's activity.
Heidegger cites Romans 11:36 and the phrases *all things* and *through him*
to justify "this direct and proximate power as first cause." Third, God's
cooperation both precedes and is simultaneous with the action of a second
cause. That is, God "predetermines it to action, . . . precedes the creature's action not in time, but in order, dignity, and surpassingness, . . .
and by the method of conjoint action . . . produces one and the same
action. . . . Finally God concurs with creatures in the mode proper to the
first cause and accommodated to the nature of second causes."[22] That is,
God operates independently, while second causes must operate according
to their nature.

If these four implications avoid the ramifications of deism, what about
the apparent danger of making God the sole agent of all causes? Heidegger asserts that second causes are not mere instruments or passive tools
that respond only when moved by a master tradesman. They are active
and voluntary as well. Furthermore, God does not act "subjectively in
second causes," but he "acts effectively, as the first cause, from which
(second causes) have received the power to act and to cause, and by the
concurrence of which they are . . . urged and applied to action."[23]

Heidegger, too, appears to understand *concursus* as a defense of God's
sovereignty while not minimizing the creature's right and duty to act
within the full boundaries of its endowed possibilities and capacities.
Hence, the hardening of Pharaoh's heart is an example of *concursus* in
which Pharaoh freely elects to oppose the Israelites, and yet God remains

20. Berkhof, *Systematic Theology*, 171f.
21. Cited by Heppe, *Reformed Dogmatics*, 258.
22. Ibid., 259f.
23. Ibid., 260f.

invincible and in command and works through Pharaoh's hardened will to the greater glory of his own redemptive activity. Or, to paraphrase Heidegger, God operates in a mode proper to his own as first cause and accommodates himself to Pharaoh's nature as a second cause, fulfilling his will through Pharaoh's.

Heidegger concludes that these two qualifications are essential to hold, else "all freedom would be destroyed in voluntary causes" and "every power with which the creatures are endued by God would be crushed, and they would have been created in vain, God being the sole operator."[24]

Berkhof maintains that there is clear and sufficient scriptural proof for the idea of concurrence and that the Bible specifically teaches that God's providence applies "not only to being but also to the actions or operations of the creature."[25] He cites the following passages: Genesis 45:5; Exodus 4:11, 12; Deuteronomy 8:18; Joshua 11:6; 2 Samuel 16:11; 1 Kings 22:20–23; Ezra 6:22; Proverbs 21:1; Isaiah 10:5. Berkhof finds support for God's predetermining concurrence in 1 Corinthians 12:6, Ephesians 1:11, and Philippians 2:13; and for God's simultaneous concurrence in Acts 17:28.

Certainly the idea of *concursus* as a divine operation that accompanies the operation and activity of God's creatures is clearly implied in many biblical passages: "For God sent me before you to preserve life" (Gen. 45:5); "The LORD said to him, 'Who has made man's mouth? Who makes him dumb, or deaf, or seeing, or blind? Is it not I, the LORD? Now therefore go, and I will be with your mouth and teach you what you shall speak' " (Exod. 4:11, 12); "for the LORD . . . had turned the heart of the king of Assyria to them" (Ezra 6:22); "Behold, my own son seeks my life; how much more now may this Benjaminite! Let him alone, and let him curse; for the LORD has bidden him" (2 Sam. 16:11); "there are varieties of working, but it is the same God who inspires them all" (1 Cor. 12:6); "work out your own salvation with fear and trembling; for God is at work in you, both to will and to work for his good pleasure" (Phil. 2:12, 13).

Barth also discusses the concept of concurrence and its biblical and theological foundations. In addition to the above passages, Barth finds others that were also frequently used by earlier Reformed theologians in their development of the idea of *concursus* (Gen. 45:8; 1 Sam. 10:26; Job 38–41; Prov. 16:1, 9, 33; 19:21; Ps. 127:1; Isa. 26:12; Jer. 10:23; Matt. 10:29; Acts 17:28; Rom. 11:36[26]).

24. Ibid., 259.
25. Berkhof, *Systematic Theology,* 172.
26. Barth, *Church Dogmatics,* 3.3:95.

However, there are Christians who may wonder with Brunner if this entire investigation into second causes and *concursus* is not a wandering into "the danger-zone" and the diminution of "the foreground"—Christ Jesus. Brunner states: "This doctrine [of *concursus divinus*] . . . seems to us to be valueless and extremely doubtful." We "must renounce all attempts to understand how the independence granted to us as created beings and God's preserving activity can be interwoven. Here we come to a full stop. We are not meant to probe any further."[27] Even the conservative Berkouwer discusses concurrence only after he has explained the meaning of *sustenance* and *government.* Moreover, he entitles his chapter "A Third Aspect?" and wonders if sustenance and government are not sufficient safeguards against deistic and pantheistic interpretations of God's providence.[28]

Nevertheless, as Barth surmises, "the problem raised by these passages is indeed a genuine one," a matter the church cannot ignore. Hence, Barth praises the efforts of earlier theologians who attempted "to do justice to the problem of a co-existence and antithesis of the divine and creaturely action which should correspond with the testimony of Scripture."[29]

Barth also asks whether the terminology of *cause* and *second causes* is appropriate to the doctrine and concludes that it is. No distortion of the biblical message occurs by resorting to this Aristotelian and Thomistic terminology. God is a *causa,* the source of all *causae* and of the whole causal series. No *causa* precedes or is above him. He is his own *causa.* Hence "all *causae* outside Him and their *causare* are not merely partly but absolutely conditioned by Him. . . ."[30]

The creature is also *causa.* It is posited absolutely by God. Without God it would neither be nor be *causa.* As a second cause the creature is both conditioned by other *causae* as well as a conditioner of other things. It is both *causa causans* and *causa causata,* a causing cause and a caused cause.

Barth cannot fault this conceptual basis of the earlier evangelical dogmatics' understanding of the *concursus Dei.* In fact, he restates it:

> As *causa prima,* or *princeps,* God co-operates with the operation of *causae secundae.* . . . The divine *causare* takes place in and with their *causare.* And this means that their operations are also His operations, and in view of the

27. Brunner, *Dogmatics,* 2:153f.
28. See Berkouwer, *Providence,* 137–72.
29. Barth, *Church Dogmatics,* 3.3:96.
30. Ibid., 98f.

difference in dignity between the two orders they are first and decisively His operations.[31]

However, Barth does object to the material content which the older dogmatics brought to this concept. There are two errors in particular that must be rejected. First, orthodoxy completely ignored the relationship between creation and the covenant of grace. It spoke abstractly of God's "general control" and presented him as a "neutral and featureless God, an Absolute," and it spoke equally "abstractly of a neutral and featureless creature." The older orthodoxy also lacked safeguards against its abstract forms.[32]

To avoid repeating these mistakes, Barth offers five conditions under which the term *causa* can be applied to a doctrine of *concursus*:

1. The term cannot apply to any operation that is automatically effective. It is not a natural cause. God is not identical with the natural order.
2. *Causa* does not mean that either God or the creature is to be understood as a "thing."
3. *Causa* does not imply that both God and the creature are subject to a "master-concept." God and the creature are radically unlike. Their absolute unlikeness must be preserved.
4. The notion of cause must not reduce theology to a kind of philosophy.
5. The term *causa* "describes . . . the operation of the Father of Jesus Christ in relation to that of the creature." God so loved the world that he became a creature to be its Savior.[33]

Barth believes that the idea of *concursus* is biblical and that it belongs to the Christian message. In developing this doctrine, Barth draws upon two theological principles to defend the place of concurrence in Christian thought. First, the starting point of all God's *operatio* is his eternal love. "The love of God is primary."[34] And it is God's love toward the creature that governs God's co-operation with the creature, so that God "co-operates with it, preceding, accompanying and following all its being and activity, so that all the activity of the creature is primarily and simultaneously and subsequently His own activity."[35]

Second, in a manner similar to that whereby patristic theology was required to defend Christ's full divinity and full humanity, without mixing

31. Ibid., 99.
32. Ibid., 100.
33. Ibid., 101–7.
34. Ibid., 107.
35. Ibid., 105.

and confusing them, by developing the theological principles of Chalcedon, so the church testifies in its doctrine of concurrence "to the problem of the co-existence and antithesis of the divine and creaturely action," without confusing and mixing them. Hence the doctrine acknowledges that "the totality of creaturely activity takes place on a level of its own" [as *causa causans* and *causa causata*], while at the same time it acknowledges that "individual activity no less than the totality of creaturely activity is wholly and utterly at the disposal of the divine. . . ."[36]

One seems compelled to conclude that a modern Reformed position on the providence of God cannot surrender this doctrine without sacrificing critical biblical and theological principles. As G. C. Berkouwer maintains, "both lines in Scripture, Divine determination and human responsibility, must be recognized and held. . . . For there are here not two competitive exclusives, as determinism would have it, but a Divine activity over and in the creaturely activity of man." For the Bible plainly teaches "the invincible power of God and our continual responsibility."[37]

Providence and the Governance of All Things

The third element in the Reformed understanding of providence is the concept of government. Reformed dogmatics referred to this as God's work of *gubernatio* ("steering"). It specifically has to do with the direction, purpose, and goal that God assigns to each component of creation and to the whole of history. This concept has been persistently maintained and advanced by many writers, both orthodox and neoorthodox:

"God's government is the act of the same providence by which God ordains, directs and executes things all and individual of every kind to the end prescribed by Himself, both the intermediates and the final one" (Heidegger).[38] Government has to do with "the ideas of design and control. It supposes an end to be attained, and the disposition and direction of means for its accomplishment" (Hodge).[39] Government is "that continued activity of God whereby He rules all things teleologically so as to secure the accomplishment of the divine purpose," which is "the glory of His name" (Berkhof).[40]

---

36. Ibid., 122.
37. Berkouwer, *Providence*, 165.
38. Cited by Heppe, *Reformed Dogmatics*, 262.
39. Hodge, *Systematic Theology*, 1:581.
40. Berkhof, *Systematic Theology*, 175.

Neoorthodox theologians embrace a similar view. Brunner compares God's work of government with his work of preservation. Whereas the latter has to do with nature, the former has to do with history. Hence, for Brunner, *gubernatio* means "that the natural course of history—of course, in its connexion with the natural order—cannot be understood in itself, but only in the light of a continued activity and presence of God, who, in this historical course, orders the whole of History towards the final goal."[41]

Barth also emphasizes the notion of aim or *telos*:

God has an aim for the creature when He preserves and accompanies it. His preservation and accompanying are as such a guiding, a leading, a ruling, and active determining of the being and activity of all the reality which is distinct from Himself. He directs it to the thing which in accordance with his good-pleasure and resolve, and on the basis of its creation, it has to do and to be in the course of its history in time; to the *telos* which has to be attained in this history. It is He Himself who has set for it this *telos,* and it is He who as Ruler guides it towards this *telos.*"[42]

Even Tillich's view reflects this line of thought, though he expresses it differently: "The concept 'the purpose of creation' should be replaced by 'the *telos* of creativity'—the inner aim of fulfilling in actuality what is beyond potentiality and actuality in the divine life. One function of the divine creativity is to drive every creature toward such a fulfilment."[43]

The concepts of guidance, direction, and lordship are clearly expressed in Scripture. The Old Testament describes Yahweh as the universal King. God is depicted as "the king of all the earth," who "reigns over the nations" (Ps. 47:7, 8); who is "King of the nations" (Jer. 10:7); and who is "the LORD of hosts" (Jer. 46:18; 48:15; 51:57).

This concept of God's universal kingship is also taught in the New Testament, where God is described as "the great King" (Matt. 5:35); "Lord of heaven and earth" (Matt. 11:25; Acts 17:24); "the King of ages" (1 Tim. 1:17); "the blessed and only Sovereign, the King of kings and Lord of lords" (1 Tim. 6:15); "the Lord our God the Almighty" (Rev. 19:6).

It is this King, who, in the New Testament, is the God and Father of Jesus Christ, who directs and guides all things toward the *telos* which he has determined for creation. And this *telos* is the uniting of all things in

41. Brunner, *Dogmatics,* 2:176.
42. Barth, *Church Dogmatics,* 3.3:155.
43. Tillich, *Systematic Theology,* 1:264.

Jesus Christ, "things in heaven and things on earth" (Eph. 1:10; see also Rom. 8:18–25; 11:36).

The Reformed tradition has taken seriously God's directing of "all things" and has seen this as pertaining to nature, all sentient creatures, mankind, and history itself.

The earlier dogmatics made a distinction between "unconscious creatures" and "intelligent creatures" or "natural things" and "voluntary things." Both categories require God's constant guidance if they are to achieve their end.[44]

According to Heidegger, "Natural things . . . [are governed] by a certain law stamped on nature or rather a force of God present in nature."[45] God actively guides the physical world through natural laws that he has established. This pertains to all biological life, animals being governed by instinct.[46]

This perception of God actively directing the physical world toward the achievement of its potential is clearly taught in Scripture: "He changes times and seasons" (Dan. 2:21); "he makes his sun rise on the evil and on the good, and sends rain . . ." (Matt. 5:45); "God . . . clothes the grass of the field . . ." (Matt. 6:30); "in his hand is the life of every living thing" (Job 12:10); "the young lions roar for their prey, seeking their food from God" (Ps. 104:21; see also vv. 27–30); "the birds of the air . . . neither sow nor reap nor gather . . . and yet your heavenly Father feeds them" (Matt. 6:26); "not one of them will fall to the ground without your Father's will" (Matt. 10:29).

Intelligent creatures and voluntary things also come under God's guidance and divine ruling. This is true of individuals: "Go from your country . . . and I will make of you a great nation" (Gen. 12:1, 2); "I AM has sent me to you" (Exod. 3:15); "I gird you, though you do not know me" (Isa. 45:5); "a man's mind plans his way, but the LORD directs his steps" (Prov. 16:9); "my times are in thy hand" (Ps. 31:15); "it is God who executes judgment, putting down one and lifting up another" (Ps. 75:7).

Nations and history are also subject to God: "And he made from one every nation of men to live on all the face of the earth, having determined allotted periods and the boundaries of their habitation" (Acts 17:26); "his dominion is an everlasting dominion . . . ; he does according to his will in the host of heaven and among the inhabitants of the earth" (Dan. 4:35); "he removes kings and sets up kings" (Dan. 2:21); "the Most High rules the kingdom of men, and gives it to whom he will" (Dan. 4:25); "Cyrus,

---

44. See Heppe, *Reformed Dogmatics,* 262f.
45. Ibid., 263.
46. Ibid.

whose right hand I have grasped" (Isa. 45:1); "you would have no power . . . unless it had been given you from above" (John 19:11); "for there is no authority except from God" (Rom. 13:1). Even the eschatological age, the future, belongs to God in which his divine work of *gubernatio* continues and is made perfect (Isa. 9:7; 11:6–9; Rev. 19:6; 21:1–4, 22–27; 22:1–5).

Furthermore, the Reformed tradition has maintained "that God exercises a controlled power over the free acts of men, as well as over their external circumstances," and that "this is true of all their acts, good and evil."[47] In support of this position, Hodge cites the following biblical passages: "The plans of the mind belong to man, but the answer of the tongue is from the LORD" (Prov. 16:1); "The king's heart is a stream of water in the hand of the LORD; he turns it wherever he will" (Prov. 21:1); "Blessed be the LORD, . . . who put such a thing as this into the heart of the king" (Ezra 7:27); "Incline my heart to thy testimonies" (Ps. 119:36). In fact, Hodge asserts that a large portion of Scripture is founded on the assumption of God's "absolute control over the free acts of his creatures."[48]

The older dogmatics[49] and modern Reformed theologians have expressed similar views, going so far so to explain *how* God's government over "free acts" operates.[50]

Brunner, however, advises caution with respect to the manner of how God directs and controls men's minds and hearts. Brunner finds the traditional solutions to this problem unsatisfactory. The notion of divine determination (i.e., God does it all) alongside that of human free choice is simply contradictory and philosophically unacceptable. The idea of divine foreknowledge (i.e., God already knows what individuals will choose) begs the question, because it favors God's omniscience over his omnipotence. It compromises his power as well as his goodness. Brunner finds the idea of permission to be equally weak, not only for the reasons he gives regarding the second solution, but because such an idea begs the question of ultimate responsibility for the universe.

Brunner asks, "What does revelation teach us . . . about Providence?" He answers:

1. The God of revelation is not the *potestas absoluta* of speculation, but the God who limits himself.
2. This God of self-limitation creates free creatures to worship him in freedom.
3. Revelation commands Christians to think of providence in personal terms.

47. See Hodge, *Systematic Theology*, 1:588.
48. Ibid., 589.
49. See Heppe, *Reformed Dogmatics*, 263.
50. See Berkhof, *Systematic Theology*, 175f.

4. God does not will sin, nor does he allow sin to eclipse his presence in human life.
5. The church is faced with the impenetrable mystery of a God who limits himself, and yet does not cease to be Lord of all that happens.[51]

Without understating the problem, the Reformed tradition can do no less than embrace Brunner's stance. That many theologians emphasize God's divine determination over his self-limitation is a principle in keeping with the older Reformed position. If it is an error, it is an error meant to uphold the *maior Dei gloria*. But, as Barth warns, the Scriptures also affirm the *minor gloria creaturae*. Reformed theology need not choose between the two. It need only affirm both, which is precisely what the Scriptures do.[52]

51. Brunner, *Dogmatics*, 2:172–75.
52. Barth, *Church Dogmatics*, 3.3:97.

Chapter Three

The Greek and Roman Philosophical Heritage

THE RUDIMENTS OF A REFORMED DOCTRINE OF THE PROVIDENCE OF God lie deeply embedded in the Western philosophical tradition. There is little point in debating this. Wisdom and truth consist in acknowledging the fact and in showing how Christian, and later Reformed, doctrines differ significantly from the older, inherited, philosophical views.

Whether or not one looks favorably upon either the Platonists or Stoics, the *logoi spermatikoi* ("rational seeds") for a doctrine of the providence of God are early and profoundly present in Greek thought.

The Homeric Perception

Beginning with Homer, one can already catch a glimpse of the Greek mind wrestling with causality and the disposition to believe that a suprahuman, supramundane force, personified by the Olympian gods, governs and oversees human fate.

Sometimes this force can be bent, or altered, to act advantageously for humankind. But, often as not, even the gods are powerless to override what is portrayed as a predetermined necessity.

The supreme example of this perception occurs in book 22 of the *Iliad*, where Zeus and the gods watch helplessly while Achilles bears down on Hector. Zeus asks, "What do you think, gods? Just consider, shall we save him from death, or shall we let Achilles beat him now? He is a brave man." But Athena objects, "O Father Flashingbolt, . . . you must never say that! A mortal man, long doomed by fate, and you will save him from death?" To which Zeus replies, "Never mind, Tritogeneia, my love. I did not really mean it. . . ." Then Homer explains, "See now, the Father laid out his golden scales and placed in them two fates of death, one for Achilles and one for Hector. He grasped the balance and lifted it: Hector's doom sank down, sank down to Hades, and Apollo left him."[1]

Although Homer is inconsistent, this dramatic scene establishes the conviction that, above the gods, an even greater force is at work, namely, Fate. The gods are as bound by this blind, merciless reality as are mortals.

Sometimes sacrifices and supplications can persuade a god or goddess to intervene in man's affairs. But throughout the Homeric epics, the chaotic and the unpredictable play a more impressive role than the orderly and the dependable. Thus, for Homer, man is called upon to bear a great burden. Much of his life is in his own hands. But, at the same time, man's ultimate fate is beyond anything prayer or action can change. It is equally beyond the power of the divine to alter—even when the divine may be disposed to act benevolently.

This perception of the way divine causality operates neither recognizes a unified, natural ordering of the universe nor a moral or personal orderer worthy of human trust. Blind fate, fickle gods, and an unpredictable natural system entrap all. There is simply the acknowledgment that one's life is in the hands of an absolute necessity, Fate.

Hesiod's Zeus

By the time of Hesiod, this perception has undergone change. Hesiod's *Works and Days* presents a different concept of Zeus and his interaction with the world. Zeus is now the indisputable ruler of the universe, a universe in which justice and right have become the standards by which he rules and overrules the affairs of men. Blind fate has been replaced by a concept of moral order, which, if not originating in Zeus, characterizes the supreme god and his will for human life.

No longer do the gods deal capriciously with mankind. "God's will" has become a central factor. Hesiod states: "Through him [Zeus] mortal

---

1. Homer, *Iliad,* trans. by W. H. D. Rouse, in *The Story of Achilles* (New York: Nelson, 1938), bk. 22. [Cited by W. T. Jones, *A History of Western Philosophy* (New York: Harcourt, Brace & Co., 1952), 28. See esp. pt. 1, chap. 1, "The Cultural Milieu." Jones's book, in many ways, is the inspiration behind the first three sections of the present chapter.] In addition, see Walter Burkert, *Greek Religion,* trans. by John Raffan (Cambridge: Harvard University Press, 1985), 129–30. Burkert disputes the traditional view that Zeus was subservient to Fate.

men are famed or unfamed, sung or unsung alike, as great Zeus wills. . . .
So there is no way to escape the will of Zeus."[2] Yet this divine will is
never arbitrary or fickle.

Hesiod explains the normative principle or criterion by which Zeus
actively and passively governs the affairs of men. This criterion is justice,
or right, and the rejection of violence and cruelty. It is a "law" that Zeus
has ordained for men.

Hesiod elaborates:

> Listen to right and do not foster violence. . . .
> The better path is to go by on the other side towards justice. . . .
> For those who practise violence and cruel deeds far-seeing Zeus, the son
> of Cronos, ordains a punishment. Often even a whole city suffers for a bad
> man who sins and devises presumptuous deeds, and the son of Cronos lays
> great trouble upon the people, famine and plague together. . . . And again,
> at another time, the son of Cronos either destroys their wide army, or their
> walls, or else makes an end of their ships on the sea.
>
> You princes, mark well this punishment you also; for the deathless gods
> are near among men and mark all those who oppress their fellows with
> crooked judgments. . . . For upon the bounteous earth Zeus has thrice ten
> thousand spirits, watchers of mortal men. . . .
>
> Lay up these things within your heart and listen now to right, ceasing
> altogether to think of violence. For the son of Cronos has ordained this law
> for men, that fishes and beasts and winged fowls should devour one another,
> for right is not in them; but to mankind he gives right which proves far the
> best. For whoever knows the right and is ready to speak it, far-seeing Zeus
> gives him prosperity; but whoever deliberately lies in his witness and for-
> swears himself, and so hurts Justice and sins beyond repair, that man's gen-
> eration is left obscure thereafter.[3]

This quotation is instructive. From a negative point of view, a number
of objections must be raised. It displays a conception of providence based
principally on divine omniscience. God acts on the basis of his knowledge
of man's response to his ordained law. Consequently, God reacts to what
humankind does; his omnipotence is bound by both his omniscience and
the perversity of men. Furthermore, God himself is absent and must rely
on intermediaries and divinely appointed "watchers" to report to him.
God can only operate from a distance.

2. Hesiod, *Works and Days*, trans. by H. G. Evelyn-White, Loeb Classical Library (Cambridge: Harvard University Press, 1926), 3. [Cited by Jones, *History of Western Philosophy*,
31.]

3. Ibid., 9, 19–25. See Jones's analysis of Hesiod's prologue in *History of Western Philosophy*, 31f.

Moreover, God himself appears as bound by his ordained law for men as are mortals. He cannot intervene to "save" man or to alter or redirect the human drama. He can only judge it and then act punitively. Hesiod's system is without grace. God can only reward or punish; he can only give man his due. To that extent he is just and upholds the criterion of justice, but the inspiring principle is one of *ad baculum,* not of *ad misericordiam.*

In contrast, as the keeper of Israel, Yahweh interjects himself into the processes of history to fulfill his purposes, in spite of an Abraham, Isaac, Jacob, or Moses and their own miscalculations and insecurities. Though the patriarchs must suffer the consequences of their misdeeds, nonetheless, the ethical and the universal do not have the final word in their lives. God has the last word and transcends the ethical and the universal in order to fulfill his ultimate and redemptive purposes. Human perversity and frailty cannot and do not bind God.

In spite of these negative observations, however, in comparison to Homer's view, Hesiod's perception of God's providential activity rescues divine causality from chaos and chance. Hesiod endows the divine operation with rational and moral elements and elevates man to a special and privileged place in the eyes of Zeus. Man is different from the other creatures and possesses immense capacities for moral interaction and development. Hence, Hesiod's system replaces Homeric caprice and fate with order and hope.

Hesiod's efforts, however, were not confined to the clarification of divine causality. Hesiod was also concerned to establish order in nature. In his *Theogony,* Hesiod brings what reform he can to the role of the gods and their function in "the house of Olympus." Again, his criterion is order, and he endeavors to explain how the gods came about, how they are related, and how the world came into being. All in all, Hesiod makes a noble attempt to anchor man in an orderly world, governed by a pervasive, uniform, and dependable law that resounds in the halls of Olympus itself.

The Dawn of a New Age and the Night of the World

The long progression in Western philosophical and religious thought, which spans the period from Hesiod to Plato, is beyond the confines of this chapter to trace in depth. Nevertheless, there are two observations that are essential to this discussion.

First, beginning with Thales and continuing through the first half of the fifth century B.C., the Greek impulse was characterized by an attempt to

develop a theory of natural causation. The importance of mythology re-
cedes, and natural causes for natural effects are theorized and explored.
Divine operation is neither denied nor refuted during this period; rather
the quest is for an empirical explanation of causality.

For example, Thales' *Urstuff* ("water") is the natural substratum and
causa of all else. True, Thales recognizes that all things are filled with
gods. But his subject is scarcely the gods or divine will and causation.
The same may be said of Heraclitus's "fire," or universal *logos,* which is
also divine. Heraclitus is not so much offering a theological explanation
as a rational explanation for a natural world of becoming and change.[4]

The result of such explorations is a further demythologization of the
real force pervading the universe. All things are held to be physically
interrelated. And this interrelatedness is universal, orderly, and regular.
It is even rational in character, inasmuch as reason can grasp it, although
this discovery seems not to have occurred until the time of Parmenides
and its significance not realized until Plato's day.

Yet this concept of natural causation is impersonal. The *causa omnium
causarum* ("cause of all causes") is neutral. It does not even wear the
robe of a hoary Zeus, let alone the mantle of Hesiod's moral and "far-
seeing son of Cronos."

Morality, in this system, as in its modern counterparts, is a function of
physics, or is subordinate to physics, as Epicurus would see. Religion is
reduced to a psychological, or, at best, a sociological phenomenon, in
which the individual in his solitude, or collectively *en masse,* yearns to
buoy his finite and fragmentary existence with a spiritual significance his
very humanness requires him to seek. The Greeks yearned for precisely
this meaning, this significance. This yearning is found in the Dionysian
movement of the seventh and sixth centuries B.C., and surfaces again at
the time of Euripides and Socrates.[5]

The Dionysian cult hungered for more than the Homeric gods could
deliver. It yearned for a vitality that came from participating in the secret
rites of union with the divine. The Dionysian cult was equally a profound
expression of discontent with this life. Participating in the rites and fes-
tivals revived one's sense of belonging to that which is most enduring and
fulfilling. It restored union with that hidden primordial power and being
which the soul longs to feel. That it could also be "intoxicating" in the

4. For an in-depth survey of Thales's and Heraclitus's positions, see Frederick Copleston,
A History of Philosophy (New York: Image Books, 1962), 1.1:38–40, 54–63. See also Jones,
History of Western Philosophy, 32–34, 38–41.

5. See Jones, *History of Western Philosophy,* 20–25. See also Friedrich Nietzsche, *The
Birth of Tragedy* (New York: Vintage Books, 1967), 33–89.

dark, bacchanalian sense, seems to be the high price that human efforts toward self-salvation ultimately involve.

By the time of Euripides, such yearning becomes a form of despair. (In retrospect, Euripides saw its nihilistic dimensions, while Socrates and Plato surmounted their despair by clinging to the rational.) The yearning that has become despair is a philosophical despair, rooted in the disastrous war between Athens and Sparta. It is a profound despair spawned by defeat, extreme suffering, and the collapse of order. Euripides witnessed the tragedy, and his plays reflect a loss of faith in God and faith in any moral order.

Euripides' Hecuba, the Trojan queen mother, says it best as she laments the fall of Troy:

> Ye Gods—Alas! Why call on things so weak
> For aid? Yet there is something that doth seek,
> Crying, for God, when one of us hath woe.[6]

Then, toward the end of *The Trojan Women,* Hecuba's despair takes on a universal dimension:

> O vain is man,
> Who glorieth in his joy and hath no fears:
> While to and fro the chances of the year
> Dance like an idiot in the wind! And none
> By any strength hath his own fortune won. . . .
> Lo, I have seen the open hand of God;
> And in it nothing, nothing, save the rod
> Of mine affliction. . . .[7]

From a Reformed perspective, one is scarcely surprised by this Euripidean despair. The "death of God" whenever experienced by any culture in any century, brings humanity to the precipice. The defeat, disillusionment, and hopelessness that accompany such a staring into the abyss, is more than a simple, tragic disorientation that inexorably results in judgment upon all human pride, violence, and passion. It touches the very nerve of that humanness, for it witnesses to something profoundly intrinsic to humankind: even human despair requires a view of man that belies all

6. Euripedes, *The Trojan Women,* trans. by G. Murray, in *The Complete Greek Drama,* ed. by Whitney Oates and Eugene O'Neill, Jr. (New York: Random House, 1938), 977.

7. Ibid., 1003 and 1005, respectively.

nihilistic and godless definitions of him. Man's "incomprehensibility," as Pascal refers to it, can only be made "comprehensible" when our humanness is sustained, accompanied, and guided by the eternal God.

As Pascal explains:

> Man finds his lasting happiness only in God. Without Him, there is nothing in nature which will take His place; neither the stars, nor heaven, nor earth, nor the elements; not plants, . . . war, famine, vices, adultery, incest. Since man has lost track of his true happiness, all things appear equally good to him, even his own destruction, though so contrary to God, to right reason, and to the whole course of nature.[8]

Only if God exists and actively maintains, sustains, and guides his universe toward purposes that fulfill all that can be fathomed as good and true, can human beings have hope and, delivered from their estrangement, have ground for courageous and moral activity. That, in part, is what the Reformed doctrine of the providence of God defends and testifies to in response to its biblical foundations. And the Greek antecedents, though tenuous, fragile, and incomplete, ought to be grasped, appreciated, and understood by a wise, thoroughly biblical Reformed theology.

Plato's Concept of God

One can certainly appreciate Plato's anguish as well as the true depth of his thought when he states in the *Laws*:

> It is a matter of no small consequence, in some way or other to prove that there are Gods, and that they are good, and regard justice more than men do. The demonstration of this would be the best and noblest prelude of all our laws. And therefore, without impatience, and without hurry, let us unreservedly consider the whole matter, summoning up all the power of persuasion which we possess.[9]

In a religious and theological sense, the entire work of Plato is dedicated to this end. His understanding of God and divine causality stands

---

8. Blaise Pascal, *Pensées*. [Cited by A. Castell, *An Introduction to Modern Philosophy: Examining the Human Condition*, 4th ed. (New York: Macmillan, 1983), 186.]

9. From *Laws 10*, in *The Dialogues of Plato*, trans. by B. Jowett (New York: Random House, 1937), 2:629. [Unless otherwise noted, further references to the dialogues of Plato are to this edition. Dialogue, book, volume number (Random House), and page(s) will be cited.]

apart from the biblical view, but his understanding of God's nature, his attributes, and the ultimate purposes which the divine favors, attracted the early church fathers and was assimilated into their theologies. Plato has also influenced Reformed theology, inasmuch as theology is required to respect rationality and cannot exist without it.

What, then, is Plato's concept of God? How does God operate causally and providentially among men, if indeed he does? Obviously, Plato never treated these questions in the form in which our study is forced to propose them. But an attempt to explore his relevant ideas is both warranted and necessary.

There is considerable debate about Plato's precise understanding of God. In the *Timaeus,* Plato presents a myth in which he describes the divine as a Demiurge, or Craftsman, who creates a world-soul, which is then diffused throughout the world.[10] This world-soul is both the world's animating principle and the seat of the rational. The world-soul is the "ruler and mistress" over all that is corporeal. The Demiurge next creates the celestial gods and the immortal aspect of human souls. Finally, the remainder of creation is turned over to the gods, who form all else that is mortal and corporeal, including the corporeal in man.

Some students of Plato argue that his Demiurge is nothing more than a symbol for divine reason, which permeates the universe and works toward good. F. M. Cornford holds this view and concludes that Plato's God is "not really a creator," never an "object of worship," and occasionally indistinguishable from the celestial gods.[11] G. M. A. Grube maintains a similar position, holding that Plato's Demiurge is "the personification of the active principle of movement and causation, of the love of good which belongs to all the gods, as to all good souls."[12]

George F. Thomas is skeptical of these positions and suggests that Plato's Demiurge represents more than the rational ordering of the universe. Thomas favors and quotes Ian Crombie's assessment:

> I think it would be contrary to the whole spirit of the doctrine to say that the craftsman is no more than a symbolic expression of the fact that the universe is rationally ordered. Corresponding to the timeless intelligible natures there exists the timeless mind which eternally comprehends them.[13]

10. See the *Timaeus,* 2:14–17.

11. F. M. Cornford, *Plato's Cosmology* (New York: Humanities Press, 1952), 38. Cited by George F. Thomas, *Religious Philosophies of the West* (New York: Charles Scribner's Sons, 1965), 13.

12. G. M. A. Grube, *Plato's Thought* (London: Methuen, 1935), 169. [Quoted by Thomas, *Religious Philosophies,* 13.]

13. Ian Crombie, *An Examination of Plato's Doctrines* (London: Routledge, 1930), 391; Thomas, *Religious Philosophies,* 13.

Crombie's reference to the "timeless intelligible natures" raises still an-other issue—the problematic relationship between Plato's God and the eternal forms.

Plato's theory of the forms is vulnerable to oversimplification. The pop-ular understanding of Plato's theory of forms involves the notion that far transcending, in reality and worth, the Heraclitean world of becoming, there exists, at least objectively for the mind, an enduring, perfect realm of rational patterns. This intelligible realm of forms, when grasped by the mind, has the power to illuminate and motivate human existence, provid-ing it with purpose, direction, and true being. God is not the creator of these forms; he is co-eternal with them.

Herein lies the problem: there is outside of God a rival organizing principle, that is, the forms. God has not created them, but he uses them for the purpose of creating an orderly world. To the extent, therefore, that God is the highest being, his espousal of the forms elevates them to the status of the universe's highest values. But the converse of this can be equally true. For if the forms are the highest values and exist inde-pendently of God, then his espousal of them is what gives his own being value and meaning. Plato's failure to subordinate the forms to the divine has often been seen as a kind of slippery theological rug under his other-wise quite convincing Demiurge.

Plato does resolve some of this tension. The highest form is the idea *Good,* that is both an end in itself as well as a characteristic of God. Insofar as it is a characteristic of God, there is at least one form which God possesses and that does not lie outside him. However, this concept of an Absolute Good serves as the primary principle of organization, and so ambivalence remains, for this principle is inseparably linked with the whole "beingness" of the eternal God.

Whatever the case, it is clear in Plato's mind that God must be under-stood as "good," and that this "goodness" embodies both moral virtue and philosophical perfection. This is one of Plato's central themes in the *Republic.* Plato criticizes the Homeric and popular Greek concept of God precisely because it fails to see that God must be good and unchanging. Plato writes:

> God is always to be represented as he truly is. . . . And is he not truly good?
>
> [Moreover] surely God and the things of God are in every way perfect? . . . . And will he then change himself for the better and fairer, or for the worse and more unsightly?
>
> If he change at all he can only change for the worse, for we cannot suppose him to be deficient either in virtue or beauty. . . .

Then it is impossible that God should ever be willing to change. . . .[14]

This perception of God dominates Plato's philosophy. God is good; he is supreme, intelligent, and the orderer of the universe. He is perfect, and he indwells a world of perfect forms that he freely uses to fulfill his purposes, in accordance with his will.

What, then, is God's will? And how is his will related to divine causality in the world?

According to the *Timaeus,* it was the will of God "that all things should be as like himself as they could be. . . . God desired that all things should be good and nothing bad, so far as this was attainable." Realizing that no creature could be good who lacked "soul" (life) or "intelligence," God then "put intelligence in soul, and soul in body." Hence, the "world became a living creature truly endowed with soul and intelligence by the *providence* of God."[15]

Several of Plato's insights are worth noting. First, God's goodness is the motivating principle of his activity or operation. Although much of creation is carried out by the celestial gods in Plato's schema, it is done so by God's guiding will. It is not the result of blind chance. Therefore, the central motivating *causa* in God is not caprice or an arbitrary will, but a will subservient to divine goodness. Second, it is the will of God that all things should be as much like him as is appropriate to their nature and that each should attain the highest good it can. With regard to humanity, this means that the *telos* of mankind transcends history, that is, humanity's meaning is given to it from beyond itself. Humankind's meaning can never be self-imposed or self-given. Its meaning is divinely ordained. Finally, to attain this, life and intelligence are necessary, and both are created for this purpose. Neither evolved by chance; both are servants of the divine will.

Such insights can, with modest alteration, be taken up into a Christian doctrine of the providence of God. The problematic area is how the divine purpose is actually attained. For at this point in Plato's thought the divine ceases any direct activity or causality. He continues to uphold his purposes for man—the attainment of "God-likeness" and the "good"—but God seems powerless to redirect a perverse will and unable to alter or override the actual events of history. Plato's God is as limited by what mankind does or fails to do as is Hesiod's Zeus. Nevertheless, Plato does credit God with whatever good comes about in human life:

> Then God, if he be good, is not the author of all things, as the many assert, but he is the cause of a few things only, and not of most things that occur

14. *Republic,* bk. 2, 1:643, 645.
15. *Timaeus,* 2:14; emphasis added.

to men. For few are the goods of human life, and many are the evils, and the good is to be attributed to God alone; of the evils the causes are to be sought elsewhere, and not in him.[16]

Plato denies that God could ever be the cause of evil or sin. But he never explains how God can be the cause of the few good things that occur to man. Plato wrestles with this problem in most of his dialogues. He never ceases to ask how virtue is to be attained, how the good is to be realized, and how truth is to be appropriated. And his answer combines both theory and metaphor.

To theory belong his doctrine of the preexistence of the soul and its cosmic fall, the doctrine of recollection, and the need for a Socratic teacher, who, because he is in possession of the truth, can, by means of the dialectical method, awaken a recollection of the truth in his pupils. Once reawakened to the truth, or to the forms, the soul can be improved and attain its divinely ordained goodness.

To metaphor belong the allegory of the cave and the figure of the charioteer. The "Allegory of the Cave" describes how prisoners in a cave, whose lives are limited by the shadows they mistake for forms, are finally forced into the light. The figure of the charioteer portrays human nature as a tension of reason, will, and appetite. The chariot (the soul's life) runs its course best when the charioteer (reason) restrains his steeds (will and appetite) to run the course as reason dictates. Only then can virtue prevail, the good life be achieved, and God's will be fulfilled.

The direct hand of God in any of this appears to be totally absent. Yet God is closer than most Platonists may dare to realize or care to admit. And this is true even for Plato, for, in the final analysis, Socrates himself (Plato's mentor and model) is a phenomenon who can only be comprehended as an extension of the activity of God. As Plato has Socrates declare, "It is God who has given me to your city." It is God who "has sent me."[17] Indeed, Socrates even speaks of a divine sign from God. "I have had it from childhood," he explains. "It is a kind of voice, which whenever I hear it, always turns me back from something I was going to do, but never urges me to act. . . .[18] The prophetic sign, which I am wont to receive from the divine voice, has been constantly with me all through my life, . . . opposing me in quite small matters if I were not going to act rightly."[19]

16. *Republic*, bk. 2, 1:643.

17. From the *Apology*, cited by Oliver A. Johnson, *The Individual and the Universe: An Introduction to Philosophy* (New York: Holt, Rinehart & Winston, 1981), 15. Cf. the Jowett translation, *Apology*, 1:413f.

18. Ibid., 16; cf. *Apology*, 1:414.

19. Ibid., 20; cf. *Apology*, 1:421.

Far from being absent, then, divine causality is active in this world, but active in the form of a restraining conscience. Hence, God's guiding influence operates, at least, at the level of conscience. Man must still choose and act and is accountable for those choices and actions, but through the power of the conscience, whenever wrong is contemplated, the very awareness of wrong (which is itself a form of the Good) never abandons man.

On the positive side, no classical philosopher's perception of God rivals Plato's. A modern Reformed theology can rightly applaud the high moral and rational attributes with which Plato endows God. Plato's supreme Demiurge is appealing, for he is a god who unselfishly wills and guides an ordered world into being; he creates life and intelligence to the end that all things might attain their highest good, becoming as much like him as is possible and appropriate; he himself is this Good and wills only this Good; he is without evil nor causes evil; and his "voice" is implanted in the very phenomenon of human conscience.

Yet Plato's God can never simply be equated with the "God of Abraham, Isaac, and Jacob." One is forced to suspect with Cornford, if not conclude, that Plato's God is a symbol for all that is rational, beautiful, and good. He is a myth which functions in a metaphorical way to attest to the phenomenon of the power and possibility of an ideal Good. To this extent, Plato's God and his divine operation are subordinate to the absolute Good that the divine serves and promulgates.

Aristotle reports that crowds often came with enthusiasm to hear Plato talk about the Good, only, to their astonishment, to hear instead lectures on arithmetic and astronomy.[20] As Barth has wisely noted, the divine *causa* cannot imply that either God or man is subject to a "master concept," or that theology (and especially Reformed theology) can ever be reduced to a kind of philosophy. That would deny the entire biblical revelation of God and the Judeo-Christian encounter with him.

Aristotle's Unmoved Mover

In comparison to Plato's Demiurge, Aristotle's Unmoved Mover is disappointing to many theists. That supreme, intelligent Craftsman, who wills to share his universe out of profound admiration for the Good, and who fills that universe with life and intelligence, is not far from Augustine's neo-Platonic deity and pulsates with an almost self-giving, moral, personal dynamism totally absent in Aristotle's *theos*.

20. See Copleston, *History of Philosophy,* 1.1:155.

Yet Reformed theology cannot ignore Aristotle's view. His concept of God as the "final cause" is, indeed, a significant one. Thomistic theology would not have been articulated without it, and the Reformed understanding of man as having a chief and highest end is, in its own way, a tacit acknowledgment of Aristotelian formal and final causes. What must be seen, however, is that the Aristotelian concept of divine operation is sharply limited and any possibility of divine providence put in jeopardy.

Aristotle conceives of God as the Prime Mover of a universe that has existed from eternity.[21] The universe and its entire system of motion, or series of motions, requires a mover or moving agent that, of necessity, is itself self-moving or unmoved. This eternal self-mover must be pure actuality, for any potentiality and change would suggest imperfection; hence this god must also be incorporeal and without perishable qualities. Thus, the Prime Mover is without sensation or desire.

The Unmoved Mover does not move the universe by "starting it" or by "creating" anything; rather the universe turns on its own in response to the Prime Mover's perfection. Inspired by this perfection, the universe cannot help but desire to become perfect and good like God. And what is his unique quality? Insofar as he is perfect, his self-consciousness is alone worthy of his attention. He is perfect thought contemplating itself. Therefore, he is without knowledge of anything imperfect (i.e., everything else), and, hence, is indifferent toward man and the world.

As George Abernethy sums it up:

> Such a theology is not religious in the usual sense of the term. It is inconsistent with divine providence, for Aristotle's God does not know or care about the universe. Such a god is not an object of worship or mystical union. It performs a metaphysical function for a system which requires an unmoved mover, a completely actual and fully realized form. It makes the world an intelligible order. And in a sense it also determines Aristotle's account of man's end, for if God's happiness lies in thinking, so does man's.[22]

As important as his metaphysical views is Aristotle's understanding of the human *telos*. The question of human purpose was an ancient one already in Aristotle's time. But Aristotle's reflections give the problem a clear focus and provide an answer that continues to influence Western thought.

21. For discussions of Aristotle's Prime Mover or Unmoved Mover, see Jones, *History of Western Philosophy,* 192–94; Copleston, *History of Philosophy,* 1.2:56–59; Thomas, *Religious Philosophies,* 34–37.
22. G. L. Abernethy and T. A. Langford, *Introduction to Western Philosophy: Pre-Socratics to Mill* (Belmont, Calif.: Dickenson, 1970), 54.

For Aristotle, every substance, every class, serves a unique function; everything has its own entelechy, or contains within itself its peculiar and particular end. This end is a good that is unique to each class (its formal cause), and which it has the potential to fulfill. When it has actualized this potential, then its good has been achieved; its *telos* has been reached; its final cause has been realized.

What, then, is the unique cause, the unique good and end that man is meant to achieve? Man's chief and highest end is to achieve *eudaimonia,* well-being or true happiness. But *eudaimonia* can be achieved only to the extent that one rightly discerns what the human aim is and, correspondingly, lives it out or fulfills it.[23]

What is this highest aim? For Aristotle, it is the life of reason, an activity of the soul. It is a life pursued under the dictates of rationality. But reason contains a twofold polarity: a practical and a cognitive dimension. Practical reason dictates that one should lead a virtuous life, free of excess and defect. Hence, the cardinal virtues of wisdom, courage, moderation, and justice are practical. In doing them one experiences *eudaimonia*; one fulfills the human aim.

But the end of man is not simply virtuous activity. The human aim is also to think. Man is both an active and a reflective creature. He desires to know; he cannot help but ask questions. And what he desires most to know is the truth. Thus man is lifted toward the divine, where truth contemplates itself, eternally and without interruption.

And, so, the Prime Mover, without knowing or caring about it, inspires man to attain his highest aim. This is strictly a human striving—there is no divine *sustentatio, concursus,* and *gubernatio.* It is an aim, a "good," a *telos,* neither willed nor blessed by the divine. What happens to mankind is entirely a human problem. What man does with his life and intelligence, neither of which (in contrast to Plato's Craftsman) God willed or created, is entirely a human matter. Men seek to interpret the mystery of their *telos* with no "voice" to guide them from above or beyond history.

Accordingly, the entire Aristotelian anthropology is an outstanding example of the modern attitude that regards the mystery of human existence, as well as its destiny, as a problem to be solved by each individual. It is a problem to be solved on empirical grounds, without the consolation of metaphysical systems or theological foundations to shed light on the profoundest and potentially most rewarding question of all. And that is the question involving the meaning of human existence vis-à-vis the reality of the living God.

23. For excellent analyses of Aristotle's understanding of the human *telos,* see Jones, *History of Western Philosophy,* 218–34; Copleston, *History of Philosophy,* 1.2:74–91.

Stoicism

The Early Stoics

The early Stoic understanding of the providence of God is inseparable from the school's perception of reality. According to Zeno's ablest successors, Cleanthes and Chrysippus, two principles underlie and constitute reality—an active principle and a passive principle.[24] These two principles are material in being and form a single whole. According to Copleston, the passive principle is something akin to "matter devoid of qualities," while the active principle is "immanent Reason or God."[25]

As Copleston explains, beauty in nature attests to the presence of a principle of thought in the universe. This presence or principle is the logos or God, who, in his wisdom or providence, has arranged everything for the good of man. Since man, who is the highest phenomenon of nature, possesses consciousness, then (arguing from what is true of the universal to what must be true of the particular—as the reverse of this is considered invalid) nature itself, which is greater than the part, must possess consciousness. Hence, God possesses consciousness and becomes the consciousness of the world.

At the same time, God is also the source of nature and of its baser elements. Thus God is the soul of the universe while the universe is his body. As the soul of the world, God is the logos, or the active principle "which contains within itself the active forms of all things that are to be, these forms being the *logoi spermatikoi*."[26] Through these active forms all things subsequently come into being.

To this concept of God and the world, the Stoics added their doctrine of the universal conflagration. God both forms the world and takes it back into himself. Thus "there is an unending series of world-constructions and world-destructions"[27]—a kind of protoscientific recurring "big bang."

This concept of nature as both constituting and regulating all things through its active and passive principles inevitably raises questions about causation and free will, or determinism and human freedom. In such a tightly interconnected world, in what sense, if any, are events sufficiently "free" from the causal series to allow for chance or choice, or, as in the case of human beings, freedom to will and act otherwise?

---

24. See Cicero's summation in *De Natura Deorum,* bk. 2, trans. by H. Rackham, Loeb Classical Library (Cambridge: Harvard University Press, 1970), 212. [Further references to *De Natura Deorum* are to this edition.]

25. See Copleston, *History of Philosophy,* 1.2:132.

26. Ibid., 133.

27. Ibid.

A. A. Long in *Hellenistic Philosophy*[28] explores this problem and argues that the Stoics were the first philosophers to maintain, in any systematic way, the law of universal causation. This position is mirrored in many of their statements, such as the following:

> Prior events are causes of those following them, and in this manner all things are bound together with one another, and thus nothing happens in the world such that something else is not entirely a consequence of it and attached to it as cause. . . . From everything that happens something else follows depending on it by necessity as cause.[29]

As Long explains, the presupposition of Stoic determinism is the conviction that every event has its set of causes. In other words, there are no uncaused events. Hence, "chance is simply a name for undiscovered causes."[30] Furthermore, since the logos is all-pervasive, then the logos or nature is both the final and immanent intelligent director behind all events or all antecedent causes. Hence nothing is without a cause or falls outside of nature or God's province.

While maintaining a rigorous determinism, the Stoics also espoused divine providence, by which they clearly meant nature's capacity to bring about good in spite of physical and moral evil. Chrysippus was especially intrigued by this problem and was one of the first philosophers to explore the ramifications of causation in any depth. He did so by making a distinction between external and internal causes. A rolling drum requires a causative agent to set it in motion, but it rolls only because of its intrinsic shape. This means that "every natural substance has a structure which is a causal component of anything predicable of it. In order for anything to act some external stimulus is required. But the manner in which a natural substance reacts to such a stimulus is necessarily determined by its intrinsic structure."[31]

If this theory accounts for physical causation, what is one to make of human freedom or the human possibility of responding to the causal series? Chrysippus sought to resolve this problem by distinguishing between external stimuli and the mental response to them. For Chrysippus, any deliberate act is a combination of an external impression and an internal response. One's internal response is automatically subject to universal

28. A. A. Long, *Hellenistic Philosophy: Stoics, Epicureans, Sceptics* (London: Duckworth, 1974).

29. Cited by Long, *Hellenistic Philosophy*, 164.

30. Ibid.

31. Ibid., 166.

causation, insofar as one's character has been determined by one's heredity and environment. Hence, one is free to assent to an external stimulus but not really free to act. All-pervasive reason or the all-pervasive
logos has already determined both external events and internal capacities.
As Chrysippus explains:

> Since the management of all there is directs things in this way, it is necessary
> that we should be as we are, whatever that may be, whether we are sick,
> contrary to our own natural condition, or maimed, or have become scholarly
> or artistic. . . . Consistently with this we shall speak in the same way about
> our virtue and our wickedness and in general about our crafts or lack of
> them . . . for no detail, not even the smallest, can happen otherwise than in
> accordance with universal nature and her plan.[32]

If nature or God so orders all things, then how is one to account for
physical and moral evil? Chrysippus acknowledges that both exist, but he
denies that either undermines nature's providence or capacity to achieve
the harmonious good of the whole. With respect to physical evil, Chrysippus explains:

> The evil which occurs in terrible disasters has a rationale (logos) peculiar to
> itself; for in a sense it too occurs in accordance with universal reason, and
> so to speak, is not without usefulness in relation to the whole. For without
> it there could be no good.[33]

In other words, any event must be seen *sub specie aeternitatis*. Or as
Long observes: "If Nature's providence is all-embracing then any event
which causes injury or suffering has to be interpreted as something which,
if all the facts were known, would be recognized as beneficial by rational
men."[34] Long, however, is somewhat jolted by this Stoic optimism and
offers the following criticism:

> This optimistic attitude towards natural events, no matter how terrible they
> may seem, is one of the least palatable features of Stoicism. It is one thing
> to say that human vision is limited, unable to grasp the full cosmic perspec-
> tive. But even at its noblest, . . . there is something chilling and insensitive
> about the Stoic's faith that all will turn out well in the end.[35]

32. Cited by Ernst Niermann in the *Encyclopedia of Theology: The Concise Sacramentum
Mundi*, ed. by Karl Rahner (London: Burns & Oates, 1975), 101f.
33. Cited in Long, *Hellenistic Philosophy*, 169.
34. Ibid., 170.
35. Ibid.

If physical evil has its rationale and place within the whole, what is one to make of moral evil? Does it, too, have its place? Chrysippus answers by claiming that no act in itself is evil. It is only the intention of the agent that makes it evil.[36] To be sure, the logos cannot be made to be the source or cause of evil. But what the logos allows for is both the logical truth of and the ontological reality of opposites. (This follows from the Stoic conviction that the real is rational and the rational real.) Contraries logically imply one another. Truth implies falsehood, pain pleasure, courage cowardice, justice injustice. Otherwise, contraries would be empty or meaningless. Hence, contraries are part of the logos and, accordingly, contribute to the causal series.

It is, thus, to this principle of contraries that Chrysippus appeals in order to justify his distinction between external causation and the intentions of agents.[37] Nature or the logos (God) does not will evil. But evil is always there as a definite (truly real in the Stoic sense) possibility to which anyone may give assent. Therefore in giving assent, one is nonetheless willing and acting in a manner dictated by the laws of universal nature. Thus, although nature does not will morally evil acts, these acts can be harmonized with the logos and the whole.

Copleston both praises and faults this view:

> If the possession of moral freedom is a good thing for man and if it is better to be able to choose virtue freely (even though it implies the possibility of vice) than to have no freedom at all, no valid argument against Divine Providence can be drawn from the possibility, or even the existence, of moral evil in the world. But in so far as Chrysippus implies that the presence of virtue in the universe necessarily implies the presence of its contrary, . . . he is implying what is false, since human moral freedom, while involving the *possibility* of vice in this life, does not necessarily involve its actuality.[38]

A. A. Long similarly praises Chrysippus's position.

36. See Copleston, *History of Philosophy,* 1.2:135.
37. Chrysippus states:
   Nothing is more foolish than the opinion of those persons who think that there could have been good things without there being bad things at the same time. Since good things and bad are opposites, they must be set against one another and as it were buttress one another. Of two opposites neither exists without the other. How could there be any conception of justice unless it is an absence of injustice? How could bravery be understood except by the juxtaposition of cowardice, or self-control except by that of license? How could there be good sense without folly? Why do these foolish men not demand that there should be truth and no falsehood? (From *On Providence*; cited by F. H. Sandbach in *The Stoics* [New York: W. W. Norton, 1975], 105.)
38. Copleston, *History of Philosophy,* 1.2:135f.

In giving man reason Nature makes him, from the perspective of the part, an autonomous agent. The character which a man develops, though it falls under the law of cause and effect, is his own character, not Nature's. For the environment in which a man finds himself he is not responsible. But the way in which a man acts in relation to this environment is attributed to him.[39]

But herein lies a crucial difficulty.

Many of the things which befall a man during the course of his life cannot be isolated from his own intentions. The Stoics often write as if all external circumstances are beyond the individual's power to alter. But if the notion of an appointed life is to be compatible with moral judgment, then it only makes sense to regard a very limited set of circumstances as the dispensation of God or Nature.[40]

Hence, "the desire to attribute everything to a single principle" is what produces a "fundamental incoherence" in Stoic thought.[41]

It is this fundamental incoherence of attempting to unite rigorous determinism with human freedom that also nags aspects of Calvinism and orthodoxy when carried to their logical extremes. For this reason an appreciation of Chrysippus's attempts to harmonize these logically incompatible views sheds light on Reformed efforts to do the same in its own doctrines of the providence of God. Hence, it will be especially necessary to explore the manner in which Calvin approximates this Stoic effort while avoiding its crass pantheism and its justification of the existence or necessity of evil.

Lucius Annaeus Seneca

Chrysippus's view best illustrates the rigor with which an early Stoic explores the problem of causation and human freedom and in doing so brings substantive philosophical inquiry to bear on the subject of the providence of God. On a more popular and morally relevant level is Seneca's essay entitled *De Providentia*. It too is important from the standpoint of Reformed interest in God's providence as conceived by the Stoics. It offers a clearly defined and bold theodicy with a minimum of philosophical jargon. Its temper and call to patience and courage is appealing, and, one might even dare argue, surfaces again in Calvin's call to these virtues.

39. Long, *Hellenistic Philosophy,* 183.
40. Ibid.
41. Ibid., 182.

Seneca subtitles his work "Why, though there is a Providence, some Misfortunes befall Good Men."[42] Seneca does not doubt that providence presides over the universe, and that God concerns himself with man. But he opens with a passage in which he first asserts the centrality of universal law. He affirms that the world is ruled by an eternal law, that its regularity is a governed one, and that nothing moves at random or by chance (a denial of Epicurean physics). Even "irregular" phenomena (such as tempests, volcanic eruptions, and tremors) occur because of a reason and are the result of "special causes."[43]

Having established the centrality of such an all-pervasive law, Seneca next addresses the question of how evil can befall good men in a world governed by such rational, ordained causes. He answers, in essence, that adversity is necessary for character building, without which the human race would be less than human.[44] In fact, it is God's will that the world should be this way: "Toward good men God has the mind of a father, he cherishes for them a manly love, and he says, 'Let them be harassed by toil, by suffering, by losses, in order that they may gather true strength.' "[45] And what is the most worthy spectacle the divine can behold as God "contemplates his works"? Seneca answers: "A brave man matched against ill-fortune, and doubly so if his also was the challenge."[46]

As a consequence of the necessity of adversity, "no evil can befall a good man."[47] Evil is only apparent. For hardships and adversities contain a twofold benefit in disguise. Hardships are opportunities "for the good of the persons . . . to whom they come" (occasions for character building), as well as opportunities "for the good of the whole human family" (occasions for civilization building). These hardships "happen by destiny" and "rightly befall good men by the same law which makes them good."[48] In other words, "good" implies both strength of character and moral virtue, and neither is possible in the absence of free choice and demanding existential conditions.

Hence, one ought wisely, patiently, courageously, and willfully accept whatever Fortune and Fate (as encountered in the causal nexus of the world) dispose. In fact, one ought to consider it a divine favor to be rigorously tested. For in doing so, one has the enviable opportunity "to

42. Seneca, *De Providentia,* in *Seneca: Moral Essays,* trans. by John W. Basore, Loeb Classical Library (Cambridge: Harvard University Press, 1963), 1:3.
43. Ibid., 5.
44. Ibid., 7ff.
45. Ibid., 9–11.
46. Ibid., 11.
47. Ibid., 7.
48. Ibid., 15.

achieve the highest possible virtue. . . ."[49] As Seneca explains: "God hardens, reviews, and disciplines those whom he approves, whom he loves."[50]

Accordingly, the purpose of human life is character building. It is a purpose willed and blessed by God. And for character building to be possible, adversity and antagonists are essential to the structure of the universe. Otherwise, man could never realize his highest and happiest potential. God is the immanent *causa* behind all this, the supreme tester and judge, all in one. Seneca offers his own summary of this position in the following statement:

> Fate guides us, and it was settled at the first hour of birth what length of time remains for each. Cause is linked with cause, and all public and private issues are directed by a long sequence of events. Therefore everything should be endured with fortitude, since things do not, as we suppose, simply happen—they all come. Long ago it was determined what would make you rejoice, what would make you weep, and although the lives of individuals seem to be marked by great dissimilarity, yet is the end one—we receive what is perishable and shall ourselves perish. Why, therefore, do we chafe? Why complain? For this were we born. Let Nature deal with matter, which is her own, as she pleases; let us be cheerful and brave in the face of everything, reflecting that it is nothing of our own that perishes.
>
> What, then is the part of a good man? To offer himself to fate.[51]

Marcus Tullius Cicero

While Cicero accepted the Stoic doctrine of the providence of God, he rejected the notion of Fate or necessity. With regard to the providence of God, he defended the Stoic view against Epicurean attacks and the skepticism of the Academics. Book 2 of *De Natura Deorum* is dedicated to this defense. It is a lengthy argument in which Cicero affirms the following broad Stoic tenets:

1. The universe is of higher worth than any of its parts.
2. The ruling principle of the universe is reason or Logos (which is seen in all its parts).
3. The world is also a living being (inasmuch as the parts possess life and, if the universal is greater than the particular, then the world must also possess sensation or life).

49. Ibid., 27.
50. Ibid., 29.
51. Ibid., 37–39.

4. "The world is a living being and possesses sensation, intelligence, and reason; and this argument leads to the conclusion that the world is god."[52]
5. The world is governed by a providential prudence.

Such being the nature of the world-mind (*mens mundi*), it can therefore correctly be designated as prudence or providence . . . ; and this providence is chiefly concentrated upon three objects, namely to secure for the world, first, the structure best fitted for survival; next, absolute completeness; but chiefly, consummate beauty and embellishment of every kind.[53]

In another series of arguments, Cicero articulates additional specifics of the doctrine. He insists that "the world and all its parts were set in order at the beginning and have been governed for all time by divine providence."[54] As a consequence:

1. The world continues to be governed by a divine rational ordering (as seen in the world's capacity to perpetuate itself).
2. The world exists expressly for the purpose of serving gods and men.
3. Man, above all, manifests this divine ordering, both in his physical form and mental abilities, by virtue of which his "mind arrives at a knowledge of the gods, from which arises piety, . . . justice and the rest of the virtues," and ultimately "happiness" (*vita beata*).[55]
4. The providence of God is "extended to individuals." For the gods not only care about humanity but "individual citizens"[56] as well.

Cicero makes it quite clear, however, that his espousal of these tenets is limited. He will not press the system for a hard determinism. The world of causal nexus is always open. Hence, victims of misfortunes and life's inevitable struggles are not to be viewed as objects of divine hatred or neglect; rather, "the gods attend to great matters; they neglect small ones."[57]

Cicero pursues this matter in two additional works: *De Divinatione* and *De Fato*. In both Cicero rejects Stoic necessity in favor of a modified determinism. Of especial interest in *De Divinatione* is the fact that Cicero rejects the claim that God has foreknowledge of future events. He argues that if God knows in advance all future events then these events must occur as God foresees them. Otherwise, God's capacity as a perfect

52. *De Natura Deorum*, bk. 2, 167.
53. Ibid., 179.
54. Ibid., 195–97.
55. Ibid., 270–71.
56. Ibid., 281.
57. Ibid., 283.

knower of future events is compromised. But if God does know everything that is to happen, then nothing can happen other than what he foresees, which, in Cicero's mind, compromises human freedom.

This problem is obviously a relevant one. Augustine cites it in *The City of God* and offers a solution to it. The question reappears in medieval and Reformed theologies, and, most recently, has been scrutinized by process theologians, who (with Cicero, but for different reasons) consider omniscience a "mistaken" attribute of God.

Cicero's *De Fato* is significant, because in this treatise he wrestles with the problem of causation and argues for what contemporary philosophers would call a form of "soft determinism." This principle may be defined as Adolf Grünbaum states it: "Rules for managing individuals and nations can be based only on causal laws which tell us that *if* such and such is done, it is likely that the outcome will be thus and so. . . ."[58] Note how open-ended this form of causation is. Grünbaum elaborates: "Determinism should never be identified with the prescientific and primitive doctrine of fatalism. The fatalist says that regardless of what we do, the outcome will be the same. By contrast, the [soft] determinist says that *if* we do such and such, *then* the effect will be thus and so."[59] This is, in essence, Cicero's position.

Cicero asks, "What is the point then of harping on fate, when everything can be explained by reference to nature and fortune without bringing fate in?"[60] Cicero appeals to the example of environment; it may influence a person's personality but cannot account for all of a person's choices: "For it does not follow that if differences in men's propensities are due to natural and antecedent causes, therefore our wills and desires are also due to natural and antecedent causes, for if that were the case, we should have no freedom of the will at all."[61]

All this leads Cicero to challenge the Stoic concept of Fate or necessity. What his predecessors have championed, thinks Cicero, is not a principle of necessity, but a principle affirming that events are rightly the results of antecedent causes, but not necessarily the results of unalterable, predetermined *causae*.

Cicero is quite willing, therefore, to concur with Chrysippus that "all things that take place take place by precedent causes." But what he is

58. Adolf Grünbaum, "Causality and the Science of Human Behavior," *American Scientist* 40 (1952):666; emphasis added.

59. Ibid., 671; emphasis added.

60. From *De Fato*, in *Cicero: De Oratore, Book III*, trans. by H. Rackham, Loeb Classical Library (Cambridge: Harvard University Press, 1982), 199.

61. Ibid., 203.

not prepared to grant is that "all events are caused by fate."[62] All events have their causes, but some of these causes involve the free choices of men and many others are due to the random possibilities of fortune.

This, then, is what is meant by claiming that Cicero favors a form of soft determinism. Barth's insistence that man is a *causa* as well as a recipient of *causae* has obvious affinities with Cicero's modified Stoicism. The same is true of Brunner's emphasis on the divine "Orders," by means of which God sustains and governs his universe. This observation is offered not in any pejorative sense; rather, it is meant as a humble acknowledgment that a Reformed theology can appreciate and build on the philosophical insight of a system which correctly recognizes that any rejection of the providence of God, or unwillingness to think critically about the problem of causation and freedom, does more to beg the question of the meaning of our existence than to solve it.

Epicureanism

Finally, a word about Epicurean thought is in order. Its perception of the divine and the divine's impingement on the world was adamantly opposed by the Stoics.[63] More significantly, Epicurean physics, on which the whole system rests, is sufficiently close in outlook to modern, nontheistic, empirical interpretations of the world so as to allow Epicurean view to be held up as a paradigm, or an unacceptable alternative that Reformed theologies must repudiate.

Epicurean theology is based on the atomism of Democritus. Epicurus accepted this premise and, hence, taught that the world consists of an infinite number of atoms (material in form) that are falling freely through the universe, through an infinite, boundless space.[64] To avoid having to acknowledge any rational or ordering principle (Cicero's charge[65]), Epicurus accepted the hypothesis that of their own accord some of these atoms swerved and thus initiated the cause-and-effect system that rules mechanical causation. Hence, the world at best is a transitory cluster of a fortuitous collection of atoms, that will break up in time to form other clusters and worlds. These, too, will be equally devoid of any plan, purpose, or ordering principle (logos). Gods exist but are also random col-

---

62. Ibid., 217.

63. See Cicero's attacks against Epicurean physics in both *De Natura Deorum* and *De Fato*.

64. See "Epicurus to Herodotus," in *The Stoic and Epicurean Philosophers*, ed. by Whitney J. Oates (New York: Modern Library, 1940), 3–15.

65. *De Natura Deorum*, bk. 1, 67.

lections of extremely fine atoms. Moreover, the gods are neither concerned with the universe nor direct the system of mechanical causation. They exist in a state of bliss, ignorant of and indifferent to man, and indwell the *intermundia,* or the empty spaces between clustered worlds. Cicero finds this position both philosophically contradictory and absurd. Perhaps Tennyson in his poem *Lucretius* says it best:

> The Gods, who haunt
> The lucid interspace of world and world,
> Where never creeps a cloud, or moves a wind,
> Where never falls the least white star of snow,
> Nor ever lowest roll of thunder moans,
> Nor sound of human sorrow mounts to mar
> Their sacred everlasting calm![66]

It should be quite apparent, therefore, that Epicurean theology has no place for divine causation or divine providence of any kind. Its acceptance of the gods, or its acknowledgment of a divine principle, is purely academic or pragmatic (for all men believe in the gods and every city-state has its patron deities). Thus, the fate of the world and the fate of men are subject to irrational forces and purposeless events. Hence, man's only hope is to pursue a life in which he prudently selects among pleasures and attempts to cultivate the higher potentials of his humanity (which is of course absurd, inasmuch as such a system lacks a normative principle for designating anything as "higher").

That such a mode of thought is equally operative in the modern world is common knowledge. That it vies for man's allegiance is equally obvious. But what does not seem to be grasped is that this mode of thinking is as vulnerable as Epicureanism was and for almost identical reasons. For, as the Stoics saw, any system of thought that attempts to find a meaning for human existence while denying a meaningful cause in the universe is self-contradictory.

---

66. Quoted by Long, *Hellenistic Philosophy,* 48.

Chapter Four

Late Classical and Patristic Formulations

The bridge between the Graeco-Roman world and the early centuries of Christian theology is a broad one. It was broad enough for many church fathers to carry over, in a metaphorical sense, carts laden with philosophical concepts. Many of these they would adopt (e.g., ideas of order, harmony, perfection, and the unchangeableness of God). Others they would reject (e.g., polytheistic concepts of God, Epicurean physics and chance, the Stoic identification of God with the world-soul or cosmos, and the eternity of matter.) Still others they would modify to suit their specific doctrines (e.g., ideas of the logos, nous, or reason, ideas of the soul and being, as well as the four cardinal virtues [wisdom, courage, moderation, and justice]).

Philo

In the first century A.D., no finer bridge existed between the Hellenistic world and Judaism than that both constructed and crossed by Philo Judaeus of Alexandria. His attempt to harmonize the Torah of Moses with Platonic and Stoic philosophy is a perspicuous characteristic of his system. But in spite of this continuity with Hellenistic philosophy, Philo emphasizes the transcendence of God and makes the logos (mind or reason) subordinate to God while assigning Platonic ideas to the logos.[1] This

---

1. See *De Opificio Mundi*, in *Philo*, trans. by B. H. Colson and G. H. Whitaker, Loeb Classical Library (Cambridge: Harvard University Press, 1971), 1:9, 15, 115. [All further references to Philo's works are to this series, and will be cited by treatise, volume (Loeb), and page number(s).]

allows him, therefore, to urge his readers to live in conformity with the logos while giving their highest allegiance to the logos-giver, God.

For Philo, one should always choose the rational over the irrational and a disciplined and orderly life over an undisciplined and disorderly life; yet ultimately transcending the rational is the ineffable God of revelation. Philo minces no words in propounding this distinction:

> So then it is best to trust God and not our dim reasonings and insecure conjectures: "Abraham believed God and was held to be righteous" (Gen. xv. 6); . . . because to trust God is a true teaching, but to trust our vain reasonings is a lie.[2]

> For wisdom is a straight high road, and it is when the mind's course is guided along that road that it reaches the goal which is the recognition and knowledge of God.[3]

It is this simultaneous continuity and discontinuity with ancient thought that distinguishes Philo's mediating position. This contrast between the Greek and biblical understanding of reason and reason's place in the cosmos was not actually discerned by the Greeks until the time of Galen (ca. . . 130–200).[4] For, as Albrecht Dihle explains, since the time of Parmenides, reason and being, nous and ontos, had been perceived as identical. Hence, there was no need to posit a reality higher than reason or "no need for assuming behind or apart from the entirely rational programming of reality a will of which the impulse or manifestation is unpredictable."[5] Philo's ineffable One, however, who creates the Platonic ideas as archetypes for all else, is precisely this step "behind or apart from" the rational as the highest ordering principle.

Philo's work on providence, *De Providentia,* is notably brief in comparison with his treatment of other subjects. But, in his other works, Philo sufficiently elaborates on God's foreknowledge and the free will/determinism controversy to permit us to reconstruct his general position regarding the providence of God.

In *De Providentia,* Philo's concern is simply to establish the fact that providence does exist, in spite of evil. In other words, this little treatise is an examination of the problem of theodicy.

Philo is asked by his interlocutor, a certain Alexander, to justify provi-

---

2. *Legum Allegoria,* 1:457.
3. *Quod Deus Immutabilis Sit,* 3:83.
4. See Albrecht Dihle, *The Theory of Will in Classical Antiquity* (Berkeley, Calif.: University of California Press, 1982), 1.
5. Ibid., 2.

dence in light of the fact that "the worst and vilest of men" rise to power, wealth, and success, "while the lovers and practisers of wisdom . . . are almost universally poor. . . ."[6] In reply, Philo adopts the following position:

1. God both governs and guards, in accordance with the immutable laws of nature (i.e., the created logos), the whole heaven and earth.
2. God, in accordance with his merciful nature and loving-kindness, is patient with the vile in the hope that they will eventually seek reformation.
3. God, whose tribunal is to be preferred to man's, nonetheless, makes effective use even of tyrants, using them to punish the wicked.[7]
4. God, from time to time, allows earthquakes and tempests to occur in order to promote virtue (the Stoic character-building motif).
5. Such natural phenomena must always be seen *sub specie aeternitatis*. That is, God's ordering of the cosmos is for the good of all, which occasionally may cause discomfort for a few. This is simply the way nature works. No fault, thereby, need be attributed to God; God is good and causes no evil.
6. Finally, one must preserve the distinction between primary and secondary causes, or antecedents and their consequences.

Adopting a Ciceronian perspective, Philo explains and concludes:

Earthquakes, pestilence, . . . and the like though said to be visitations from God are not really such. For nothing evil at all is caused by God, and these things are generated by changes in the elements. They are not primary works of nature but a sequel of her essential works, attendant circumstances to the primary. . . .[8]

Secondly providence or forethought is contented with paying regard to things in the world of the most importance, . . . not to some chance individual of the obscure and insignificant kind.[9]

Philo's interest in providence is hardly exhausted, however, by this brief treatment in *De Providentia*. The subject and related themes often occur elsewhere. For example, in his other works, Philo frequently stresses God's omniscience, or forethought and foreknowledge. In each case, the Greek term is either a form of the verb *pronoeō* ("to think of beforehand, to foresee, to care for, or provide for"), or is the noun *pronoia* ("providence, foresight, or forethought"). Philo uses both the verb and the noun to explain his understanding of the divine operation. On the whole, he leans in the direction of making God's providential activity dependent on

6. *De Providentia*, 9:459.
7. Ibid., 485f.
8. Ibid., 493.
9. Ibid., 495.

God's foreknowledge of all events. Philo's central point, however, is that both God's foreknowledge and forethought are compatible with his nature and are inseparable from the way God exercises providential care.

By the term *forethought,* Philo tends to mean that God rightly exercises concern for the cosmos, its maintenance and functions, and its inhabitants. By the term *foreknowledge,* he clearly means that God knows everything that happens—past, present, and future—and governs the world accordingly.

For example, with respect to God's forethought, Philo states: "God also exercises forethought (*pronoei*) on the world's behalf. For that the Maker should care for the thing made is required by the laws and ordinances of Nature. . . ."[10] And he "that has begun by learning these things . . . and that He ever exercises forethought (*pronoei*) for His creation, will lead a life of bliss and blessedness. . . ."[11]

As for God's foreknowledge (i.e., in the sense of foreseeing events), Philo explains:

> For a mere man cannot foresee the course of future events, or the judgments of others, but to God as in pure sunlight all things are manifest. For already He has pierced into the recesses of our soul, and what is invisible to others is clear as daylight to His eyes. He employs the forethought (*promētheia*) and foreknowledge (*pronoia*) which are virtues peculiarly His own, and suffers nothing to escape His control or pass outside His comprehension. For not even about the future can uncertainty be found with Him, since nothing is uncertain or future to God.[12]

In addition to these themes, Philo also explores the free will/determinism problem, inherited from the Stoic-Epicurean debates that were still being waged. Again, his position is similar to Cicero's, insofar as he maintains a soft-deterministic connection between antecedent causes and their effects, while insisting on man's freedom of choice, unimpaired by any antecedent causes. Philo adopts this view as the only one capable of holding mankind morally accountable before God:

> For it is mind [nous] alone which the Father who begat judged worthy of freedom, and loosening the fetters of necessity (*tēs anankēs*), suffered it to range as it listed, and of that free-will (*dōrēsamenos*) which is his most peculiar possession and most worthy of His majesty gave it such portion as it was capable of receiving. For the other living creatures . . . have been com-

10. *De Opificio Mundi,* 1:137.
11. Ibid.
12. *Quod Deus Immutabilis Sit,* 3:25.

mitted under yoke. . . . But man, possessed of a spontaneous and self-determined will, whose activities for the most part rest on deliberate choice, is with reason blamed for what he does wrong with intent, praised when he acts rightly of his own will. . . . But the soul of man alone has received from God the faculty of voluntary movement, and in this way especially is made like to Him, and thus being liberated, as far as might be, from that hard and ruthless mistress, necessity, may justly be charged with guilt, in that it does not honour its Liberator.[13]

On the whole, then, Philo retains concepts dear to both the Platonists and Stoics. But he reworks them so as to subordinate the rational in the universe to the merciful in the nature of God. Thus God, whose goodness and grace transcend the power of the logos or nous, alone provides the true ordering principle behind the universe. This principle, hidden in the ineffable depths of God ("He is not apprehensible even by the mind, save in the fact that He is"[14]), can only be accepted and trusted in faith. But far from being an arbitrary principle, it is always governed by God's goodness and grace. "So that if anyone should ask me what was the motive for the creation of the world, I will answer what Moses has taught, that it was the goodness of the Existent, that goodness which is the oldest of His bounties and itself the source of others."[15] "For 'God' is the name of the goodness pertaining to the First Cause, and is so used that thou mayest know that He hath made the inanimate things also not by exercising authority (*exousia*) but goodness. . . ."[16] For "the righteous man exploring the nature of existence makes a surprising *find,* in this one discovery, that all things are a *grace* of God. . . ."[17]

Hence, we see how Philo proves uniquely faithful to his Jewish heritage by maintaining a principle of discontinuity (i.e., God cannot be equated simply with the nous or logos in the world), while at the same time paying homage to the philosophical traditions of his age by grounding God's transcendence in his goodness (echoes of Plato) and perceiving God as the Creator of the logos and the orderly.

Justin Martyr and Irenaeus

Elements of a Christian understanding of the providence of God can be gleaned from almost any of the early Greek fathers. Certainly, nuances

13. Ibid., 33f.
14. Ibid., 41.
15. Ibid., 65.
16. *Legum Allegoria,* 1:349.
17. Ibid., 353; emphasis added.

are to be found in apologetic works (e.g., *Epistula ad Diognetum;* Athenagoras's *Plea*). Owing, however, to the position Justin Martyr has enjoyed as an apologist and as one who frequently draws upon his own training as a Platonist (even commenting about it), his views on the providence of God perhaps best represent early second-century thought.

Justin Martyr

At no point in his writings does Justin actually discuss providence, but throughout his works, he deals with a cluster of related aspects. Four, in particular, attract notice: (1) his anti-Marcion statements; (2) his understanding of the logos; (3) his emphasis on free will; and (4) his references to God's foreknowledge.

Anti-Marcion statements

Second-century Gnosticism posed an ominous threat to Christianity. Its denial of God's direct participation in creation, concomitant with its understanding of matter as evil, and its espousal of vast spiritual distances that separate a lost humanity from a holy God, did much to militate against any sense of God's providential care for *his* world (which it clearly was not) or *his* children (many of whom obviously were not).

Over against Gnosticism, Justin draws upon the teachings of the Old and the New Testaments, as well as the Christian traditions he has received, to argue the contrary. Against Marcion, whom he names explicitly, he reiterates the biblical position and acclaims God as the Creator and Ruler of all. Justin's appellations for God confirm this view: "God the Father of all," "the unchangeable and eternal God, the Creator of all," "all things have been produced and arranged into a world by God."[18] Justin's anti-Marcion statements, however, express his position best: "And, as we said before, the devils put forward Marcion of Pontus, who is even now teaching men to deny that God is the maker of all things in heaven and on earth, . . . and preaches another god besides the Creator of all. . . ."[19] In his struggle against Gnosticism, Justin affirms God's sovereignty as divine Father, Ruler, and Creator of all.

The logos

Justin builds on the concept of the logos to explain how God operates in the universe. In this respect, Justin draws upon his philosophical and

18. See *The First Apology of Justin,* in *The Ante-Nicene Fathers,* ed. by A. Roberts and J. Donaldson (Buffalo: Christian Literature Publishing Co., 1885), 1:166–67, 169. [Unless otherwise noted, all further references to this series will be cited by treatise, *ANF,* volume, and page number(s).]

19. Ibid., 182; see also ibid., 171.

Platonist background to demonstrate that Christianity is both a reasonable and worthy religion, and, in particular, that it witnesses precisely to what the finest philosophers had already come to know and experience about the divine. Hence, like Philo before him, Justin utilizes a mediating motif to emphasize the continuity between the biblical message and the Hellenistic experience of God and of how God functions in the world. Only Justin's aim is hardly apologetic. It is also to clarify, correct, and deepen man's understanding of God and the logos.

To this end, Justin speaks of the logos as "the first-born of God," the very "Logos of God," who "is even God," who was "with God when he created and arranged all things by Him, . . . ordering all things through Him," who was "partially known even by Socrates," because "He was and is the Logos who is in every man," "of whom every race of men were partakers; and those who live reasonably [*meta logou*] are Christians, even though they have been thought atheists."[20] This logos has taken on flesh and become man in Jesus Christ for the sake of the whole human race.

Free will

Justin teaches that God exercises his lordship over creation through his gift of free will to men. Justin underscores the centrality of free will and rejects Stoic necessity:

> In the beginning He made the human race with the power of thought and of choosing the truth and doing right, so that all men are without excuse before God; for they have been born rational and contemplative. . . .[21] Since if . . . all things happen by fate, neither is anything at all in our own power. . . .[22] And again, unless the human race have the power of avoiding evil and choosing good by free choice, they are not accountable for their actions. . . .[23]

In a section reminiscent of Cicero's and Philo's solutions to the free will/determinism controversy, Justin similarly adopts a form of soft determinism in which he maintains that nature, in general, is subject to cause-effect occurrences while man is not. "For not like other things, as trees and quadrupeds, which cannot act by choice, did God make man; for neither would he be worthy of reward or praise did he not of himself choose, but were created for this end."[24]

20. Ibid., 170, 184, 190, 191, and 178, respectively.
21. Ibid., 172.
22. Ibid., 177.
23. Ibid.
24. Ibid.

At the same time, however, Justin rejects any thoroughgoing Stoic position (as did Cicero) that would equate all events with operation of the logos and thereby denigrate any personal acts as one's own, as well as reduce God to the world process, or that would minimize the distinction between good and evil, on the supposition that all events are divine actions. As Justin argues:

> The Stoics . . . maintained that all things take place according to the necessity of fate. . . . [But] if they say that human actions come to pass by fate, they will maintain that God is nothing else than the things which are ever turning, and altering, and dissolving into the same things, . . . or that neither vice nor virtue is anything. . . .[25]

God's foreknowledge

Justin touches on the issue of God's foreknowledge. He understands it to be the means whereby God foresees what actions and choices mankind exercises, in light of which God then distinguishes the elect from the nonelect. Thus God delays the final act of history "until the number of those foreknown by Him as good and virtuous is complete."[26] "For the reason why God has delayed to do this, is His regard for the human race. For He foreknows that some are to be saved by repentance, some even yet that are perhaps not born."[27]

We have, then, in Justin the rudiments of an early Christian perception of the providence of God. It is a position which Gnosticism, on the one hand, and the state's persecution of the church, on the other, have forced him to clarify. It is based, in part, on an idea that he adopted from classical philosophy (i.e., an all-pervading logos), and it displays affinities with a Ciceronian and Philonian rejection of fate. But it is equally founded on biblical revelation, with a christological emphasis at the center.[28]

Irenaeus

It is in the writings of Irenaeus that a more biblical and deliberately constructed statement on the providence of God is formulated. Irenaeus's position is articulated in book 3, chapter 25, of *The Detection and Refutation of False Knowledge,* better known as *Against Heresies.* It is a brief but powerful statement. However, it must be seen in its context to be properly understood.

25. Ibid., 191.
26. Ibid., 178.
27. Ibid., 172.
28. Ibid., 193.

In books 1–3 of *Against Heresies,* Irenaeus describes at some length a
heretical system that he associates with a certain Valentinius and his dis-
ciples. The system is rich in myth and wildly complex. Irenaeus method-
ically explains the role of each of thirty deities (the Aeons, or Pleroma),
the functions of Achamoth (a heretical Christ), and the Demiurge. Irenaeus then rejects this false replacement of the true God of Scripture with
the absurd world of the Aeons, along with its docetic view of Christ. This
"abyss of madness,"[29] as he calls the system, is neither biblical nor a
faithful representation of what the church consistently teaches.

In book 3, chapter 24, Irenaeus recapitulates his arguments. Then, in
chapter 25, he comes to the heart of the issue, which he defines as a
question of the providence of God. If Valentinian Gnosticism were correct, then God would be neither knowable nor present in his universe.
But, on the contrary, what biblical Christianity clearly teaches is that God
is knowable ("not with regard to His greatness, or . . . essence"), but
knowable insofar as God gives himself to be known both in his creation
and by means of his Word, and that he is the unquestionable "Framer and
Maker of this universe, the only true God and Lord of all."[30] Consequently, God's providence, presence in his world, goodness and justice,
and lordship over all may be gratefully and confidently affirmed. First:

> God does . . . exercise a providence over all things. . . . It follows then
> . . . that the things which are watched over and governed should be ac-
> quainted with their ruler; . . . [as] they have understanding derived from the
> providence of God. And, for this reason, certain of the Gentiles, . . . being
> moved, though slightly, by His providence, were nevertheless convinced that
> they should call the Maker of this universe the Father, who exercises a
> providence over all things, and arranges the affairs of our world.[31]

Irenaeus also affirms God's governing presence. This is demonstrated
by the fact that not only does God arrange the affairs of our world, but
"He also gives counsel; and when He gives counsel, He is present with
those who attend to moral discipline."[32] This passage is faintly reminiscent of Socrates' "voice," if not Hesiod's criterion of justice, but in it
Irenaeus espouses the position that wherever humankind lives in accordance with what God has established as moral, then God is not only
present, but is actively governing his world through the "moral sphere."

Irenaeus confirms God's goodness and justice, along with his wisdom.

29. See *Against Heresies, ANF,* 1:315.
30. Ibid., 460.
31. Ibid., 459.
32. Ibid.

Gnosticism divides God, for it separates his goodness from his justice and thereby begs the question of his wisdom. This follows from the Gnostic decision to distinguish between two Gods: the "wrathful" or "judicial" God of the Old Testament, and the God and Father of Jesus Christ in the New. Irenaeus rejects this bifurcation of divinity and sees through its philosophical weaknesses:

> Marcion, . . . by dividing God into two, maintaining one to be good and the other judicial, does in fact . . . put an end to deity. For he that is the judicial one, if he be not good, is not God, because he from whom goodness is absent is no God at all; and again, he who is good, if he has no judicial power, suffers the same . . . , by being deprived of his character of deity. And how can they call the Father of all wise, if they do not assign to Him a judicial faculty?[33]

In the final analysis, however, Irenaeus favors God's goodness over his justice (as did Philo and Plato), anchoring God's principle of motivation in his goodness. "Nor does He show Himself unmercifully just; for His goodness, no doubt, goes on before, and takes precedence." Irenaeus cites two sources to justify his position: Matthew 5:45 and the fact that Plato in the *Timaeus* argues both for God's justice and goodness but establishes "the goodness of God, as the beginning and the cause of the creation of the world" (not Aeons, or Achamoth, or defect, or some other god).[34]

Hence, the one true God of biblical Christianity, whom even the best ancient philosophers were blessed to know, albeit it incompletely, is the Lord, Judge, and Ruler of all. He is the Maker and Framer of the universe.

Irenaeus succinctly and powerfully upholds the providence of God. This section (bk. 3, chap. 25) of *Against Heresies* provides a fitting conclusion to Irenaus's long refutation of Valentinian Gnosticism, with its denial of God's sustentation, accompaniment, and governance of the world.

In *Aganist Heresies*, Irenaeus introduces two additional themes that are also integral to his doctrine of the providence of God: man's freedom of choice and God's foreknowledge.

Irenaeus vigorously maintains that man possesses free will. As he explains, the Scriptures clearly

> set forth the ancient law of human liberty, because God made man a free [agent] from the beginning, possessing his own power, even as he does his own soul, to obey the behests of God voluntarily, and not by compulsion.

33. Ibid.
34. Ibid.

For there is no coercion with God. . . . And in man, as well as in angels, He has placed the power of choice. . . .[35]

Moreover, Irenaeus rejects any concept of fate or predetermination that would assign human goodness or evil to causes external to the human will. Such appeals simply compromise human accountability:

But if some had been made by nature bad, and others good, these latter would not be deserving of praise for being good, for such were they created; nor would the former be reprehensible, for thus they were made [originally]. But since all men are of the same nature, able both to hold fast and to do what is good; and, on the other hand, having also the power to cast it from them and not to do it,—some do justly receive praise . . . ; but the others are blamed. . . .[36]

Irenaeus cites numerous biblical passages in defense of this position, rather than arguing from a philosophical perspective.

Irenaeus then poses an interesting question: "Could not God have exhibited man as perfect from the beginning?"[37] He answers affirmatively but points out that "as [man] was only recently created, he could not possibly have received [perfection], or even if he had received it, could he have contained it, or containing it, could he have retained it."[38] Hence, God has made mankind to "progress day by day," endowing him with the "mental power" to distinguish between good and evil, until in time he "should see his Lord"[39] (something of the character-building motif of Seneca's Stoicism).

This is God's plan for the universe, claims Irenaeus, and this is precisely what the various stages of biblical history, Christ himself, and the apostles show—this movement of God's Spirit, in which God draws mankind toward himself and his glory:

God thus determining all things beforehand for the bringing of man to perfection, for his edification, and for the revelation of His dispensations, that goodness may both be made apparent, and righteousness perfected, and that the Church may be fashioned after the image of His son, and that man may finally be brought to maturity at some future time, becoming ripe through such privileges to see and comprehend God.[40]

35. Ibid., 518.
36. Ibid., 519.
37. Ibid., 521.
38. Ibid.
39. Ibid., 522.
40. Ibid., 520–21.

For Irenaeus, God foreknows all things, and on this basis he distinguishes between the elect and the reprobate. "But God, foreknowing all things, prepared fit habitations for both, kindly conferring that light which they desire on those who seek after the light . . . ; but for the despisers and mockers . . . darkness. . . ."[41]

Hence, we have in Irenaeus a staunch opponent of a Gnosticism that would deny God's lordship over and redemptive presence in his world. Irenaeus perhaps saw this more clearly than Justin. Certainly, Irenaeus debates the issues with greater candor and astuteness and more clearly perceives the theological ramifications at stake. Moreover, rather than relying on a principle of continuity with the classical age, Irenaeus builds his doctrine of the providence of God primarily on biblical sources and addresses the central issues in terms of biblical considerations and categories.

Clement and Origen

As we have seen, Justin and Irenaeus's concepts of divine providence were worked out in conflict with Marcionite and other heretical views. At the same time, Justin and Irenaeus drew upon the Hellenistic ideas of their day to demonstrate the continuity between the message they proclaimed and the truth (logos) pervading the universe.

Clement and Origen, both Alexandrian theologians, also construct their theological positions in opposition to heretical movements and the persecution of the state. But in contrast to the two earlier apologists, they pursue their projects in a manner that draws far more favorably and knowledgeably on classical and Hellenistic sources; their theologies are also more speculative and esoteric in style and substance. These tendencies are understandable, as Alexandria was a major center of philosophical inquiry and instruction, as well as the home of Philo, whose allegorical method of interpreting Scripture inspired, not only Clement and Origen, but many church fathers for generations to come.

Clement

Clement's doctrine of the providence of God can be pieced together only tenuously at best; nevertheless, in books 5–7 of *The Stromata,* Clement articulates sufficient information to enable us to reconstruct his theory of divine providence.

41. Ibid., 523.

First, God is the Creator of the world. It is neither self-originating nor self-existent.[42] Hence, God may be rightly acclaimed as the "Father of the universe,"[43] "God of all, and truly Universal King,"[44] "Father . . . and Maker of all things."[45]

Second, God is universally recognized and known as God; he is "apprehended by all."[46] All the earth's inhabitants are "imbued with the faith of a superior being," "since the most universal of His operations equally pervades all."[47]

Third, God created the world outside of time, for "how could creation take place in time, seeing time was born along with things which exist"?[48]

Fourth, the universe is under God's providence.[49] God exercises this governance through a complex network of means that includes the orders of nature, secondary causes, human cooperation, heavenly administrative agents, free will, God's omniscience and foreknowledge, and the divine Son.

The orders of nature. Clement maintains that God has established "the order of created things," and has commanded that they "should be preserved inviolate,"[50] that is, God has created the orders of nature, which are able to operate, of themselves, in their own right.

Secondary causes. As a consequence of the orders of nature, God now governs through the "medium of secondary causes," in which "the operative power is propagated in succession to individual objects."[51] Or, as Clement explains elsewhere, "He no longer now creates, on account of his having granted once for all to man the power of generating men."[52] Or, as he states again, God rules "through natural sequence and order."[53] Hence, through the natural propagation of the species and the phenomenon of causation, God's providential oversight of creation is carried out.

Human cooperation. God also governs through human cooperation, in which the "exercise of human reason" (as a gift of God to all) produces beneficial effects for humankind.[54]

42. See *The Stromata, ANF,* 2:514.
43. Ibid., 515.
44. Ibid., 474.
45. Ibid.
46. Ibid.
47. Ibid.
48. Ibid., 513–14.
49. Ibid., 514.
50. Ibid., 513.
51. Ibid., 515.
52. Ibid., 584.
53. Ibid.
54. Ibid., 517.

Heavenly administrative agents. In addition, God governs the universe through "administering angels," whom he has appointed to rule over the various kingdoms and nations of the earth. These angels may well have some distant affinity with Hesiod's "watchers of men," but Clement bases their activity and appointment on the Septuagint rendering of Deuteronomy 32:8: "When the Most High divided the nations, as He separated the sons of Adam, He set the bounds of the nations according to the angels of God."[55]

Free will. Central to all of God's governance, however, is free will. For Clement, the human soul is "self-determined."[56] "Self-determining choice and refusal" belong to man.[57] But through the free will of good men, "God's will is especially obeyed," for in their cooperation with the divine, God's gifts are maximized and human life is blessed.[58]

God's omniscience and foreknowledge. Through his omniscience and foreknowledge, God is able to control his universe, preserving its unity and wholeness. But Clement does not explain this idea at length and gives the impression that God's omnipotence is limited by his omniscience, and that his "control" of the universe is at best a passive one:

> For God knows all things—not those only which exist, but those also which shall be—and how each thing shall be. And foreseeing the particular movements, "He surveys all things, and hears all things," seeing the soul naked within; and possesses from eternity the idea of each thing individually. . . . For in one glance He views all things together, and each thing by itself. . . .[59]

The divine Son. It is through the person and work of the logos, however, that God most intimately guides and provides for the entire universe. Drawing upon Paul's Christology in the Book of Colossians, Clement explains that Christ

> is the highest excellence, which orders all things in accordance with the Father's will, and holds the helm of the universe in the best way, with unwearied and tireless power, working all things in which it operates, keeping in view its hidden designs. For from His own point of view the Son of God is never displaced; . . . being always everywhere; . . . seeing all things; knowing all things; . . . scrutinizing the powers.[60]

55. Ibid., 517, 524.
56. Ibid., 527.
57. Ibid., 349.
58. Ibid., 517.
59. Ibid.
60. Ibid., 524.

Moreover, Christ cares for all men (including the Greeks and barbarians) and governs all persons: some through knowledge, some through hope, some through corrective discipline. Consequently, God's providence is in private, in public, and everywhere.

Finally, God has created the world for a specific *telos*—the "growth and perfection of all things"[61] (the Irenaean and Stoic character-building motif) and the assimilation of everything as close to the likeness of God as possible (Platonic motif). Hence, the task of the true believer is to imitate Christ in his own pilgrimage toward the Father as he seeks to become as God-like as possible.

> Subsequently, therefore, the Gnostic at last imitates the Lord, as far as allowed to men, having received a sort of quality akin to the Lord Himself, in order to assimilation to God.[62]

> And as Godliness (*theoprepeia*) is the habit which preserves what is becoming to God, the godly man is the only lover of God, and such will he be who knows what is becoming, both in respect of knowledge and of the life which must be lived by him, who is destined to be divine (*theoi*) and is already being assimilated to God.[63]

To this end, philosophy itself was given to the Greeks and barbarians "as a preparatory discipline for the perfecting which is by Christ."[64]

Thus we have in Clement a synthesis of Christian and Hellenistic motifs. On the positive side is Clement's insistence that God exercises providential care for his world that is rooted in the very orders of nature. However, these orders never totally rule man in a deterministic sense, for the human race is always subject to self-determination. Furthermore, Clement's providential scheme has a christological focus. The divine Son is the primary agent of providential activity. Hence, Clement replaces any abstract, metaphysical concept (i.e., the logos or nous) with the personal presence and power of Christ.

Nevertheless, Clement's position retains some questionable aspects. His emphasis on "assimilation to God" and the esoteric quest to achieve this goal inevitably places man at the center. In particular, it reduces Christ's role from that of being the Savior of the world (the only Mediator between God and man) to that of being an archetype and guide. That is, a gnosis as to how to become God-like has replaced God's grace and election in Christ Jesus. Furthermore, history loses its significance as the

61. Ibid., 515.
62. Ibid.
63. Ibid., 524.
64. Ibid., 516, 525.

theatre of God's activity, for in Clement's system, history exists primarily for the sake of individual souls who are slowly winding their way toward union with the divine. Clement's system even lacks the Stoic sense of "civilization building," for rather than God's logos existing as the bond that unites all rational creatures as brothers, the logos is made subservient to the private quest of the individual soul.

Origen

If Clement's understanding of God's providence is at best tenuous and characterized by a minimum of philosophical analysis and biblical exegesis, Origen's approach is just the opposite. For Origen provides ample philosophical development and striking biblical exegeses in his efforts to justify his views. This accounts for his originality and, in the final analysis, his shortcomings.

Origen's doctrine of the providence of God is far-ranging and, as in the case of Clement's, must be pieced together from a number of sources. In general, Origen's discussion of the world and of the end of the world—subjects that are frequently examined in *De Principiis*—offer the richest sources for recovering his views.

Origen develops, without equivocation, a system of divine providence, or a schema of "dispensations of Divine Providence."[65] These dispensations include all events—from before the creation of the world, to during and since, to what will occur "after the end."[66]

Origen postulates a prefall community of souls who enjoyed a "primal unity and harmony" with God.[67] In this unity, "they existed undoubtedly from the very beginning in those [ages] which are not seen, and are eternal."[68] For reasons owing to each soul's own choosing, a descent took place from a higher to a lower condition. God then created the world as the necessary abode for these fallen souls and populated it with other beings and entities necessary to the order of the whole.[69]

All rational creatures, however, were originally created "of one nature" (i.e., equal in nature), as God cannot be accused of having created some better or higher or more rational than others. Therefore, "every one has the reason in himself, why he has been placed in this or that rank in life."[70] For "it was owing to preceding causes, originating in free-will, that this variety of arrangement had been instituted by God."[71]

65. See *De Principiis, ANF*, 4:268.
66. Ibid.
67. Ibid.
68. Ibid., 342.
69. Ibid.
70. Ibid., 343.
71. Ibid.

Hence, the created world exists as a consequence of the cosmic fall of these rational souls. In fact, Origen argues, this is precisely what the Bible teaches, as a proper exegesis of *katabolē* substantiates. According to Origen, Matthew (24:21) and Paul (Eph. 1:4) both refer to the beginning and the foundation of the world as a *katabolē*, a "casting downwards." Moreover, he finds additional support for this view in a notion preserved in the Septuagint text of Ecclesiastes 1:9–10: "Who shall speak and declare, Lo, this is new? It hath already been in the ages which have been before us."[72]

From the very beginning God foresaw these events. Consequently, having clearly perceived the reasons and causes of each soul's fall, and seeing in advance what kind of world would be required for every soul's restoration, God arranged and appointed things as they exist today. Origen maintains that the world is now a "training" center for all the ranks of souls that indwell it. To aid them, God has provided "powers which were prepared to attend, and serve, and assist them."[73]

The highest of these powers is the only begotten Son of God, whom God has appointed to redeem and assist all souls. This Christ has done, first, by accomplishing in himself that level of obedience and discipline that the Father wills of all, and, second, by calling, subjugating, and embracing all humanity in himself.

Origen insists that the ultimate purpose of creation and of God's activity is the final restoration of all lost souls, that God might be "all in all."[74] Origen cites 1 Corinthians 15:28 as the principal biblical justification for this view.

Such restoration, however, requires time, patience, and "training":

And this result must be understood as being brought about, not suddenly, but slowly and gradually, seeing that the process of amendment and correction will take place imperceptibly in the individual instances during the lapse of countless and unmeasured ages. . . .[75]

Furthermore, God will not use force to accomplish his purposes, but "word, reason, and doctrine," "the best systems of training,"[76] and in a manner "consistent with the preservation of freedom of will in all rational creatures."[77]

The goal of restoration is to become as much like God as possible. For

72. Ibid., 342.
73. Ibid.
74. Ibid., 343.
75. Ibid., 347.
76. Ibid., 344.
77. Ibid.

Origen, the image-of-God motif in Genesis accounts only for man's potential capacities and dignity, whereas the likeness motif refers to man's realized goal or end. As Origen explains: "the *possibility* of attaining to perfection [is] granted him at the beginning through the dignity of the divine image, and the perfect *realization* of the divine likeness [is] reached in the end by the fulfilment of the (necessary) works."[78] Origen, however, stops short of any assimilation or Stoic absorption into the divine. God never becomes "all things." Rather, when the soul is finally purified, God is "all in all"; he totally becomes the measure and standard of all its thought and action.[79]

This restoration will include "all rational souls."[80] "For nothing is impossible to the Omnipotent, nor is anything incapable of restoration to its Creator: for He made all things that they might exist, and those things which were made for existence cannot cease to be."[81] Thus, in time, "all things [principally all rational souls and their transformed bodies] shall be re-established in a state of unity, . . . when God shall be all in all."[82]

Each of the above motifs receives frequent elaboration throughout *De Principiis*. This is especially true of the freewill theme, for like Clement, Irenaeus, and Philo before him, Origen is a stalwart proponent of free will. It is always the use of one's will that determines one's fate, rank, or station in life.[83]

Origen also appeals to God's foreknowledge as a central factor in God's governing and arranging of his world. But Origen is careful to distinguish between God's foreknowledge of an event and the actual causes of that event.

Origen underscores this distinction in *Contra Celsus* and *On Prayer*. He explains that God is always the knower of all choices but never their cause. Thence, on the basis of knowing all choices, he is able to "arrange" the universe into a harmonious whole. God alone sees the whole picture. What we see is veiled and dim. But in time God will grant us an understanding of what presently eludes us:

I think, therefore, that all the saints who depart from this life will remain in some place on the earth, which holy Scripture calls paradise, as in some place of instruction, and, so to speak, classroom or school of souls, in which they are to be instructed regarding all the things which they had seen on earth, and are to receive also some information respecting things that are to

78. Ibid, 344; emphasis added.
79. Ibid., 345.
80. Ibid., 345f.
81. Ibid.
82. Ibid., 347.
83. Ibid., 240, 261, 265, 267, 290, 292, 323, 324, 328.

follow in the future, . . . all of which are revealed more clearly and distinctly to the saints in their proper time and place.[84]

There is much that is appealing in Origen's doctrine of God's providence. There is his uncompromising support of the principle of free will and his insistence on human accountability. Hence, he allows for a world of incalculable interplay and variety.

Moreover, the Creator, through his foreknowledge, has clearly foreseen the full range of this interplay and has arranged his universe to be able to accommodate every possible human action. In addition, God has made the restoration of all the universe's "lost souls" his principal goal, and has committed himself to restoring every single soul. Finally, Origen's speculation about other worlds at least emphasizes the sovereignty of God and his ineffable greatness, as well as his goodness, and sets the finite present into the context of eternity, governed and loved by a God who wills to lose nothing he has made.

At the same time, there is much that is questionable. A prefall community of cosmic souls, whose fall from grace necessitates a created world, makes creation an afterthought; it certainly compromises the biblical emphasis on the goodness of creation and God's profoundest hopes for beings created in his own image. Moreover, the speculative thrust of Origen's theology undermines God's providential activity and purposes.

However, more alarming is Origen's insidious determinism—in spite of his denials to the contrary. Origen's man is hardly free to exercise anything other than a fallen will. If every soul's rank and status in this life has been predetermined by choices and causes in an eternity before time, then is anyone truly free (even in Origen's sense) to achieve a life of one's own here and now? The fall of Adam is paled by this cosmic fall, and history, as in the case of Clement, is made subservient to mystery and myth. Must one not conclude that an unaccountable cosmic perversity among preexistent souls has become the tragic presupposition of creation and providence, rather than God's gracious election in Jesus Christ? Perhaps Origen's novelty at this point serves a purpose often glossed over in philosophy's general fascination with classical, Platonic thought. For the cosmic fall of the soul and its descent is crucial to Plato's world view, in spite of that view's otherwise attractive features.

Plotinus

Philo, Clement, and Origen were three representatives of the Hellenistic, Gnostic, and Middle Platonic environment of Alexandria. Equally rep-

---

84. Ibid., 299.

resentative of that intellectual center, and a contemporary of Origen's, was Plotinus, "the philosopher of our times," as Porphyry describes him.[85] He and Origen both attended lectures by the philosopher Ammonius Saccas, but Plotinus's perceptions far surpass Origen's speculations.

Plotinus's tractates on fate and providence are deliberately constructed treatises, designed to explore the problem of causation and the nature of universal governance. Plotinus's tractate on fate is a critical analysis of causation and of various philosophical positions. Plotinus openly acknowledges one of his working principles—"the assumption that all happens by Cause,"[86] that there are no uncaused events. A second (but unacknowledged) principle is his espousal of free will. In any event, the primary intent of his treatise is to discover that principle which serves as the central cause of all causes, particularly with regard to the destiny of mankind.

Plotinus opens this tractate with a rejection of the Epicurean solution, which denies any originating cause. Plotinus argues that "order, reasoning, and the governing soul" are all manifestations of "order." Their existence cannot be accounted for by appealing to an original "disorderly swirl." Sounding almost modern in his charge, Plotinus asks, "Would anyone pretend that the acts and states of a soul or mind could be explained by any atomic movements?"[87]

Plotinus does, however, adopt the modified Stoic position that causation is an operating principle governing "soulless" entities. Nevertheless, he contends that "material forces . . . can be causes of nothing that is done in the sphere of mind or soul: all this must be traceable to quite another kind of Principle."[88]

Plotinus rejects the Stoic idea of a single logos or nous ("Soul," as he prefers) that permeates the universe and acts as the "Cause of all things and events." Plotinus considers this view "the extremity of determination" and rejects it on two grounds. It destroys any sense of "the mind [being] itself . . . the prime mover" of an individual's act or actions,[89] and it also obliterates distinctions between the One and the many, thereby effacing the unique sense of the self.[90] Plotinus asserts that "each several thing must be a separate thing; there must be acts and thoughts that are

85. See Porphyry's "On the Life of Plotinus and the Order of His Books," in *Plotinus*, Loeb Classical Library (Cambridge: Harvard University Press, 1978), 1:3.

86. See *The Six Enneads*, vol. 17 of Great Books of the Western World, trans. by S. MacKenna and P. S. Page (Chicago: Encyclopedia Britannica, 1952), 78.

87. Ibid., 79.

88. Ibid.

89. Ibid.

90. Ibid., 80.

our own; the good and evil done by each human being must be his own; and it is quite certain that we must not lay any vileness to the charge of the All."[91]

Plotinus dismisses the answer of astrology: that one's destiny is governed by the stars. Heredity and environment are more accurately the determinants, not the constellations. (In fact, his answer has close affinities with Augustine's refutation of astrology.[92])

Plotinus rejects the Stoic *logoi spermatikoi* theory, or the position that seminal reason-forms are the determinants of all causes. He compares this principle to the single Soul pervading all. He calls this theory "the most rigid of universal Necessity." For where it is assumed to be true, then "all our ideas will be determined by a chain of previous causes; our doings will be determined by those ideas; personal action becomes a mere word."[93]

What, then, is the only adequate cause that accounts for the orderliness of nature while preserving the freedom of the will? Plotinus answers: "Soul: we must place at the crest of the world of beings, this other Principle, not merely the Soul [i.e., World-Soul] of the Universe but, included in it, the Soul of the individual: this, no mean Principle, is needed to be the bond of union in the total of things. . . ."[94]

The precise character of the individual Soul, however, is complex; Plotinus endows it with a higher and a lower nature. The higher nature of the Soul is able to lead a well-ordered life, as well as achieve contemplation with the Nous, from which it has emanated, and ultimately contemplation with the One. In this regard, an element of the human Soul has escaped corruption and remains unfallen. But the lower nature of the Soul falls prey to the physical world and its laws of causation. Hence, the lower nature of the Soul is no longer unbounded but becomes subject to passions and the necessity of causal interactions. Consequently, the lower nature of the individual Soul leads to a disorderly life, beset by miseries and mistaken choices: "All things and events are foreshown and brought into being by causes; but the causation is of two Kinds; there are results originating from the Soul and results due to other causes, those of the environment."[95]

Plotinus's two tractates on providence are more difficult to summarize and lack the explicit organization of his treatise on fate. In general, Plo-

91. Ibid.

92. See the *Confessions,* in *Confessions and Enchiridion,* vol. 7 of Library of Christian Classics, trans. by A. C. Outler (Philadelphia: Westminster, 1955), 77–79, 140–42.

93. *Enneads,* 81.

94. Ibid.

95. Ibid., 82.

tinus's aim is twofold. He wants to establish "the process by which . . . individual things . . . have come into being, and how they were made," and how one can justify belief in "a Universal Providence," in light of all that is "undesirable."[96]

Plotinus believes in providence but rejects a creation in time that God deliberately planned. With Aristotle, Plotinus believes in the eternity of the universe. Hence, he must establish a providential principle (in distinction from a God who acts providentially) on a basis quite different from one founded on a Creator who personally creates, sustains, accompanies, and governs his world:

> But since we hold the eternal existence of the Universe, the utter absence of a beginning to it, we are forced, in sound and sequent reasoning, to explain the providence ruling in the Universe as a universal consonance with the divine Intelligence to which the Kosmos is subsequent not in time but in fact of derivation, in the fact that the Divine Intelligence, preceding it in Kind, is its cause as being the Archetype and Model which it merely images, the primal by which, from all eternity, it has its existence and subsistence.[97]

To explain the process by which creation has occurred, or continues to occur, Plotinus appeals principally to the concept of "emanation." He then supplements this concept by appealing to a cluster of secondary but equally significant principles. The latter include the noetic ideas of "contrariety," "multiplicity," "harmony," "gradation," "choice" (i.e., the principle of the individual Soul), and, above all, "necessity."[98]

Necessity is especially important, for, in a manner similar to the Soul's higher and lower nature, it has a twofold function. By "necessity" Plotinus sometimes means nothing more than cause-and-effect interactions; but, more importantly, "necessity" often refers to the metaphysical realization that in the process of emanation itself, as phenomena radiate out from the One, there occurs a kind of "descent" in the perfection and being of entities. What would be interesting to know is if there is any connection between Plotinus's "descent" and Origen's "casting downwards" (*katabolē*). In all likelihood, both positions are direct echoes of Plato's *Timaeus*.

What is true of the world of becoming also sheds light on the problem of evil. Evil, both moral and natural, can be accounted for by appealing to the above principles or noetic ideas. Good, of necessity, implies the possibility of evil, but even more importantly, the process of emanation

96. Ibid.
97. Ibid.
98. See ibid., 83–84, 91.

requires that as entities emanate, matter will always pull things downward. Moreover, the multiplicity of souls, their higher and lower natures interacting with one another, cannot help but engender variety and conflict, as well as noble and ignoble persons with their corresponding noble and ignoble actions. Still, all, of necessity, are parts of the harmonious whole.

> The Souls are in harmony with each other and so, too, are their acts and effects; but it is *harmony* in the sense of a resultant unity built of *contraries*.[99]

> This Universe is good not when the individual is a stone, but when everyone throws in his own voice towards a total *harmony*, singing out a life—thin, harsh, imperfect, though it be.[100]

> Thus, every man has his place, a place that fits the good man, a place that fits the bad. . . .[101]

Hence, for Plotinus, this is the best of all possible worlds. "All stands as well as the nature of things allows." he declares, "Matter dragging [mankind] down." Yet "given the plan as we know it, evil cannot be eliminated and should not be;" for "Matter making its presence felt is still not supreme but remains an element taken in from outside to contribute to a definite total, or rather to be itself brought to order by Reason."[102] "Man is, therefore, a noble creation, as perfect as the scheme allows; a part . . . in the fabric of the All. . . ."[103]

This summary hardly exposes more than the mere tip of the Plotinian iceberg, but it should be apparent why a Reformed theology, and above all a biblical theology, cannot substitute an abstract process for a personal God. Plotinus clearly replaces the God of Abraham, Isaac, and Jacob with a philosophical and purely conceptual principle. More so than ever, history is swallowed up in endless cycles of becoming. All distinctions between good and evil fade, since both are materially equivalent in an order that bestows value on the necessity of (rather than the possibility of) diversity, conflict, and discord. Above all, the soul's fate is entirely in one's own hands; there can be no redeemer in this system. And the soul is ultimately destined for reassimilation into the All.

There is, in Plotinus's system, an incredible accommodation to human wretchedness and misery. Yet, his thought is equally characterized by an

---

99. Ibid., 93; emphasis added.
100. Ibid., 92; emphasis added. Cf. Augustine's *De Gratia Christi, et De Peccato Originali,* bk. 2, chap. 38, where echoes of this Plotinian idea reappear.
101. Ibid., 91.
102. Ibid., 89f.
103. Ibid., 87.

incredible optimism about man's future. It is this residual optimism that is of importance today. As J. M. Rist explains:

> The great difference between Plotinus and Christian thinkers [lies in] Plotinus' optimistic view of human capabilities. When man is produced in the Plotinian world, he is a being capable . . . of returning to his origins, of attaining ὁμοίωσις. He can attain it precisely because part of his soul has not fallen . . . but remains above in the Intelligible World.[104]

> It is essential to realize that here, in the matter of how far man's nature is corrupted, lies a major challenge of Plotinus' thought. It does not greatly matter whether he subsumes knowledge and will under the general heading of νοῦς. . . . It does matter, however, whether his estimation of the divine nature of the human spirit answers to the facts of psychology and morality as we understand them.[105]

In this sense, then, Plotinus's optimism is an argument for the reality of the power and presence of the divine in human life, although its form, as articulated by Plotinus, is unacceptable. To this extent, it also lends credence to Tillich's theme of the "ontological awareness of the unconditional," which he identifies as one of the strengths of Augustine's system.[106]

Augustine's Predecessors

Tertullian

One of the most notable features of Tertullian's theology is its discontinuity with classical and Hellenistic philosophy. In this regard, his affirmations of God's providential oversight are based more on Scripture and deductive reflection on the same than on any quasi common ground between Jerusalem and Athens. Therefore, his approach from its inception precludes the vain conjectures and speculations of the Platonists, Epicureans, and Stoics.[107]

Tertullian's aim is fivefold: (1) to establish God's providence over against Stoic and Epicurean misconceptions; (2) to uphold God's goodness and

104. J. M. Rist, *Plotinus: The Road to Reality* (Cambridge: Cambridge University Press, 1967), 137.

105. Ibid., 138.

106. See Paul Tillich's "Two Types of Philosophy of Religion," *Union Seminary Quarterly Review* (May 1946): 3–13.

107. See Tertullian's *Ad Nationes, ANF,* 3:130, 132–33.

justice against Marcionite criticisms; (3) to defend God's goodness, omniscience, and omnipotence in the light of evil's presence in the world; (4) to argue for the central place that human liberty deserves in God's total plan for mankind's destiny; and (5) to distinguish between God's "active" and "passive" will. In addition, Tertullian appeals to God's foreknowledge as the positive attribute that enables God to govern and guide his universe.

Tertullian poses the question most often raised by Marcion and his followers. It has to do with the goodness, omniscience, and omnipotence of God in light of the reality of evil, a problem that challenges any glib affirmations of divine activity. Tertullian phrases it well:

> If God is good, and prescient of the future, and able to avert evil, why did He permit man, the very image and likeness of Himself, and, by the origin of his soul, His own substance too, to be deceived by the devil, and fall from obedience of law into death? . . . Since, however, it has occurred the contrary proposition is most certainly true, that God must be deemed neither good, nor prescient, nor powerful.[108]

Tertullian's answer is as forthright as the question. He affirms and defends the central role God has bestowed on man by virtue of free will; he also emphasizes God's trustworthiness in holding to what ultimately promotes human welfare and his own purposes.

Tertullian explains that God foresaw that man would fall, yet would not rescind the liberty he had given to man. If he had rescinded it, or had interjected himself into the process in order to prevent the fall, then he would have destroyed man's moral and spiritual integrity, as well as undermined his own purposes in creating human life. That God refused to protect man or to rescind his liberty, accordingly, does more to vouch for God's goodness, wisdom, and omnipotence than it does to mitigate them. God "does not change His judgments through inconstancy or want of foresight, but dispenses reward, according to the deserts of each case with a most unwavering and provident decision."[109] Furthermore, the fact that God responded to man's predicament after the fall with patience and mercy only magnifies God's power and goodness.

Tertullian also examines the active and passive will of God and evaluates their significance. His purpose is to reaffirm the accountability of man as a moral agent and to defend God against a shallow fatalism that would identify God with morally questionable and ambivalent causal events:

108. *Against Heretics, ANF*, 3:300f.
109. Ibid., 315.

> It is not the part of good and solid faith to refer all things to the will of God in such a manner . . . that each individual should so flatter himself by saying that "nothing is done without His permission," as to make us fail to understand that there is a something in our own power.[110]

If the passive will of God is appealed to in order to explain every occurrence, then God is made to will things contrary to his will, and moral distinctions between events simply become irrelevant.

Tertullian carefully distinguishes between what God "permits" and what God "absolutely wills." To equate the two under a theology of "permission" commits one to a naive and irresponsible position. "For, albeit some things seem to savour of 'the will of God,' seeing that they are *allowed* by Him, it does not forthwith follow that everything which is *permitted* proceeds out of the mere and absolute will of him who permits."[111]

Lactantius

Lactantius, one of the fourth century's foremost Latin apologists, loved the Roman culture, so much so that he has been called the "Christian Cicero," and is recognized today as one of the major founders of Christian humanism.[112] He united reason and faith using his rhetorical skills, preconversion erudition, and knowledge of classical philosophy.[113] His aim was to win educated pagans, which, in part, accounts for his numerous citations of classical sources as opposed to his few references to Scripture.

Lactantius views his work as a series of reflections on the providence of God, for "there is nothing which we can discuss that is not at the same time a discussion of providence."[114] Three of his foci warrant attention.

First, in a manner similar to that of the pagan philosophers and church fathers who precede him, Lactantius argues for the providential character of the universe. Again, it is the Epicureans who must be repudiated in favor of the Platonists and Stoics, whose ideas more nearly approximate the biblical truth of God's oversight of creation. For God has "both established all things and . . . governs them with that same power with which He established them."[115] Even now he "sustains them by His spirit and governs them by His power."[116]

---

110. See *On Exhortation to Chastity, ANF,* 4:50–51.
111. Ibid., 51; emphasis added.
112. See the general introduction to *The Divine Institutes,* vol. 49 of The Fathers of the Church, trans. by M. F. McDonald (Washington, D.C.: Catholic University of America Press, 1964), x–xi.
113. Ibid., xii.
114. Ibid., 20.
115. Ibid., 21f.
116. Ibid., 38.

Lactantius uses the word *providence* often in his *Divine Institutes,* but he never specifically defines it. Instead, he provides metaphors and offers broad illustrations of providential action in general. For example, Lactantius draws upon the Stoics' favorite stock illustrations to explain how God rules ("as a lord directs a household, a pilot a ship, a charioteer a chariot"[117]). In general, however, his references to providence are references to the orders of nature and the superb way in which everything fulfills its *telos* while serving the greater good of the whole.[118]

In addition to his support of the providential character of the universe in his *Divine Institutes* is Lactantius's development of the theme in his earliest extant work, *De Opificio Dei (The Workmanship of God).* Here too he vindicates God's providence against the ancient schools that question it, emphasizing man's psychological and physical framework (especially his rationality) as the key manifestation of order and design in the world.

A second focus of Lactantius's theology is the problem of purpose and of how God's providential rule is related to purpose. Lactantius notes that the world was created for the sake of the creatures living in it. And, "in order that these may live . . . , all necessities are provided for them at fixed times."[119] As for man and his *telos,* Lactantius agrees with Plato and the Stoics (mainly Cicero), insofar as the philosophers are right, that "God made the world for man and man for Himself."[120] Man's highest purpose, however, is to win immortality for himself.[121]

Finally, Lactantius grapples with the problem of evil, articulating what some have called a "subordinate dualism,"[122] coupled with the Stoic motif of character building amidst the adversities of life. In all of this, he assumes freedom of the will.

Lactantius explains the presence of evil on the grounds that vice is a necessary condition for virtue (a principle similar to the Plotinian and Chrysippian emphases of "opposites" and "contraries"). This principle is endemic to the order of creation and dictated (if not limited) God's creative act.

Coupled with this is Lactantius's appeal to the Greek concept of probation and its character-building motif. Joining his classical predecessors, Lactantius espouses the virtues of suffering and of winning immortality through one's own conquest of life's barriers:

117. Ibid., 437.
118. Ibid., 480.
119. Ibid., 481.
120. Ibid., 484.
121. Ibid., 484, 486, 487.
122. Ibid., xxii n. 39.

From diverse and repugnant principles, therefore, man has been made as the world itself from light and darkness and from Life and death. The Creator charged these two principles to struggle with each other in man, so that if the Soul should win, which is of God, he may be immortal and live in perpetual light. . . .[123]

[For] reason itself and necessity demand that both goods and evils be set before [man]; goods which he may use, evils which he may shun and avoid. It is for this that wisdom [i.e., free-will] has been given to man. . . .[124]

Of especial interest is Lactantius's personal endorsement of Seneca's *De Providentia*. If anyone seriously wishes to know how providence works, then Lactantius urges him to read Seneca's "wisely and almost divinely" inspired explanation.[125] Lactantius reflects the patristic appreciation, in general, for the Stoic understanding of the activity of the logos (i.e., God) in world events and demonstrates how the church fathers viewed Stoic thought as a *praeparatio evangelica*.

Ambrose

One could argue that Ambrose offers nothing new and that his contribution is too meagre to warrant attention. He also emphasizes the providential character of the universe,[126] champions free will,[127] and wrestles with issues involving God's goodness, omniscience, and omnipotence.[128] All in all, his position is similar to Tertullian's and does not require elaboration here.

What is unique, however, about Ambrose's ideas is the context in which they appear and the use to which he puts them. His major references to the providence of God are preserved in his homilies. Hence, his comments on God's providential activity are guided by Scripture and are intended to uplift, support, and bring moral guidance to his congregation. Granted, he follows Philo's allegorical method, and is fond of typologies; nonetheless, his views are highly practical and free of those esoteric and specu-

123. Ibid., 147.

124. Ibid., 482, 485.

125. Ibid., 387f.

126. See Ambrose's *The Prayer of Job and David,* in *Seven Exegetical Works,* vol. 65 of The Fathers of the Church, trans. by M. P. McHugh (Washington, D.C.: Catholic University of America Press, 1972), 376–85. [Further references to this volume will be cited by *FC*, volume, and page number(s).]

127. See *Jacob and the Happy Life, FC,* 65: 119, 125, 153.

128. See Ambrose's *Paradise,* in *Hexameron, Paradise, and Cain and Abel,* vol. 42 of The Fathers of the Church, trans. by J. J. Savage (New York: Fathers of the Church, 1961), 319f. [Further references to this volume will be cited by *FC,* volume, and page number(s).]

lative interests of the Alexandrian apologists. Moreover, his practical concerns foreshadow Calvin's insistence that theology must edify the church and illumine the Christian life. But, above all, the biblical context of his approach prevents Ambrose from turning his understanding of the providence of God into a purely abstract philosophical system.

Two specific aspects of Ambrose's thought are noteworthy. One is his reiteration of the Bible's emphasis on God's work of *sustentatio*. As Ambrose explains: "The majesty of God holds [the earth] together by the law of His own will, so that what is steadfast should prevail over the void and unstable."[129] Or again, "by the will of God . . . the earth remains immovable. . . . It does not therefore continue to exist because of its own foundations. It does not stay stable because of its own props. The Lord established it by the support of His will, because 'in his hand are all the ends of the earth' (Ps. 95:4)."[130]

Ambrose also emphasizes God's role as Creator. His famous *Hexameron*, or *The Six Days of Creation*, is a valiant defense of the principle of *creatio ex nihilo*. These Lenten homilies demonstrate how the legacy of Plato, Aristotle, the Stoics, and the Epicureans continued to dominate, haunt, and challenge major Christian views. Ambrose makes it sufficiently clear, however, that any theological scheme that accepts the eternity of matter, or allows matter to exist co-eternally with God, raises grave questions concerning God's nature and aims. In the final analysis, the church's primary source for refuting rival claims is and must be Scripture, plus the life of the mind in service to God.

Marius Victorinus

Victorinus is Augustine's link to neo-Platonism as the translator of Plotinus's and Porphyry's treatises. Also, owing to his significance as a philosopher, Victorinus formed an important intellectual link between the late Roman Empire and the Middle Ages.[131] His distinction between Being and existence (the "To Be" of the Godhead versus the "to be" of existents) and his use of Porphyry's triad—*esse* ("to be"), *vivere* ("to live"), and *intelligere* ("to understand")—were influential in shaping not only Augustine's thought (such as his gradations of being in *De Libero Arbitrio*), but also in determining the ideas of Boethius, Bede, Alcuin, Hincmar, and others.[132]

129. *Hexameron, FC,* 42:21.
130. Ibid., 22.
131. See introduction to *Theological Treatises on the Trinity,* vol. 69 of The Fathers of the Church, trans. by M. T. Clark (Washington, D.C.: Catholic University of America Press, 1981), 3.
132. Ibid., 3–18.

Augustine

What Lactantius says about his own work ("there is nothing which we can discuss that is not at the same time a discussion of providence") pertains in large measure to Augustine's work as well. For Augustine, God's activity as an omnipotent Creator extends to everything that is; and there are few theological topics among his writings in which he does not touch on some aspect of the doctrine.

Moreover, as in the case of Justin, Irenaeus, Clement, and Origen, Augustine's work is drafted in response to specific philosophical and religious movements of his day that inevitably determine the foci of his theology and shape much of his thought. Hence, many of Augustine's specific ideas concerning God, evil, free will, and providence are formed in response to Manichean, neo-Platonic, and Pelagian challenges.

In addition, Augustine acknowledges that his theological views are the result of a long process of reflection and development.[133] Hence, any summary of Augustine's doctrine of the providence of God must acknowledge this progression of his thought.

Augustine's interest in the providence of God revolves around four major themes: (1) the freedom of the will; (2) the problem of evil (along with its corollary, God's omnipotence and goodness); (3) the function of God's foreknowledge; and (4) the meaning of creation and history. Quite frequently, the themes are so interconnected as to render the analysis of any one practically impossible apart from an analysis of the others.

Augustine's understanding of the function of the will developed in two overlapping and complex stages, principally before and after Pelagius.

Prior to his conflict with Pelagius, Augustine defended the freedom of the will with an argument common to his Greek and Latin predecessors. The central work of this period is his *De Libero Arbitrio (On Free Will)* although he had explored the subject earlier in a shorter treatise, *De Ordine.*

In *De Libero Arbitrio,* Augustine first of all affirms the necessity of free will. Without it, man sins either by virtue of his nature or contrary to the will of God. Either alternative compromises God's nature, as it erodes both his goodness and his power. Augustine denies that God's foreknowledge of future events is, in any sense, a causal condition of sin or evil. That God foreknows what sinful beings will do does not necessitate their doing it. What they intend to do will certainly come to pass, but not because God's foreknowledge makes it inevitable; rather, it comes to pass because men have elected so to act.

---

133. Augustine's *Retractations* sufficiently indicate this; see also *On the Gift of Perseverance,* chap. 55.

Furthermore, Augustine argues that voluntary sinfulness, or moral evil, far from frustrating God or his purposes, has its fitting place in God's moral order and is, therefore, justly punished. In one of the most celebrated passages of the treatise Augustine explains:

> Neither the sins nor the misery are necessary to the perfection of the universe, but souls as such are necessary which have power to sin if they so will, and become miserable if they sin. . . . Sin and its punishment are not natural objects but states of natural objects, the one voluntary, the other penal. The voluntary state of being sinful is dishonourable. Hence the penal state is imposed to bring it into order. . . . So, whatever a soul may choose, ever beautiful and well-ordered in all its parts is the universe whose Maker and Governor is God.[134]

In still another anti-Manichean and neo-Platonic work (*Enchiridion*), Augustine explores the problem of natural evil and its place in the universe. He concludes that evil, rather than being a "substance," results from "the privation of good."[135] God creates all things good. However, there is an infinite distinction between the triune Creator, who is "immutably good," and all created "mutable goods." Hence, gradations of "greater" and "lesser" goods come into being, each with its proper place:

> All of nature, therefore, is good, since the Creator of all nature is supremely good. But nature is not supremely and immutably good as is the Creator of all. Thus the good in created things can be diminished and augmented. . . .[136]

> Still, each single created thing is good, and taken as a whole they are very good, because together they constitute a universe of admirable beauty [i.e., the idea of harmony].[137]

Augustine even draws upon the principle of opposites or contraries to justify the place of evil in the universe; however, he cites Scripture to support this clearly Greek theme.[138]

The Pelagian debates required Augustine to formulate a critical new understanding of free will and its function in God's providential scheme

---

134. *De Libero Arbitrio*, trans. by J. H. S. Burleigh, in *Earlier Writings*, Library of Christian Classics (Philadelphia: Westminster, 1953), 6:187.

135. *Enchiridion*, chap. 3, 342f.

136. Ibid., chap. 4, 343.

137. Ibid., chap. 3, 342.

138. *The City of God*, bk. 11, chap. 18, in the *Nicene and Post-Nicene Fathers*, ed. by P. Schaff (Grand Rapids: Wm. B. Eerdmans, 1979), 2:215. [All further references to material in this series will be cited by *NP-NF*, volume, and page number(s).]

and activity on mankind's behalf. The older traditional view, so often espoused, that God "elected" souls on the basis of his foreknowledge of their free moral choices would no longer suffice. Clearly for Augustine, this view failed to grasp the radical alteration of human nature that original sin caused and largely denied biblical emphasis on God's grace, election, predestination, perseverance, and the gifts of faith. Hence, toward the end of his career, Augustine argues for a highly active role on the part of the omnipotent Creator, who, out of the mystery of his unsearchable will, graciously elects to redeem some of Adam's posterity, while allowing the rest to suffer the punishments of sin, which they justly incur as a fitting consequence of Adam's fall and in which they continue willfully to concur by virtue of their own free will.

In two works dating from the last years of his life (*On the Predestination of the Saints; On the Gift of Perseverance*), Augustine develops this view with unwavering consistency. In justification of his position, he cites mainly those Johannine and Pauline passages that discuss election and predestination and couples this with insight from Cyprian and Ambrose. He never tires of quoting, first from Cyprian, "that we must boast in nothing, since nothing is our own";[139] and from Ambrose, "our hearts and our thoughts are not in our own power."[140] Consequently, Augustine builds a tight case for an omnipotent, gracious Creator, whose work of predestination provides the conclusive presupposition of providence and, ultimately, the meaning of creation and human history.

> Therefore God chose us in Christ before the foundation of the world, predestinating us to the adoption of children, not because we were going to be of ourselves holy and immaculate, but He chose and predestinated us that we might be so.[141].

> Neither are we called because we believe, but that we may believe.[142]

Between the early years of Augustine's philosophical reflections and his stormy altercations with Pelagius occurred Alaric's sack of Rome. This unimaginable strike at the heart of the empire shook the nerves of its proud inhabitants and raised troubling questions about the meaning of history, Rome's place in it, and the true character of the Christian message. Augustine responded with his monumental philosophy of history,

139. See *On the Predestination of the Saints,* chap. 7, *NP-NF,* 5:500.
140. See *On the Gift of Perseverance,* chap. 48, *NP-NF,* 5:545.
141. *On the Predestination of the Saints,* chap. 37, *NP-NF,* 5:516.
142. Ibid., chap. 38, 517.

The City of God, in which he brilliantly explores the providential nature of civilizations and God's governance of world history.

A complete discussion of *De Civitate Dei* is beyond the scope of this study, but in it Augustine argues persuasively for the universal providence of God. In an effort to calm the uneasiness of his age, Augustine reiterates the goodness of God's creation and the purpose of man both to seek after and to know his Creator.

In book 5, Augustine rejects all those views, both classical and contemporary, that account for historical events on the basis of fortune, fate, or astrological phenomena. Such positions undercut divine governance and thus must be rejected.

At the same time, he challenges and refutes Stoic, hard-deterministic interpretations that minimize, if not eliminate, the role of the human will. Such determinism empties God's governance of its meaning, since it mitigates the moral and personal character of mankind and history. "There are some . . . who define fate, not as the arrangement of the stars . . . , but as the total series of causes which bring about all that happens." They "attribute to the will and power of God the order and dependence of causes. They are perfectly right in believing that God allows all things before they come to pass." But what they fail to understand is that what God allows in the moral order includes the free choices of men. Hence, Augustine is willing to concede that God "is the Cause of all causes," but "not of all choices."[143]

Furthermore, Augustine denies that God's foreknowledge (contrary to Cicero's opinion) vitiates human accountability. Augustine argues:

> Our main point is that, from the fact that to God the order of all causes is certain, there is no logical deduction that there is no power in the choice of our will. The fact is that our choices fall within the order of the causes which is known for certain to God and is contained in His foreknowledge—for human choices are the causes of human acts.[144]

However, Augustine's main point in book 5 is to establish that God governs the entire universe—including individual souls and all the political societies they engender. As Augustine puts it, "God is the Lord of both stars and men. But, what kind of rule over men's actions is left to God if men are necessarily determined by the stars?"[145] Furthermore, seeing that God is the Author of all measure, form, and order, "how,

---

143. See *The City of God,* bk. 5, chap. 8, trans. by G. G. Walsh, D. B. Zema, G. Monahan, and D. J. Honan (Garden City: Image Books, 1958), 102f.
144. Ibid., bk. 5, chap. 9, 106f.
145. Ibid., bk. 5, chap. 1, 100.

then, can anyone believe that it was the will of God to exempt from the laws of His providence the rise and fall of political societies?"[146]

Hence, the Roman Empire, as well as all preceding kingdoms, have come into existence under the will and by the power of God and are governed by the same. Both their temporal glory and great leaders are products of God's providence. Consequently, Augustine explains:

> The conclusion from all this is that the power to give a people a kingdom or empire belongs only to the same true God who gives the Kingdom of Heaven with its happiness only to those who believe in Him, while He gives the earthly city to both believers and unbelievers alike, according to His Will which can never be unjust.[147]

> The one true God, who never permits the human race to be without the working of His wisdom and His power, granted to the Roman people an empire, when He willed it and as long as He willed it. It was the same God who gave kingdoms to the Assyrians and even to the Persians.[148]

Augustine also devotes a chapter to the phenomenon of Christian emperors, in which he emphasizes the beneficial ramifications of political orders when wisely and piously directed by devout leaders.

Finally, Augustine develops his celebrated view of the two cities, which together constitute a theological model for understanding the meaning and purpose of history. Beginning with book 11 and continuing through book 22, Augustine traces the origin, development, and final end of the two cities, or two societies, the one being ultimately the community of the elect, the other the society of those who willfully aspire to the highest honor, glory, and power of man.

From a positive point of view, Augustine's synthesis (for it is a synthesis), brings to an end the patristic period, with its attempts to formulate adequate doctrines of the providence of God. First, with his predecessors, he retains the necessity of free will, for its absence clearly destroys the moral integrity of man as well as jeopardizes God's goodness and omnipotence. But unlike his predecessors, Augustine recognizes that the will is in bondage, a slave to concupiscence and ignorance. Hence, he rightly rejects the older tradition, stretching as far back as Hesiod's "far-seeing son of Cronos," which posits that God's election is based on his foreknowledge of man's free choices. This view is inadequate. Thus his explorations of nature and grace compel Augustine to attribute a profounder

146. Ibid., bk. 5, chap. 11, 111.
147. Ibid., bk. 5, chap. 21, 116.
148. Ibid.

divine activity in the salvific process than his predecessors deemed necessary to acknowledge.

Second, Augustine's personal need to refute a Manichean dualism and his astute sensitivity to the political crises of his time allow him to embrace a distinctly linear (and therefore less cyclical and Hellenistic) view of creation, history, and time.[149] Certainly, this view is more biblical and has the power to deepen our appreciation of history as history and of history as the realm of God's activity and presence.

Third, Augustine's allegiance to Scripture as the highest source of the church's authority keeps his theology biblical in substance and helps him contain his philosophical and speculative interests within necessary bounds.

Furthermore, there is Augustine's own genius, aided by a love of truth, wisdom, and reason, the highest rational elements of the soul, which are marshalled to serve the truth and wisdom of God. Such gifts in service to God help account for the eloquence, persuasiveness, and logical rigor with which he pursues his tasks. They do not substitute for the biblical foundations on which Augustine builds his understanding of God's providence. But, without them, his interpretations and applications would lack their intellectual and psychological credibility, spiritual illumination, and moral and political relevance.

Finally, Augustine's development as a theologian and his unflinching attempt to grapple substantively with the major crises and intellectual movements of his day are reminders of the demanding and humble nature of theology, and of the need for contemporary Reformed theology to formulate its doctrines of God's providence in ways that are relevant to the intellectual challenges and historical conditions of the twentieth century.

149. See Langdon Gilkey's analysis of Augustine's concepts of time, history, and providence in *Reaping the Whirlwind* (New York: Seabury, 1976), 159–75.

Chapter Five

Scholastic, Medieval, and Renaissance Views

REFORMED THEOLOGY TENDS TO NEGLECT THE PERIOD WHICH THIS chapter explores. There is a preference, instead, to focus on Calvin, or Augustine, or both (see B. B. Warfield [*Calvin and Augustine*] and Reinhold Niebuhr [*The Nature and Destiny of Man*]). Except for the christological debates and Anselm's legacy (see Barth's *Anselm: Fides Quaerens Intellectum*), the theology of this period is often viewed as tainted by the corrupt doctrines of the medieval papacy and church, monasticism, sacramentalism, scholasticism, and mysticism. Nevertheless, over nine hundred years separate Augustine's *De Civitate Dei* from Calvin's *Institutio Christianae Religionis*. These nine hundred years cannot be casually brushed aside.

From Proclus to Erigena

Before considering the views of Dionysius and Boethius, who historically belong to the late patristic and classical periods but whose perspectives, foci, and works generate considerable interest during the scholastic age, brief attention ought first be given to the last important neo-Platonist of the classical world, Proclus Diadochus of Lycia (A.D. 410–485).[1] He inspired the philosophical imagination of medieval theologians as well as

1. See Thomas Whittaker, *The Neo-Platonists: A Study in the History of Hellenism,* 2d ed. (Freeport, N.Y.: Books for Libraries Press, 1970).

107

gave impetus to their scholastic and mystical bent. This he appears to have done indirectly through two of his admirers, Dionysius and Boethius.[2] It is also fitting to give some emphasis to Proclus, as this period is dominated by neo-Platonic principles, so much so that the biblical and Christian bases for understanding the providence of God are made captive to the abstract, mystical, and speculative elements of philosophy in general.

Proclus Diadochus of Lycia

Proclus is described by modern historians as a condenser of Plotinian doctrines.[3] However, whereas Plotinus embraced a metaphysical order of being, intellect, and life, Proclus chose to emphasize being (*ousia*), life (*zōē*), and mind (*nous*), thus ascribing a vitality to the universal order often neglected by Plotinus.

Proclus begins with the One and the Good, which is the primal and principal cause of all. From the divine One flow divine "henads," gods who are above being, life, and mind; "all the gods are hyper-being, hyper-life, and hyper-mind."[4]

From the primal One also flow the first intellect, the first soul, and nature: "Beyond all bodies is the essence of Soul, and beyond all souls the intellectual nature, and beyond all intellectual existence the One."[5]

The henads, intellect, soul, and nature represent distinct universal series, each with its own causal chain. Each particular chain is governed by a monad or universal that brings order to all its members. In turn, each member within a chain strives to return to its cause and to its highest good (a blending of Plotinian, Aristotelian, and Platonic themes).[6]

It is from the divine henads, however, that the providential ordering of being, life, and mind descends. This is due in part to the fact that Proclus defines providence as that which is "prior to intellect" or "mind" (*pro nou*).[7] For this reason, as Proclus explains, "providence is therefore primarily among the gods, for where could an activity prior to intellect be if not in super-essential things? Providence, as its name implies, is an activity 'prior to intellect.' "[8]

---

2. Ibid., 186, 187f., 238.
3. Ibid., 163.
4. Ibid., 173 n. 1.
5. Ibid., 165.
6. Ibid., 165–66.
7. See Stephen Gersh, *From Iamblichus to Eriugena* (Leiden: E. J. Brill, 1978), 117. Gersh notes that Proclus defines πρόνοια on the basis of πρὸ νοῦ—an activity preceding the intellect.
8. Ibid.

According to Proclus, the goodness and power of the One is communicated first to the henads, from the henads to mind, from mind to soul, and from soul to body. Hence, the primal One, through this downward process, participates in or penetrates all levels of being.[9] As Thomas Whittaker explains: "At each stage of remission, the divinity is present, not only in the manner peculiar to each causal order, but in the manner appropriate to the particular stage."[10]

In Proclus's schema, everything comes under divine providence and is pervaded by the presence of the Good. This does not mean, however, that every particular good is "good" in the same sense as the All. In neo-Platonic thought, absolutes always take precedence over relatives, and cause is always superior to effect. Besides, Proclus's All is beyond being, as "hyper-being" or "super-essential."

In two separate treatises (*De Providentia et Fato* and *De Decem Dubitationibus*), Proclus explores the problem of evil and distinguishes between providence and fate. For Proclus, external and mechanical causes often elude our intellectual grasp; as such, they remain factors of blind fate.[11] But when we examine the whole, we are enabled to understand the reasonableness of their occurrence. Henry Chadwick explains that this distinction is one that neo-Platonists drew from Plotinus; providence concerned the higher realm, while fate was "the unalterable chain of cause and effect in this inferior and determined world."[12]

Proclus, however, is unwilling to explain mental occurrences as flowing merely from mechanical determinants. Living beings shape their world precisely through their "mental imaginations" and "vital rational nature" (*incorporabiliter phantasia et vitaliter . . . rationem*).[13] In other words, "the metaphysical universe of mental realities is wider than the physical universe."[14] Proclus goes on to state that "many things escape Fate; nothing escapes Providence."[15] Hence, the primal One and primal Good, which is able, through intellect and soul, to penetrate all levels of being, is thereby enabled to bring order to all causal chains of beings, whether rational or corporeal.

Proclus also works out a scheme (similar to Origen's) for explaining one's present status in the world. It is due in part to the soul's former

9. Whittaker, *Neo-Platonists*, 174f.

10. Ibid., 175.

11. Ibid., 238.

12. Henry Chadwick, *Boethius: The Consolations of Music, Logic, Theology, and Philosophy* (Oxford: Clarendon, 1983), 242.

13. From Proclus's *De Providentia et Fato*, cited by Whittaker, *Neo-Platonists*, 238 n. 4.

14. See Whittaker, *Neo-Platonists*, 239.

15. Ibid.

deeds. But it is also the result of the causal way in which particular races (*geni*) are bound to the fate of their political institutions (*civitates*), so that what any political state's specific generation does influences its inhabitants for good or ill, besides making or breaking its people's moral fiber (the Greek character- and civilization-building motifs).[16]

Dionysius the Areopagite

Dionysius's theology incorporates many Proclusian and Plotinian themes. These are readily evident in his discussion of God, the world, and God's providential care of that world.

Like Proclus, Dionysius defines God as "Hyper-being" and "Hyper-mind."[17] God is the "Cause exalted above all," "the good Cause of all," the "Unknown" (*Agnosia*), the primal "Good," "Being," "Life," and "Wisdom."[18]

The universe is a manifestation of God (a theophany). It emanates from God and flows back into him in a series of descending and ascending hierarchies.[19] "Hierarchy is . . . a sacred order and science and operation, assimilated, as far as attainable, to the likeness of God, and conducted to the illuminations granted to it from God, according to capacity, with a view to the Divine imitation."[20]

Dionysius identifies God with the Good and the Beautiful. Hence, insofar as God is the cause of all Good (being, life, and mind), wherever in any capacity this Good exists, we encounter God acting providentially. Evil is an absence of the Good and has its place in the well-being of mankind (the character-building motif) and is part of the natural order:

> How . . . are there evils when there is a Providence? The Evil, *qua* evil, is not, neither as an actual thing nor as in things existing. And no single thing is without a Providence. . . . And, if no single thing is without participation in the Good, but the lack of the Good is evil, and no existing thing is deprived absolutely of the Good, the Divine Providence is in all existing things, and no single thing is without Providence.[21]

16. Ibid., 239–40.
17. See Dionysius, *On Divine Names*, in *The Works of Dionysius the Areopagite*, trans. by John Parker (Merrick, N.Y.: Richmond, 1976), pt. 1, 9. [Further references to Dionysius's works are to this collection and will include the work's title, part, and page(s).]
18. See Dionysius, *Mystical Theology*, 1:131, 132, 134, and 137, respectively.
19. *On Divine Names*, 1:79ff.
20. *On the Heavenly Hierarchy*, 2:13.
21. *On Divine Names*, 1:70.

Consequently, the world and all its hierarchies, or causal chains, are under divine providence.[22]

God as love is the "unifying power" of all things, for divine love exists for the purpose of restoring all things to God. "For . . . Love . . . is assigned to the Divine Wisdom, for the purpose of leading back and restoring [humankind] to the knowledge of the veritable Love. . . ."[23]

Finally, life's highest purpose is to ascend the chain of being, as one contemplates the divine exemplars, until one arrives at that knowledge of God which is beyond knowing God (*agnosia*).[24] This occurs when one has transcended all subject-object levels of consciousness and has been "made one with the super-luminous rays" of "the unsearchable depth of wisdom."[25]

Toward the end of the classical and patristic periods, neo-Platonic concepts came to dominate the Christian world view. It was a world view in which creation as a unique event was replaced by a cyclical view of history. It was a view in which mystical union with the All and schemes to ascend the chain of being downplayed the work of the Redeemer, and one in which the very elements of creation became divine exemplars, which, although not identifiable with the divine in either a Stoic or a pantheistic sense, became the first steps toward that possibility, ultimately surfacing in the mysticism of the Middle Ages (i.e., Bruno, and ultimately Spinoza and Hegel).

Boethius

Boethius's principal work on the providence of God is his *Consolation of Philosophy*. This is a philosophical work, not a theological one, drawing heavily on Aristotle, Plato, and the neo-Platonists. But it is more than a simple rehearsal of classical views. Boethius has so internalized the positions of his predecessors as to make them uniquely his own.[26]

Chadwick, in his rigorous and impressive work on Boethius, describes the *Consolation* as an argument for providence based exclusively on natural reason, in which the author provides "an impassioned discussion of the logical problems of providence, freedom, and evil."[27]

22. See ibid., chap. 5, sect. 2; ibid., 74.
23. Ibid., chap. 4, sect. 12; ibid., 47.
24. Ibid., chap. 7, sect. 3; ibid., 91f.
25. Ibid.
26. See Boethius, *The Theological Tractates and the Consolation of Philosophy*, trans. by H. F. Stewart, E. K. Rand, and S. J. Tester, Loeb Classical Library (Cambridge: Harvard University Press, 1973), xii–xiii.
27. Chadwick, *Boethius*, 54.

Boethius wrote the *Consolation* while in prison, awaiting his death. Separated from his library and classical sources, he consoled himself with the philosophical synthesis he had been working on throughout his life. In an effort to find meaning in his own suffering, Boethius attempts to reconcile divine providence with evil and human freedom. According to Chadwick, Boethius achieves this by "ascend[ing] from a Stoic moralism to a Platonic metaphysical vision of the divine ordering of an apparently chaotic world."[28]

Boethius maintains that God has created the orders of nature and given them their stability.[29] Moreover, God has granted free will to mankind and will neither rescind it nor interfere in human actions.

> With a sure purpose ruling and guiding all,
> Man's acts alone
> You will not, though you rightly could, constrain.[30]

This does not mean, however, that man falls "outside the sphere of God's watchful care."[31]

For Boethius, man is more than Aristotle's "mortal, rational animal." He can neither understand himself nor be understood apart from God's highest purposes for him. Neither can man be understood apart from God's governance of the world (the denial that human destiny is shaped by "the randomness of chance events" alone, that always seem to favor the wicked).[32]

Boethius acknowledges that human life is bounded by cause and effect. There is no escaping this kind of "fortune," or soft determinism. This is true from both an empirical point of view and an ethical viewpoint. "If you spread your sails for the wind, you must go where the wind takes you."[33]

Happiness, which Boethius defines as "the highest good of a rational nature," cannot be attained aside from the eternal.[34] There is a natural dimension to human life, the pursuit of which is largely satisfying. But man is a transcendent creature, whose very capacity to rise above self requires a self-concept that surpasses naturalistic explanations: "For the nature of man is such that he is better than other things only when he

---

28. Ibid., 228.
29. See *Consolation of Philosophy*, 161, 167.
30. Ibid., 161.
31. Ibid., 167.
32. Ibid., 169.
33. Ibid., 179.
34. Ibid., 197.

knows himself, and yet if he ceases to know himself he is made lower than the brutes. For it is natural for other animals not to have this self-knowledge; in man it is a fault."[35]

This insight, of course, is not only Platonic, but also deeply Augustinian. It compares with Calvin's insistence that all "true and sound wisdom, consists of two parts: the knowledge of God and of ourselves."[36]

Boethius identifies the highest ordering principle as Love (*amor*). Behind eternal law (*Foedus perpetuum*) and regular harmony (*stabili fide*) looms Love.

> What binds all things to order,
> Governing earth and sea and sky,
> Is Love. . . .
> O happy race of men,
> If the love that rules the stars
> May also rule your hearts![37]

Chadwick explains that this principle of "providential equilibrium," interpreted as "the love that binds together the cosmos to prevent its disintegration," was a characteristic Stoic theme, rhapsodized by the Latin poets, and absorbed in time by the Platonists.[38]

In the *Consolation*, Boethius de-rhapsodizes this theme and views the principle of equilibrium as pointing directly to the power and goodness of God. For Boethius (in somewhat of a Tillichian sense), the phenomenon of equilibrium is a manifestation of the universe's "ground of being." As Boethius explains: "And whatever this is by which created things continue in being and move, I call by the name used by all, God."[39]

Boethius believes that much human evil and unhappiness can be explained as the result of ignorance and confusion about life's highest aim. Most men must first awaken to the emptiness of their pursuits before life's "true goods" can be sought or recognized.[40]

God as the highest Good is the source of the highest or perfect happiness. Boethius's position is based on the premise that "all perfect things are prior to the less perfect"[41] and on other more general Platonic motifs. Following Plato's lead, Boethius emphasizes that the well-ordering of hu-

---

35. Ibid., 205.
36. Calvin, *Institutes*, 1.1.1.
37. *Consolation of Philosophy*, 227.
38. Chadwick, *Boethius*, 232.
39. *Consolation of Philosophy*, 249.
40. Ibid., 263.
41. Ibid., 277.

man life is inseparable from participation in the highest vision of life, which, in turn, is rooted in God.

Boethius argues that evil is caused when any existent good ceases to participate in the Good. Once the Good, which constitutes anything's unity, is lost sight of, disunity, division, and disintegration set in.[42] It is for this reason that Boethius defines God as that which is able to hold created things together.[43] Hence, the unifying good, or the principle of equilibrium, which the supreme God communicates to all things by virtue of their existence, is the providential principle preserving the world's order.[44]

However, can God's goodness and power be defended in a world in which evil exists and even goes unpunished? Must not one "complain" and "wonder" that "this should happen in the kingdom of God who knows all, and is all-powerful, but only wills the good"?[45]

Boethius's answer contains a mixture of Aristotelian and Platonic motifs. He emphasizes that man is confused primarily about his ultimate *telos* and, in having to endure the consequences of his own misconceptions and misdeeds, he experiences justice, which is a form of good. Insofar as this occurs, evil does not fall outside the province of divine governance.[46]

Boethius adopts the Platonic distinction between providence and fate. Providence involves the universal, fate the particular. Providence is the divine master plan; fate is the subordinate and finite manner in which that plan is particularized. This subordinate realization of what the divine mind wills includes many agents or efficient causes:

> Now whether fate works by certain divine spirits acting as servants of providence, or whether the course of fate is woven by the service of the soul or of the whole of nature [i.e., both free will and cause-and-effect interactions], or by the celestial motions of the stars; . . . or by any or all of these, this surely is clear, that the unmoving and simple form of the way things are done is providence, and fate is the movable interlacing and temporal ordering of those things which the divine simplicity has disposed to be done.[47]

From the human, finite side, things may appear "in random flux," "confused and disordered"; but insofar as the divine has disposed this

42. Ibid., 289.
43. Ibid., 299.
44. Ibid., 301.
45. Ibid., 313–15.
46. Ibid., 345.
47. Ibid., 361.

ordering of life, everything has been arranged toward some good and "nothing . . . is done for the sake of evil."[48]

In the course of fate, providence often favors good men to come to power "that luxuriating wickedness may be beaten back." Others may face a life mingled with prosperity and hardships, but through the practice of patience great strength is won (the familiar character-building motif). Psychological fears and social pressures often cause some to reform. And evil men can even cause other evil men to become good, as the latter so hate their oppressors as to want to be unlike them.[49]

Boethius, in a Ciceronian manner, affirms free will as an ordained order by means of which providence is exercised. Granted, the universe is ruled by a "close-linked series of causes"; nevertheless, "this chain of fate" does not bind "the motions of men's minds."[50]

For Boethius, freedom of the will is a necessary condition for rational creatures. It is the quality that makes the human race human. But Boethius is aware that the human will is hardly free. To the extent that the human soul ceases to contemplate the divine mind, it becomes less free:

> Human souls must indeed be more free when they preserve themselves in the contemplation of the divine mind; less free, however, when they step down to the corporeal, and still less free when they are bound into earthly limbs [i.e., the Plotinian "descent" into Matter that pulls one downward].[51]

Nonetheless, God sees this condition, and depending on what each soul makes of its life, governs it accordingly. Boethius maintains that providence "looks forth on all things from eternity, sees this and disposes all that is predestined to each according to his deserts"—a position that favors the traditional view of the will and salvation instead of Augustine's.[52]

Finally, Boethius raises the question of God's foreknowledge and human freedom. How can God foreknow all that man will do without determining, from eternity, the future choices man thinks he freely makes? Any argument that attempts to solve this problem by answering that God only *foresees* what choices men will make must still wrestle with the problem that future temporal events, although not chosen by God, are known to God as events before they occur. Hence, they either happen because they are "coming or happen because they are foreseen."[53]

48. Ibid., 363.
49. Ibid., 369f.; see also 371.
50. Ibid., 391.
51. Ibid., 393.
52. Ibid.
53. Ibid., 397.

Boethius realizes that, logically speaking, to embrace either solution begs the question. For "the occurrence of a thing foreknown cannot be avoided."[54] Nor can true divine foreknowledge exist if nothing necessarily occurs as it is foreseen. In other words, the dilemma is rift with logical contradictions. "For," argues Boethius, "foreknowledge and not-necessary outcomes . . . [are] incompatible."[55] Hence, the Augustinian solution, however appealing, is by no means the sole philosophical answer.

Boethius is uneasy with a philosophical standoff and is loathe to concede that all human actions and choices have been predetermined by the foreknowledge of God. Consequently, he proposes that one way to grasp the horns of the dilemma is to recognize that God's manner of foreseeing differs from the human perception of how this must occur, thus removing the sting of necessity while preserving definite foreknowledge.[56] For God's knowing is in accordance with the divine nature, and man's in accordance with his human nature.[57]

Since the clue to what and how God "knows" lies in his nature, what is its fundamental essence? Since God is eternal and eternity is "the whole, simultaneous and perfect possession of boundless life," God "comprehends and possesses at once the whole fulness of boundless life," in which nothing "future is lacking from it" and nothing past has "flowed away." Therefore, God holds "as present the infinity of moving time."[58]

Boethius concludes, then, that it is wiser to conceive of God's foreknowledge "not . . . [as a] foreknowledge as it were of the future but knowledge of a never-passing instant." It should not be confused with prevision (*praevidentia*) but understood as genuine providence (*providentia*). After all, if our seeing present events in no way confers necessity on them, then why suppose that God's comprehending of the "eternal present" confers necessity on it?[59] Any necessity, therefore, that pertains to God's foreknowledge is of the present, for "if providence sees anything as present, that must necessarily be." Nevertheless, future events that God foresees presently are events that happen because of free will.[60]

Boethius's position is clearly superior to Cicero's and is not altogether unlike the one maintained by contemporary process theology, in which God knows all that can be known at any moment of being and in whom everything past is now presently remembered. But whereas Boethius was

54. Ibid., 399.
55. Ibid., 409.
56. Ibid., 419–21.
57. Ibid., 423.
58. Ibid., 423–25.
59. Ibid., 423.
60. Ibid.

trying to reconcile foreknowledge with free will, process theology wants to eliminate the former altogether.[61]

John Scotus Erigena

Between Augustine and Anselm, no figure emerges in the Western church with as powerful an intellect as Erigena.[62] His arrival at the court of Charles the Bald took place in a specific theological milieu. Alcuin of York had already wrestled with the problem of universals and in his *De Vera Philosophia* had drawn freely upon Boethius's *Consolation* and Aristotelian logic.[63] This was also the era of the bitter predestination controversy, involving Gottschalk, Rabanus Marus, Hincmar, and Ratramnus. Gottschalk and Ratramnus had taken a strict Augustinian view, Rabanus the more traditional position, and Hincmar had opposed the first two and had sought Erigena's support. But Erigena's *De Praedestinatione* created more problems than it solved, as he pleaded in his treatise for the supremacy of reason in theological debate.

From our perspective, it is Erigena's *Periphyseon: On the Division of Nature* that commands attention. In it Erigena attempts to explain God's relationship to creation, the fall of man, Christ's redemptive work, and the return of all things to God. It is a theological work, which, in John Marenbon's estimation, is indebted to the Platonic and Dionysian idea of procession from God and return to him.[64]

Erigena distinguishes between being (*ousia*) and nature (*physis*). *Being* refers to a thing's essence, *nature* to any concrete spatiotemporal manifestation of being. Erigena recognizes four divisions of nature: (1) nature that creates and is not created (God as the ultimate principle of things); (2) nature that is created and creates (the archetypal or eternal Ideas, that are created but also create things); (3) nature that is created and does not create (the effects of God's creative Ideas); and (4) nature that does not create and is not created (God as the goal or *telos* of all things).[65]

Etienne Gilson, who is somewhat sympathetic toward Erigena's Platon-

61. See Charles Hartshorne, *Omnipotence and Other Theological Mistakes* (Albany: State University of New York Press, 1984), 26–27; see also *The Logic of Perfection* (La Salle, Ill.: Open Court, 1962), chap. 10.

62. See *John the Scot, Periphyseon: On The Division of Nature,* trans. by Myra L. Uhlfelder (Indianapolis: Bobbs-Merrill, 1976), ix.

63. See John Marenbon, *From the Circle of Alcuin to the School of Auxerre* (Cambridge: Cambridge University Press, 1981), 31.

64. Ibid., 70.

65. See Etienne Gilson, *History of Christian Philosophy in the Middle Ages* (New York: Random House, 1955), 116.

ism, denies that Erigena's "divisions" are pantheistic or can only be interpreted in a pantheistic manner: "We should not imagine 'nature' as a whole of which God and creatures would be parts. . . . God is not all things, nor are all things God. . . . The division of nature signifies the act by which God expresses and makes himself known in a hierarchy of beings which are other than, and inferior to, him."[66]

What is important to understand, however, is that for Erigena, following Dionysius's lead, God is "hyperousios."[67] God is more than anything we can predicate of him. He simply supersedes all the categories that can be predicated of the corporeal.[68]

Following both Dionysius and Plotinus, Erigena maintains that God is the One, in whom all Ideas and potential existences reside in unity. He is their cause and principle.[69] Thus creation is a "theophany," "an apparition of God," a manifestation of all the Ideas that reside in him.[70] This is how God reveals himself.

The first theophanies are God's Ideas. In them, God begins to emerge from his own secret nature and becomes known to himself. As the Ideas, which are the universal causes of all things, are in turn externalized, the world as we know it comes into being. Consequently, every visible and corporeal thing is a light (Dionysius's "divine exemplars") that displays the divine phenomenon. In Erigena's judgment, "there is nothing among visible and corporeal things which does not signify something incorporeal and intelligible."[71]

God is present in all these beings, insofar as the universal always comprehends its particulars and includes them; but no created thing is an actual part of God. God is always "hyperousia," or "super-essential." If this distinction is maintained, then Erigena's "pantheism" dissolves. As Gilson explains: "Erigena only means that each and every creature is essentially a manifestation, under the form of being, of what is above being. The *esse* of a being is but a light radiated by the *superesse,* which is God."[72]

Man, too, is a theophany in Erigena's hierarchy of beings. Authentic man is to be found in the eternal Idea or Image of man in God. This image "is both goodness and a good image by participation in the Highest Good

66. Ibid., 117.
67. *Division of Nature,* 24.
68. Ibid., 27.
69. Ibid., 123–33.
70. Ibid., bk. 1, chap. 7; bk. 2, chap. 23.
71. Ibid., 277.
72. Gilson, *History of Christian Philosophy,* 121.

and Highest Goodness, of which it is the reflection."[73] Generated man
fell from this Highest Good when he ceased to participate in it by an act
of his own will. He abandoned "the knowledge and wisdom implanted
within" and slipped "into deep ignorance."[74] [Note here that the fall is
explained purely in Platonic and neo-Platonic terms. It was not man's
pride or disobedience that caused his fall but his failure to "participate"
intellectually in the highest principle. His sin was not disbelief in the
living God but neglect of an abstract good.]

In Erigena's system, however, God is not merely the source of all things,
or life's formal cause. God is also life's final cause and the end to which
all things return. Hence, death initiates the first stage of man's return to
God; the second stage involves the resurrection of the body; in the third
stage the soul and its resurrected body are reunited; in the fourth stage
the soul returns to its Idea in God; finally, in the fifth stage, all nature is
returned to God and God alone is left.[75]

Erigena's ideas were condemned repeatedly during the Middle Ages: in
1210 by Peter of Corbeil; in 1225 by William of Auvergne; again in 1241.
They were put on the *Index* in 1684 and, more recently, were condemned
in the *Index Librorum Prohibitorum* of Rome (1924).[76]

Gilson's assessment of Erigena is an accurate one:

> No one, after him, has ever dared to take up as a whole a doctrine so little
> suited to the sober teachings of the Latin tradition, but it was to remain as
> a sort of permanent temptation against which, from century to century, doc-
> trinal authorities were never to cease struggling, without ever succeeding in
> killing it.[77]

Erigena's system is an astonishing deviation from the biblical understanding of God's governance of the world. It represents a neo-Platonic
conquest of theology and clearly replaces the God of Abraham, Isaiah,
and Paul with an abstract principle.

In our time, however, Erigena's system provides subject matter for quiet
reflection. In the Western world, Eastern mystical religions (Hinduism,
Buddhism, and Taoism) have appealed to many whose Christianity has
been unable to sustain them or compel belief. Reformed theology must
rightly consider the extent to which its own cherished doctrines have
ceased to touch and heal those lonely and yearning souls who long to

73. *Division of Nature,* 252.
74. Ibid.
75. See Gilson, *History of Christian Philosophy,* 126.
76. Ibid., 613 n. 39.
77. Ibid., 128.

know the Ineffable. Is it not possible for Reformed theology to recover
the early church's sense of union with her Lord while avoiding the excesses of mystical spiritualism?

Anselm of Canterbury

Anselm is best known for his ontological argument for God's existence,
for his Augustinian interpretation of Isaiah 7:9 ("for I do not seek to
understand in order to believe but I believe in order to understand"[78]),
and for his treatise on the incarnation and atonement, the *Cur Deus
Homo*.

In addition, however, to the *Monologion, Proslogion,* and *Cur Deus
Homo,* there are other treatises, which, although they have received less
attention, are especially relevant to our study. These include *De Libertate
Arbitrii, De Casu Diaboli,* and *De Concordia Praescientiae et Praedestinationis et Gratiae Dei cum Libero Arbitrio.*

Anselm does not develop the doctrine of providence extensively in any
of these writings. However, his discussion of creation and its sustentation,
as well as the problem of how free choice can be reconciled with God's
foreknowledge and grace reveal his understanding of providence.

In the *Monologion,* Anselm maintains that God is both supremely good
and supremely great, is self-caused, and is superior to all else that exists.
Drawing largely upon the *ex nihilo* principle, Anselm argues that the world
has been created out of nothing; it did not come into being from pre-
existing matter. It previously did not exist and presently exists only through
the power of God.

Nevertheless, there is a profound sense in which the world was preexistent in the thought (*ratio*) of its Maker, so that God knew "all creatures
before . . . [he] created them."[79] In fact, creatures exist in God more
truly than in themselves. Anselm argues from a trinitarian perspective in
which the Supreme Wisdom (third person of the Trinity) and the Word
(second person of the Trinity by whom God both "expresses" himself and
"creates") contain beforehand all creatures that will come into existence.
"For before [created things] were made and once they have been made
and after they have perished or have changed in some manner, they always
are in this Spirit what this Spirit is, rather than what they are in them-

---

78. See the *Proslogion,* in *Anselm of Canterbury,* ed. and trans. by J. Hopkins and
H. Richardson (Toronto and New York: Edwin Mellen, 1975), 1:93. [All references to Anselm's works are to this series.]
79. *Anselm of Canterbury,* 1:27–29.

selves. For in themselves they are a mutable being. . . . But in this Spirit they are the primary Being. . . ."[80]

Anselm also argues that all creatures are presently sustained only because of the Creator's goodness and power. Anselm reasons that since God alone exists through himself and everything else exists through him, then God alone must be self-sustained and everything else sustained through him. Hence, "it must be the case that just as nothing was made except through the creative and present Being, so nothing is sustained except through the conserving presence of this same Being."[81]

God's creative and sustaining work, along with his spiritual knowledge of every creature, has profound repercussions for a doctrine of God's providence, as Anselm is acutely aware. In fact, he concludes the *Monologion* with a chapter in which he explores these repercussions:

> For just as we have established that all things were created through, and are sustained by, this Spirit's supremely good and supremely wise omnipotence, so it would be altogether unsuitable to think that (1) this Spirit does not have dominion over what it created by itself, or that (2) the things created by it are ruled over by some other less powerful, less good, or less wise being, or that (3) they are directed by no rational principle at all but only by a random changing, due to chance occurrences.[82]

Anselm wrote the *Monologion* around 1076.[83] Sometime between 1080 and 1085 he began writing a series of tightly reasoned treatises in which he explores language, truth, and evil. *De Libertate Arbitrii (On Freedom of Choice)* belongs to this period, and is the preamble for his reflection on foreknowledge, predestination, and grace.

Anselm defines freedom of choice as "the ability to keep uprightness-of-will for the sake of this uprightness itself," or as a willing what is right only because it is right.[84] Man retains this freedom of choice though he is no longer able to use it.[85] Anselm argues that freedom of choice belongs essentially to a rational nature. Therefore, the fact that a person may not be able to use his essential nature as he ought does not mean he has lost this nature. "Even if uprightness-of-will is absent, rational nature still has without diminution what belongs to it essentially."[86]

---

80. Ibid., chap. 34; ibid., 50–51.
81. Ibid., chap. 13; ibid., 21.
82. Ibid., chap. 80; ibid., 85–86.
83. See *Truth, Freedom, and Evil: Three Philosophical Dialogues*, ed. and trans. by J. Hopkins and H. Richardson (New York: Harper Torchbooks, 1967), 11.
84. See *Anselm of Canterbury*, 2:110 n. 8.
85. Ibid., 108.
86. Ibid., 110.

To demonstrate this truth, Anselm suggests the analogy of having the ability to see but of being placed in a dark room where, owing to the condition of darkness, that ability cannot be used. In a similar manner, when someone chooses to do evil, he places himself in an adverse condition, in that whoever sins becomes the servant of sin. The sinner still retains freedom of choice but, owing to his condition of sin, cannot exercise that choice freely.[87] So "when free will deserts uprightness because of the difficulty of keeping it, then . . . free will subsequently serves sin because of the impossibility of recovering uprightness through its own efforts."[88] Only God's grace can restore the will to will the upright thing in itself.

In a later treatise (De Concordia), Anselm returns to this problem and offers a clarifying distinction: One "abandons uprightness-of-will not because the *ability* to keep it fails him . . . but because the *will* to keep it fails him."[89] Both Jasper Hopkins and Herbert Richardson find Anselm's clarification burdened with ambiguities. They charge: "To say, 'I had the ability to do it, but didn't use my ability,' gives rise to the rejoinder: 'Why didn't you use it? Were you unwilling to or unable to?' And answers to both these questions lead to an infinite regression."[90]

Sometime between 1107 and 1108 Anselm resolved to reconcile the philosophical contradictions implied in belief in free choice and the scriptural emphases on God's foreknowledge, predestination, and saving grace. The result was his De Concordia or Harmony of the Foreknowledge, the Predestination, and the Grace of God with Free Choice.

In a manner similar to Augustine, Anselm argues that free choice and divine foreknowledge are not mutually exclusive. For when God foreknows anything, he knows whether it will be done out of necessity or by free choice:

> And thus it follows that whether you sin or do not sin, in either case it will be without necessity; for God foreknows that what will occur will occur without necessity. Do you see, then, that it is not impossible for God's foreknowledge (according to which future things, which God foreknows, are said to occur of necessity) to coexist with freedom of choice (by which many actions are performed without necessity)?[91]

Anselm also incorporates Boethius's concept of the "eternal present" and sets the problem of foreknowledge within the context of eternity and

87. Ibid., 112.
88. Ibid., 120.
89. See Anselm of Canterbury, 2:214; emphasis added.
90. See Truth, Freedom, and Evil, 32–33.
91. See Anselm of Canterbury, 2:182.

time. Thus, what God knows he knows in the "eternal present," "in which there is no past or future but . . . only a present," and what he knows herein "is immutable" (i.e., it must occur as he knows it). But time differs from eternity, and the temporal present allows for mutability and for a future in which free choice is an inescapable characteristic of rational natures.[92] Hence, God's present foreknowledge of any event in no way contradicts or determines free choice in a "temporal future."[93]

Anselm reconciles any philosophical contradictions between free choice and predestination by subsuming predestination under foreknowledge and the principle of the eternal present: "We must also realize that just as *fore*knowledge is not properly said to be found in God, so *pre*destination is not either. For nothing is present to God either earlier or later, but all things are present to Him at once."[94] Thus, in the same manner that "some actions which are going to occur as a result of free choice, are foreknown," so "some actions which are going to occur by means of free choice, are likewise predestined."[95]

In fact, Anselm cautions that wherever Scripture speaks of events of free choice as if they were done necessarily or were predestined, Scripture must be interpreted as speaking "in accordance with eternity."[96] Anselm is thinking specifically of Romans 8:29–30: "For those whom he foreknew he also predestined . . . And those whom he predestined he also called. . . ." [Note that in this passage foreknowledge is mentioned before predestination.] Anselm asks whether things that are going to happen as a result of free choice can be predestined. He concludes that as God foreknows he predestines (i.e., from the view of eternity), thus making predestination subordinate to God's foreknowledge.[97]

Besides, there is another principle to consider. For Anselm, no one can be predestined to be just who does not keep justice by means of a free will.

For although God predestines . . . things, He causes them not by constraining or restraining the will but by leaving the will to its own power. But although the will uses its own power, it does nothing which God does not cause—in good works by His grace, in evil works not through any fault of His but through the will's fault. . . . And just as foreknowledge, which is not

92. Ibid., chap. 1, sect. 5; ibid., 189.
93. Ibid., 190.
94. See *Anselm of Canterbury,* 2:197.
95. Ibid., 197.
96. See *Anselm of Canterbury,* 2:190.
97. Ibid., 197–98.

mistaken, foreknows only the real thing as it will occur—either necessarily or freely—so predestination . . . predestines only as the thing exists in foreknowledge.[98]

In Anselm's estimation, the problem of the relationship of free choice and grace exists because Scripture itself sometimes speaks of salvation as if it were the result of grace alone and at other times as if it were dependent solely on free will.[99] Anselm takes a modified Augustinian solution (a semi-Pelagian or semi-Augustinian position) in which free choice cooperates with divine grace. Divine grace, for Anselm, always precedes and accompanies the cooperating free choice. Nevertheless, "grace and free choice are not incompatible but cooperate in order to justify and to save man."[100] In this way Anselm hopes to preserve both biblical emphases while underscoring God's prevenient and subsequent grace.

We have then, in Anselm's "Christian rationalism"[101] a perception of providence that hinges on God's foreknowledge of what morally accountable agents will elect to become and do through free choice. In it, predestination is subsumed under foreknowledge, and both foreknowledge and predestination, in turn, are subsumed under the principle of the "eternal present."

What does this mean? In the final analysis, the principle of free choice prevails, assisted by divine grace. God has intended it this way, even foreseeing that man would fall. But God, who is necessarily everywhere at all times, and who always has his rational creatures on his mind, has elected to restore them to their highest uprightness by vivifying their wills to will the right thing, for which reason he did not hesitate to become man in a temporal past that serves mankind eternally.

One must grant that a strong current of neo-Platonism has been taken up into Anselm's dialectical theology. Nevertheless, it is also characterized by profound spiritual piety. For Anselm's supremely good and supremely powerful God, who never ceases to contemplate and know his rational creatures, and in whom they are preserved and sustained better than in themselves, gathers them to himself in ways that can touch and heal that intense longing of each human soul.

---

98. Ibid.
99. See *Anselm of Canterbury,* 2:199.
100. Ibid., 205.
101. See Gilson, *History of Christian Philosophy,* 139.

Thomas Aquinas

Aquinas's Sources

Aristotle's works constitute one of Aquinas's major sources. In particular, Aquinas cites sections from the *Metaphysics* and *Nicomachean Ethics* (book 6 especially) and draws widely upon logical and philosophical principles found in the *Organon*, principally *Categories* and *On Interpretation*.[102]

Aquinas incorporates in its entirety Aristotle's concept of causes (formal, efficient, and final), the principle that antecedents imply their consequents, and, above all, from the *Nicomachean Ethics*, the principle that "prudence arranges things to an end," or in Aristotle's words, "all knowledge and every pursuit aims at some good."[103] This last principle is central to Aquinas's doctrine of providence, as he ultimately conceives of providence as a function of wisdom, thus subsuming it under God's knowledge. Further, since God's knowledge is part of, or one with, his being, providence is subsumed under God's being—which is the principal objection Barth raises against the Thomistic position.[104]

In addition to Aristotle, Aquinas also draws upon the works of Augustine, Dionysius, Boethius, John Damascene (eighth century), and Moses Maimonides (1135–1204).

For John Damascene, providence is God's solicitude for all existing things. It is grounded in the will of God by means of which all things are properly guided through to their end (a concept that Aquinas will completely absorb). Any accomplished good is due to God's co-operation. God "foreknows all things but . . . He does not predestine them all." He knows what human beings will do but does not predestine them. However, things "which do not depend upon us" he "predestines in accordance with his foreknowledge." "For, through His foreknowledge, He has already decided all things beforehand in accordance with His goodness and justice."[105]

Aquinas was fond of Maimonides and often cites him favorably; how-

---

102. For an excellent discussion of Aquinas's use of Aristotelian principles, see Edward Booth, *Aristotelian Aporetic Ontology in Islamic and Christian Thinkers* (Cambridge: Cambridge University Press, 1983), esp. chaps. 1 and 6.

103. *Nicomachean Ethics*, bk. 1, chap. 3, in *The Basic Works of Aristotle*, ed. by Richard McKeon (New York: Random House, 1971), 937.

104. Barth, *Church Dogmatics*, 3.3:3.

105. See *Saint John of Damascus*, vol. 37 of The Fathers of the Church, trans. by Frederic H. Chase, Jr. (New York: Fathers of the Church, 1958), 260–66.

ever, he was opposed to Maimonides's "partial providence" and was forced to reject it.

Maimonides's views on providence are concentrated in book 3, chapters 8–24 and 51–54 of *The Guide of the Perplexed*. He draws as much upon Aristotle (in dialogue with and against Avicenna and Averroes) as he does upon rabbinic and Jewish traditions.

With Aristotle, he agrees that "every natural act has a certain final end," and that "in natural things the agent, the form, and the final end, are one and the same thing."[106]

Since everything exists for its own good end, Maimonides disagrees with the Stoics that the world exists principally to serve man.[107] From the viewpoint of the Torah, everything exists for God's glory. Hence, no other cause for God's will ought or can be sought beyond his volition as the highest end of all existing things.[108]

According to the Torah, all nonhuman creatures exist for their own specific purposes in accordance with their natural form, while man is free to do as he wills. As a result, all calamities and good things that befall him are "determined according to the deserts of the men concerned."[109]

In Maimonides's opinion, "divine providence watches only over . . . the human species" (partial providence), and what results from human decisions (good or evil) is due to "deserts." As for nature, it is entirely governed by "chance," or cause-and-effect interactions.[110] Furthermore, God does not watch over all men in an equal manner. Rather, providence is graded as their human perfections are graded.[111]

Maimonides subsumes providence under God's being. God knows all things from eternity; hence, no new knowledge can come to God. As Maimonides puts it: "His knowledge is His essence, and His essence His knowledge."[112] All things that happen, then, "follow upon His knowledge, which preceded and established them as they are. . . ."[113]

Finally, Maimonides provides an interesting study of the Jewish concept of *trial*. He rejects the popular belief that "God sends down calamities upon an individual, without their having been preceded by a sin, in order

106. See *The Guide of the Perplexed*, trans. by Shlomo Pines (Chicago: University of Chicago Press, 1963), 449–50.

107. Ibid., 452.

108. Ibid., 454.

109. Ibid., 469.

110. Ibid., 471f.

111. Ibid., 475, 624–25.

112. Ibid., 481.

113. Ibid., 485.

that his reward be increased."[114] The biblical trial passages, instead, are paradigms of what the faithful ought to believe and do, and serve to reaffirm the centrality of faith as both sufficient and useful. One ought not speculate about hidden meanings behind calamities. However, Maimonides does embrace a character-building motif with regard to suffering.[115]

Aquinas adopts Maimonides's first, second, and sixth positions, modifies his third, and rejects his fourth and fifth points.

Aquinas's Summa Theologiae

Although Aquinas draws upon many sources, his treatment of the providence of God is not merely a summary or synthesis of his predecessors' positions. Based on the revival of Aristotelian studies, Aquinas's doctrine represents a fresh and rigorous attempt to articulate a responsible theological understanding of God's providence. It is truly the first systematic and analytical discussion of providence worthy of the name, in spite of its scholastic form. Aquinas's position is most clearly articulated in his *Summa Theologiae* rather than in the expanded, less systematic, and more practical *Contra Gentiles*.

Aquinas devotes five major Questions to the providence of God: Question 23 ("On Providence"), Question 24 ("On Predestination"), and Questions 103–105 ("On Divine Government"). Providence is the eternal planned disposition of all things; predestination is a function of providence essentially concerned with salvation; and divine government is the temporal disposition and execution of what God has planned from eternity.

Providence

Aquinas examines providence only after discussing God's knowledge (Q. 14), Ideas (Q. 15), will (Q. 19), love (Q. 20), and justice and mercy (Q. 21)—all of which pertain to his being.

Aquinas argues that "God's knowledge is the cause of things."[116] In agreement with Boethius and Anselm, Aquinas explains that God knows everything from the perspective of an "eternal present." Hence all that takes place in time is eternally present to God."[117]

Furthermore, God's Ideas are inseparable from his essence; thus, the

114. Ibid., 497.
115. Ibid., 498–500. Maimonides identifies the following passages as containing the "trial" motif: Gen. 22:12; Exod. 16:4; 20:17; Deut. 8:2; 8:16; and 13:4.
116. See Thomas Aquinas, *Knowledge of God*, vol. 4 of *Summa Theologiae*, trans. by Thomas Gornall (London: Blackfriars, 1964), 31.
117. Ibid., 47.

"natures of all things," as well as their cause, reside in the divine mind.[118] So also, in the same way that God's knowledge is the cause of things, God's will is the cause of things.[119] "By one act God understands everything in his essence, and similarly by one act he wills everything in his goodness."

As for God's will, it can never be caused or motivated by anything outside God. Echoing Maimonides, Aquinas states that "God's willing is not in any way caused."[120] For to search for a volition behind God's will is philosophically pointless. As Gilby explains: "There is no causality within God, no relationship of cause to effect. . . ."[121] God, however, does not will moral evil, which is due to free will. But physical evil "he does will by willing the good to which it is attached."[122]

Aquinas's doctrine of providence has four major tenets: First, God has planned and created every goodness and ordained everything to its final end.[123]

Second, everything is subject to divine providence. Drawing upon the Aristotelian principle that universals include that which pertains to their particulars, Aquinas argues that "Providence rules all things, not only in their general natures, but also as individuals." "Since every efficient cause acts for an end, the purposed ordering of effects extends as far as the causality of the first cause engaged." "Hence everything that is real in any way is . . . directed by God to an end."[124]

God's direct ordering of every nature, however, is not incompatible with defects in nature or with free will in man (the Augustinian principle). God allows for both, as defects in nature ensure "that the complete good of the universe be disentangled" (the concept of harmony); and free will "goes back to God as its cause." Hence, whatever men do freely also falls under God's general oversight; "indeed their providing for themselves is contained under God's providing as a particular under a universal cause."[125]

Third, God "immediately" provides for all things. Since God has given creatures the power to work effects, and since he is the cause of that power, "the whole of their design down to every detail is anticipated in

118. Ibid., 67.

119. See Thomas Aquinas, *God's Will and Providence,* vol. 5 of *Summa Theologiae,* trans. by Thomas Gilby (London: Blackfriars, 1967), 19.

120. Ibid., 23.

121. See Gilby's note to this effect, ibid., 22–23.

122. Ibid., 41.

123. Ibid., 87–91.

124. Ibid., 93.

125. Ibid., 96.

his mind." God works through intermediaries, or through secondary causes, which, although they properly act in their own right, only do so because God has ordained things to function in this manner.[126]

Finally, God's providence does not impose a necessity on all things. God has provided that some things will be governed by "necessary causes" and other things by "contingent causes." Hence God cannot be charged with creating a deterministic world.

Aquinas's entire section on providence is relevant to the concept of *concursus*. Throughout Question 23, Aquinas's emphasis is on provision. God has provided for the universe to function as it does. To that extent God is not only the antecedent cause of all effects but, in the final analysis, is the complete cause of everything's power to act as it does. As Gilby explains:

> The Mainspring is the principle that God is the complete cause of all *esse* and *agere* . . . ; his creative activity continues while the whole of a being . . . is sustained . . . and extends to the whole of its acting. . . . This last function is called the divine *concursus,* an unhappy word if it implies the joint effort of two parties, for God is the complete cause of the ability to act, of the acting itself, and of the effect it may produce.[127]

This is an important distinction which Reformed theology can respect, provided it does not equate an agent's immoral acts or effects with the desired will of God (Tertullian's caution).

Predestination

While providence is the eternal planned disposition of all things, predestination has to do specifically with humankind's highest destiny and is, therefore, a function of providence. Aquinas perceives two destinies ordained for creatures. One is a natural end appropriate to natural powers (the Aristotelian motif); the other involves eternal life, which can be attained only through God's redemptive will. "Accordingly, the planned sending of a rational creature to the end which is eternal life is termed predestination. . . ."[128] Such predestining never belongs to the one predestined but only in God who predestines.[129] This means that God allows for some to fail and elects those who are saved.[130]

In an Augustinian manner, Aquinas concedes that by virtue of its very

126. Ibid., 99–101.
127. Ibid., 104. See esp. Gilby's note.
128. Ibid., 109.
129. Ibid., 113.
130. Ibid., 117.

meaning predestination presupposes election, and, in turn, a choice of love. For "when God chooses to love another and thereby wills him good, his will is the cause of the other being singled out and so endowed." In other words, love precedes choosing, and choosing precedes predestining. "Therefore all the predestined are picked loves" (*Unde omnes praedestinati sunt electi et dilecti*).[131]

Does God love and elect people on the basis of his foreknowledge of their merits? No! Are free will and good works of no avail? No! For God still works through secondary causes, which are effects of his grace. Aquinas echoes Anselm: "What is from freewill and what is from grace are not distinct, no more than what is from a secondary cause and what is from the first cause; God's Providence procures its effects through the operation of secondary causes. Hence what is through freewill is also from predestination."[132]

On what basis, then, does God love and elect those who are saved and condemn those who are lost? With Maimonides, as well as Augustine, Aquinas answers simply and soberly, "His so willing is the sole ground."[133]

Divine government

Divine government is the temporal disposition and execution of what God has planned from eternity for each creature. As far as God's government as a whole, "nothing can exist that is not created by God, so also nothing can exist that is not ruled by him."[134] This holds true even for autonomous man, through whose abilities God works interiorly and for whom God works exteriorly by drawing him toward the good through commandments, prohibitions, and the like.

Nature itself is governed directly by God. "For the *esse* of all creaturely beings so depends upon God that they could not continue to exist even for a moment, but would fall away into nothingness unless they were sustained in existence by his power. . . ."[135] God also uses secondary causes (cause-and-effect interactions) to sustain creation.

Finally, God so governs as to improve the lives of his creatures. He "moves man's mind" through its very powers of understanding and through the concepts it is able to conceive.[136] Above all, God acts in every agent cause without eroding that agent's autonomy. Aquinas explains this op-

---

131. Ibid., 120–21.
132. Ibid., 125.
133. Ibid., 129.
134. See Thomas Aquinas, *Divine Government,* vol. 14 of *Summa Theologiae,* trans. by T. C. O'Brien (London: Blackfriars, 1975), 21.
135. Ibid., 39.
136. Ibid., 69.

eration on the basis of Aristotle's causes (*Physics,* 2, lects. 5–6; *Metaphysics,* 5, lects. 2–3). For God acts as the end toward which all things strive; hence, he is "the cause of every operation whatsoever."[137] God also acts as the highest agent or efficient cause behind all the actions of other agents. Hence, "all agents act in dependence on God himself, so that he is the cause of the actions of all."[138] Finally, God provides the forms (formal essence) of every creature, and preserves and sustains these forms by his power.[139]

There is much in Aquinas that is commendable. There is the rigor and thoroughness with which he pursues the philosophical issues involved in formulating a doctrine of the providence of God. Aquinas also allows for a certain latitude in the interaction between necessary and contingent causes in God's exercise of providence. In addition, Aquinas bases God's government on noetic factors that link God logically and metaphysically with human action, but not psychologically and deterministically. God appeals to and through the intellectual framework of man's nature and accompanies man's free thought and actions with divine grace. Also, for Aquinas, God's will is inseparable from his wise, loving, and just character. Hence God's will, which is the highest principle and beyond which theology cannot go, is never arbitrary but always "sufficient" to solicit man's profoundest hopes and faith.

Nonetheless, as Barth points out, Aquinas does seem to subsume providence under God's eternal being in a manner that detracts from the scriptural emphasis on God's gracious election in Christ Jesus. But if that is the case, it must be admitted that Aquinas struggles to preserve the latter by subsuming predestination under God's love. Indeed, Barth's own inclusion of providence under predestination represents a subsumption of providence under the being of God, since, in Barth's own words, predestination is a matter "of the eternal decree without which God would not be God."[140]

A greater problem would seem to be Aquinas's dependence on the Aristotelian principles which he brings to his analysis of biblical revelation. But then we must remember that he was trying to harmonize Augustinian theology with the Aristotelian philosophy that was the intellectual *dynamis* of his day. Perhaps the most relevant criticism is that Aquinas's discussion of providence is principally a discussion of causation more than it is a study of God's governance of the world.

137. Ibid., 77.
138. Ibid.
139. Ibid.
140. Barth, *Church Dogmatics,* 3.3:5.

In the end, one could argue that Aquinas represents a brilliant example of how theology can become subservient to a philosophy that ultimately loses sight of the God of Abraham, David, and Paul, and instead leaves us with another abstract form of an Absolute Good, defined in Christian terminology. But if this position is taken, it must be offered with the profoundest respect for all that Aquinas was attempting to do.

John Duns Scotus and William of Ockham

No review of the Middle Ages, with regard to the concept of providence, would be complete without acknowledging the important work of John Duns Scotus (1265–1308) and William of Ockham (1290–1349).

John Duns Scotus

Scotus is generally acknowledged to follow the Augustinian-Franciscan tradition in emphasizing God's will over God's intellect.[141] This does not mean, however, that one should read an unwarranted divine authoritarianism into his system.

For Scotus, God is the object of theology rather than the object of metaphysics. Man's natural knowledge of God can only be gleaned through reflection on experience and is limited to univocal concepts. As a result, God's omnipotence and providence can never fully be demonstrated by metaphysics but belong more properly to the truths of faith.[142]

As for the divine Ideas, Scotus writes: "The divine intellect, precisely as intellect, produces in God the *rationes ideales,* the ideal or intelligible natures."[143] Hence God's intellect precedes his will. Since God's essence is infinite, the Ideas are also infinite, but it is God's will that ultimately determines which Ideas become "existents." In fact, will is central to God's essence. "Will in God is His essence really, perfectly and identically."[144] Because this is so, whatever God wills is in itself good.[145]

Copleston cautions, however, that "Scotus did not teach that the divine will acts in a simply capricious and arbitrary manner." Nonetheless, "the free choice of God is the ultimate reason of contingent things, and we

141. See Copleston, *History of Philosophy,* 2.2:205.
142. See Scotus's *De Primo Principio,* 4, no. 37; as cited and summarized by Copleston, *History of Philosophy,* 2.2:242–50.
143. *Opus Oxoniense,* 1, 36, no. 4; as quoted by ibid., 2.2:252.
144. *Reportata Parisiensia,* 1, 45, 2, no. 7; as quoted by ibid., 253.
145. *Opus Oxoniense,* 2, 1, 2, no. 65; cited by ibid., 254.

cannot legitimately go behind God's free choice and seek a necessary reason determining that choice."[146]

William of Ockham

In order to safeguard God's liberty and power, William of Ockham took Scotus's concept of will and turned it into an independent principle in God. It is Copleston's contention "that one of Ockham's main preoccupations as a philosopher was to purge Christian theology and philosophy of all traces of Greek necessitarianism, particularly of the theory of essences, which in his opinion endangered the Christian doctrines of the divine liberty and omnipotence."[147]

Platonic, Neo-Platonic, and medieval Christian thought repeatedly borrowed Plato's Ideas and turned them into eternal patterns in God's mind. Aquinas even identified them ontologically with the divine essence itself. In Ockham's estimation, however, these eternal Ideas limit God's power and creative activity if they are the sole norm of God's free choice. Hence Ockham rejects the "realism" of the Middle Ages, or the notion that essences or universals are real, and maintains that only individual entities possess being (whether temporally in reality or eternally in God).

We need not detail Ockham's rejection of realism, his theory of universals, or his nominalism. We need only emphasize their repercussions.

For Ockham, if only individual things exist, then our knowledge in general is based on our experience of these entities. Since God is not an observable entity, our natural knowledge of God can be based only on our knowledge of his effects in creatures. On this supposition, which Ockham shares with Scotus, metaphysical knowledge of God is always limited, and our knowledge of God's perfection, unicity, and providence must be based on revelation.

When Ockham applies this approach to creation and providence, what emerges is the pivotal role God's will plays in the creation and conservation of the world. Philotheus Boehner notes: "When dealing with philosophical problems concerning creatures Ockham never loses sight of the central idea that everything that is not God is radically contingent; for to be created means to be entirely dependent on the free will of God. That our world is what it is is due to a free decision of God."[148] Even at this, however, Boehner warns that Ockham's emphasis on God's will is an

146. Ibid., 254.
147. See Copleston, *History of Philosophy,* 3.1:60.
148. See William Ockham, *Philosophical Writings,* ed. by Philotheus Boehner (New York: Nelson, 1959), xlvi.

emphasis that also includes God's wisdom and goodness. However, God's wisdom is always a "free wisdom," and his goodness a "free goodness."[149]

Ockham maintains "that God is the mediate or immediate cause of all things,"[150] basing this contention on divine revelation (John 1:3). In fact, God may even be said to be the cause "for a wrongful action," insofar as "the same act may be caused by one cause with guilt and by another cause without guilt."[151] This is relevant to the Thomistic concept of *concursus,* in which God is the "complete cause," while an intermediate cause (such as free will in man) may be the cause of guilt. "For instance, the same act of will comes from a natural cause, viz. cognition, and from a free cause, viz. the will. Therefore the same act may have God as its immediate part-cause without His incurring guilt, and also be caused by a will that does incur guilt."[152]

Ockham also maintains that God foreknows future contingent facts or has knowledge of all individual entities and what will be true or false about them.[153] Ockham admits that he cannot explain how God knows all contingents. "Yet it can be said that God Himself or the divine essence is an intuitive cognition both of Himself and of all things which can or cannot be made, and that this intuitive cognition is so perfect and so clear that it is also an evident knowledge of past, future and present facts."[154]

Ockham pursues these themes in much greater depth in his treatise *Predestination, God's Foreknowledge, and Future Contingents.*[155] In this highly scholastic and intricately argued work, Ockham posits and defends a set of "assumptions" by means of which he attempts to clarify some of the contradictory problems related to his topic.

For Ockham, predestination signifies three things: "God [who will give eternal life to someone], eternal life, and the person to whom it is given."[156] Further, "all propositions having to do with predestination and reprobation are contingent whether they are of present tense . . ., or of past tense, or of future tense."[157] That is, the truth or falsehood about predestined persons can only be known after the event. This makes propositions about such events contingent. God, however, by virtue of his

---

149. Ibid.
150. *Quodlibeta,* 3, Q. iii; Ockham, *Philosophical Writings,* 128.
151. Ibid., 129.
152. Ibid.
153. *Ordinatio,* D. 38, Q. *unica;* Ockham, *Philosophical Writings,* 133.
154. Ibid., 133–34.
155. William Ockham, *Predestination, God's Foreknowledge, and Future Contingents,* trans. by M. M. Adams and N. Kretzmann (New York: Appleton-Century-Crofts, 1969).
156. Ibid., 45.
157. Ibid.

"intuitive cognition," knows all future contingent facts; still, his knowledge of these facts does not impose necessity on them. For events and facts about them never lose their contingency.[158]

Ockham attempts to safeguard both God's free will to predestine and man's freedom to act as a moral agent. He argues that while God ordains or predestines those who are saved, he always does so contingently.[159] He maintains "that a created will follows a divine ordinance . . . not necessarily but freely and contingently."[160]

Even future events revealed by the prophets in Scripture are contingent, though their certainty is known to God. For, explains Ockham, such events are always dependent on certain conditions that must occur before they become fact.[161] Thus not even future events happen necessarily but happen contingently.

Ockham asks, "Is there a cause of predestination in the predestinate and a cause of reprobation in the reprobate?" His answer is ambiguous: "For just as God is not a punisher before a man is a sinner, so He is not a rewarder before a man is justified by grace."[162]

In other writings, Ockham distinguishes between God's antecedent and consequent will.[163] It is right to assert that "nothing occurs contrary to the [consequent] disposing will of God."[164] Nonetheless, it is God's antecedent will that everyone should be saved. Only in so willing this antecedent, God has willed that such salvation should include the free choice of moral agents, who, under the aegis of God's antecedent will have the prerogative to deny their salvation. Thus the consequent of their rejection of God also falls under his will.

Ockham emphasizes the divine law as a consequent of the divine will (a theme that Calvin will adopt), as well as distinguishing between God's *potentia absoluta* and his *potentia ordinata* (i.e., between what God could have ordained as "right" versus what he has actually established as "right" in the moral order reflected in the Decalogue—all of which is part of God's governance of the world). Suffice it to say that Ockham's work represents a significant challenge to that long succession of Platonic thought, which the church both cherished and absorbed, so as to allow other motifs, sources, and interests to emerge and be utilized in theological reflection.

158. Ibid., 48.
159. Ibid., 41.
160. Ibid., 40.
161. Ibid., 44.
162. Ibid., 77.
163. See introduction to ibid., 18–19.
164. *Ordinatio,* D. 46, Q. 1; cited by ibid.

Renaissance and Reflection

Ernst Cassirer in *The Individual and the Cosmos in Renaissance Philosophy* argues that, prior to the Renaissance, three rival philosophical systems, all of which were absorbed by the church, vied for man's perception of himself and his universe: Platonism, Aristotelianism, and neo-Platonism. Platonism posited a sharp dichotomy between the intelligible and sensible realms and was noted for its concept of "transcendence." Aristotelianism viewed the world as "a self-enclosed sphere," in which the differences between the intelligible and sensible realms were differences of degree; it was a system characterized by "development," rather than escape or release from the sensible. Cassirer's view of neo-Platonism is highly pejorative. He criticizes it for its "bastard concept of 'emanation' " and its categories of "graded mediation" and "hierarchies" linking the transcendent to the sensible.[165]

Cassirer, along with other historians of philosophy,[166] notes that beginning at least with the fifteenth century, there occurred a revival of these three systems and that ultimately what came to prevail was a perception of man as a microcosm of the universe, the *locus classicus* for exploring all else. Philosophers like Nicholas of Cusa drew upon all three classical schools. Other Renaissance philosophers tended to favor either Platonic, Aristotelian, or neo-Platonic motifs. Among the neo-Platonists were figures like Giordano Bruno and Jokob Bohme, who embraced pantheism and speculative mysticism. Their view, in turn, later influenced Spinoza, Leibniz, Schelling, and Hegel. Pantheistic and mystical trends flourished during the Reformation, and Calvin would aim one of his bitterest polemics against the Libertines and their deterministic view of providence.[167]

Serious and worthwhile explorations of man's free will and God's relationship with the world were attempted by such notable Renaissance figures as Picco della Mirandola, Pietro Pomponazzi, and Lorenzo Valla; Valla's views, in particular, influenced both Luther and Calvin.[168]

With respect to their anthropologies, and therefore their understanding of providence, W. T. Jones explains that both classical and medieval minds were dominated by "teleological" interests and a quest for "purpose." But for modern man, all this has changed:

165. Ernst Cassirer, *The Individual and the Cosmos in Renaissance Philosophy* (Philadelphia: University of Philadelphia Press, 1983), 16–18.

166. See Copleston, *History of Philosophy,* 3.2:chaps. 13–17.

167. See *Calvin's Treatises Against the Anabaptists and Against the Libertines,* trans. and ed. by Benjamin Wirt Farley (Grand Rapids: Baker Book House, 1982), esp. chaps. 13–16 of *Against the Libertines.*

168. See Charles Trinkaus, *The Scope of Renaissance Humanism* (Ann Arbor: University of Michigan Press, 1983), 193–339.

> In place of the one supremely important vertical relationship of man to God which absorbed all of the attention and energy of the Middle Ages, we conceive a network of horizontal relations that connect every individual to his social and physical environment. For us, the good life does not consist in getting back into a right relation with God but in effecting an efficient and harmonious relation with our environment. From this view our position is Classical; but . . . the Classical mind . . . conceived all things to be subserving some purpose and aiming at some good. Hence for the Classical mind, as for the medieval, purpose was the primary mode of explanation.[169]

It is premature, if not unnecessary, to formulate an answer to Jones's implicit denial of divine providence as a meaningful modern position. Jaspers, Marcel, the Niebuhrs, C. S. Lewis, and others have adequately argued the contrary. But we may close this chapter by noting that Calvin's concern to explore the knowledge of God and the knowledge of man places him squarely in the Renaissance tradition. In addition, his rejection of speculative mysticism, pantheistic determinism, Aristotelian metaphysics, and, to a certain extent, Platonic idealism enables him to read the Scripture with clearer eyes, thus recovering those biblical foundations upon which the Reformed tradition has continued to build its doctrine of the providence of God.

---

169. Jones, *History of Western Philosophy,* 527.

Chapter Six

The Reformers' Perspectives

THE REFORMERS WERE CONVINCED THAT A PROPER UNDERSTANDING OF man and his abilities is essential to understanding God's relationship with mankind and the world. Too great a confidence in human ability and virtue is incompatible with what both Luther and Calvin, as well as Zwingli, know to be true about man from a biblical perspective. The same is true of man with regard to his political, economic, and social achievements, as they too are marred by pride and sin. Hence, it comes as no surprise to find Luther's clearest theological explorations of the providence of God embedded in his discussion of the bondage of the will, just as Calvin's views are guided by his principle of the twofold knowledge of God and man.

Martin Luther

Unlike Zwingli or Calvin, Luther does not develop a full-fledged doctrine of providence. Instead, he addresses the matter indirectly, in the context of more critical issues.

Luther views providence as a corollary of salvation; it is the twin of predestination. Barth maintains that predestination precedes providence; it is the presupposition on which providence rests.[1] Luther comes very close to subscribing to the identical principle, though not as unequivocally.

In his "Preface to the Epistle of St. Paul to the Romans," Luther writes: "In chapters 9, 10, and 11 Paul deals with the eternal providence

1. Barth, *Church Dogmatics, 3.3, 4, 5.*

138

of God. It is by this providence that it was first decided who should, and who should not, have salvation."[2] Here, providence is equivalent to predestination, if not subsumed under it. It is clear that, for Luther, providence has to do with the electing mystery of God, by which some are brought to faith.

Luther maintains that the criterion by which God acts both providentially and soteriologically is his incomprehensible will. In *The Bondage of the Will* Luther states: "He foresees, purposes, and does all things according to His own immutable, eternal and infallible will."[3] Luther cautions that "this will is not to be inquired into, but to be reverently adored. It is "the most awesome secret of the Divine Majesty."[4]

Following Ockham, Maimonides, and Augustine, Luther posits God's will as the highest cause for all causes, actions, and judgments. There is no higher criterion. Luther argues that sufficient biblical justification for this principle is found in Romans 11:33 and Isaiah 46:10. Luther maintains that "what God wills is not right because He ought, or was bound, so to will; on the contrary, what takes place must be right, because He so wills it."[5] To posit a principle higher than this would be to posit a God-beyond-God, which is absurd.

Luther also contends that God necessitates all things. This supposition follows the fact of God's incomprehensible will and is based on what Luther calls "resistless logic." He appeals to reason, the Greek concept of God's unchangeableness, and logical inference to substantiate this point.

Since God's nature is both eternal and changeless, then so are his attributes, which include his will. Moreover, since God's power cannot be impeded, his omnipotence compromised, or his wisdom deceived, it follows that whatever God has willed he has willed immutably, eternally, and infallibly. Hence, Luther concludes that "it follows, by *resistless logic,* that all we do, however it may appear to us to be done mutably and contingently, is in reality done necessarily and immutably in respect of God's will." Thus, "what is done cannot but be done where, when, how, as far as, and by whom, He foresees and wills."[6]

Luther believes that God's governing actions are a function of his foreknowledge. But unlike the patristic theologians who subsumed divine action under divine foreknowledge, or made God's operations subservient

---

2. See "Preface to the Epistle of St. Paul to the Romans," in *Martin Luther: Selections from His Writings,* ed. by John Dillenberger (Garden City: Anchor Books, 1961), 32. [All further references to this collection will be noted as *Writings.*]

3. See *Writings,* 181.

4. Ibid., 190.

5. Ibid., 196.

6. Ibid., 181; emphasis added.

to his foreknowledge of human "free choices," Luther makes God's fore-knowledge a function of his will. God's foresight and redemptive action are grounded in the divine "secret"; they are never simply a divine response to human sin and perversity.

In fact, Luther denies that the will is really "free." Rather, it "is the permanent prisoner and bondslave of evil."[7] Consequently, men are not as free to work out their individual destinies as they think they are. A fallen humanity does "everything of necessity, and nothing by 'free-will'; for the power of 'free-will' is nil, and it does no good, nor can do, without grace."[8] Human beings have "no power of freely turning in any direction, yielding to none and subject to none."[9]

However, Luther does acknowledge that man has a limited ability, tainted of course by pride and self-deception, to engage in a "lower" series of cause-and-effect interactions. But this is the only level at which "choice" exists. Man possesses free will primarily in respect to "what is below him." In this realm of external affairs, particularly with regard to money and possessions, persons may or may not use them. To this extent, the will is "always free according to its nature, but only with respect to that which is in its power and is inferior to it. . . ."[10] Short of the grace of God, the will is never free to do good or to realize righteousness. The "power of decision" only becomes free when it receives grace.[11]

Luther maintains that the purpose of the knowledge of God's providential and redemptive action is to foster and nurture Christian faith and is meant to issue in acts of courage and love. As Luther explains: "For the Christian's chief and only comfort in every adversity lies in knowing that God does not lie, but brings all things to pass immutably, and that His will cannot be resisted, altered, or impeded."[12] Above all, knowing that salvation no longer depends on free will, one can rejoice that salvation rests securely in God's merciful hands.[13]

Luther also espouses the biblical and patristic principle of eschatological justification: "There is a life after this life; and all that is not punished and repaid here will be punished and repaid there; for this life is nothing more than a precursor, or, rather, a beginning, of the life that is to come."[14]

---

7. Ibid., 187.
8. Ibid., 188.
9. Ibid.
10. See *Luther: Lectures on Romans,* vol. 15 of Library of Christian Classics, trans. and ed. by Wilhelm Pauck (Philadelphia: Westminster, 1961), 252.
11. Ibid.
12. *Writings,* 185.
13. Ibid., 199.
14. Ibid., 202.

Luther is confident that God's inscrutable ways among men can and will be justified. In the same way that God's will is incomprehensible, it is both reasonable and inevitable that his justice should also be incomprehensible. In support of this motif, Luther cites Romans 11:33: "O the depth of the riches and wisdom and knowledge of God! How unsearchable are his judgments and how inscrutable his ways!"

In the end, however, God's justice will be revealed as just. Luther admonishes the believer to "keep in view three lights, the light of *nature,* the light of *grace,* and the light of *glory.*" Luther elaborates:

> By the light of nature, it is inexplicable that it should be just for the good to be afflicted and the bad to prosper; but the light of grace explains it. By the light of grace, it is inexplicable how God can damn him who by his own strength can do nothing but sin and become guilty. . . . But the light of glory insists otherwise, and will one day reveal God, to whom alone belongs a judgment whose justice is incomprehensible, as a God Whose justice is most righteous and evident—provided only that in the meanwhile we *believe* it. . . .[15]

Until that time, however, God is actively engaged in governing the present world. This divine governance is based on the distinction between two kinds of men and the two different kingdoms to which they belong.

Luther divides the children of Adam into two classes: the elect in Christ and the nonelect. Each lives in a different kind of kingdom (Luther's parallel to Augustine's two cities) and is governed by a different kind of law.

Both the elect and the nonelect share the same temporal kingdom and are governed by its authority. But this temporal government "has laws which extend no further than to life and property and external affairs on earth."[16] Its man-made laws may never govern the soul.

This worldly government works through the sword. It represents a providential ordering ordained and administered by God, through which God exercises a righteousness over the sinful world and its prince, namely, Satan. "And although God will not reward this kind of righteousness with eternal life," explains Luther, "he still wishes peace to be maintained among men and rewards them with temporal blessings."[17] Thus even this

15. Ibid; emphasis added.
16. See Luther's *Temporal Authority: To What Extent It Should Be Obeyed,* vol. 45 of *Luther's Works,* ed. by W. T. Brandt and H. T. Lehmann (Philadelphia: Muhlenberg, 1962), 105.
17. See Luther's *Whether Soldiers, Too, Can Be Saved,* vol. 46 of *Luther's Works,* ed. by R. C. Schulte and H. T. Lehmann (Philadelphia: Fortress, 1967), 101.

world and its sinful humanity enjoy divine guidance and undeserved blessing.

The second kind of government God has established among men is a spiritual one. It has no sword, nor does it need one. It has and needs only the Word, "by means of which men are to become good and righteous, so that with this righteousness they may attain eternal life."[18] All men and women belonging to this government may freely engage in the commerce of the temporal kingdom, as well as in its politics and social structures (in which even the hangman's occupation has its place), provided only that they are governed inwardly by the dictates of the gospel.

In Luther, then, we see the triumph of Augustinian principles. In many respects, Luther's doctrine of the providence of God is a restatement of Augustine's position. Without elaborating, Luther also acknowledges the insufficiency of a principle of the foreknowledge of God which maintains that God orders his world primarily in response to human choices. In light of the bondage of the human will, such a principle is simply unacceptable. Luther also emphasizes God's necessitating will and Augustine's two-cities motif.

What is missing in Luther is Augustine's philosophical approach and the range of his reflection. The closest Luther comes to engaging in philosophical analysis is in his polemic with Erasmus. Specifically, in *The Bondage of the Will,* Luther rejects the philosophical implications of the schoolmen's distinctions between contingency and necessity, or between philosophical antecedents and their consequents.

Luther refers to this matter under the rubric of the *necessity of consequence.* The schoolmen who used this formula apparently meant that once the effect of a cause has been realized, it cannot be changed, but until that effect is caused, an outcome could be different.[19] This distinction was favored in an effort to salvage free will while claiming that the elect are necessarily saved. This would allow for God's will necessarily to be done, but to be done contingently. Luther charges that the schoolmen "maintained that all things take place necessarily, but by necessity of consequence (as they put it), and not by necessity of the thing consequent."[20] He denounces "this play on words," and with it any possibility of soft determinism (although he obviously retains the latter with respect to "free choices" in "external affairs").

Luther concludes: "So our original proposition still stands and remains unshaken: all things take place by necessity. There is no obscurity or

18. Ibid., 99.
19. See *Lectures on Romans,* 248 n. 60.
20. Ibid., 183.

ambiguity about it. In Isaiah, it says, 'My counsel shall stand, and my will shall be done' [46:10]; and any schoolboy knows the meaning of 'counsel,' 'will,' 'shall be done,' 'shall stand'!"[21]

This is sufficient for Luther. In something akin to an existentialist statement, he boasts: "If I come to exist of necessity, it does not much worry me that my existence and being are in themselves mutable; contingent and mutable as I am, . . . yet I still come to exist!"[22] All one need do is "believe" and be "willing to yield to truth without stubborn resistance."[23]

The Reformed tradition can respect Luther's position. Although he does not elaborate on God's work of *conservatio* or *concursus,* Luther clearly underscores the magnitude of God's work of *gubernatio.* He also allows man a degree of secular freedom within which personal and political destinies may be pursued. At the same time, however, Luther affirms the biblical witness to God's redemptive presence in the world and calls us to renew our faith in him. With Paul Luther summons us to temper all our cause-and-effect interactions with choices made possible by the redemptive work of Christ and by the presence and power of the Holy Spirit in all believers' hearts (see Gal. 5).

Ulrich Zwingli

Zwingli was the first Reformer to devote a critical treatise to the subject of providence. It grew out of a sermon he preached during the Marburg Colloquy (Oct. 1–4, 1529). At the request of Philip of Hesse, he reproduced the sermon in writing under the title *On the Providence of God.* It is dated August 20, 1530.

Zwingli's *On Providence* is tightly and logically argued, and spans many subject areas. Samuel Macauly Jackson has referred to this treatise as "the most abstruse as well as the most penetrating Latin work of Zwingli."[24] In it, Zwingli develops a concept of the providence of God that is both rationalistic and biblical. Tillich describes it as a doctrine "colored by a rational determinism."[25]

For Zwingli, God's nature determines the character and extent of his providential activity. Zwingli defines God primarily along rationalistic lines,

---

21. Ibid.
22. Ibid.
23. Ibid., 202f.
24. See *On Providence and Other Essays,* ed. by William John Hinke (Durham, N.C.: Labyrinth, 1983), 130.
25. See Paul Tillich, *A Complete History of Christian Thought,* ed. by Carl E. Braaten (New York: Harper & Row, 1968), 258.

but the attributes he assigns God are, in his view, compatible with biblical revelation. In many instances, after having argued his point philosophically, Zwingli cites numerous biblical texts in support of his position.

Zwingli defines God as supremely good (citing Plato), simple, pure, complete, omniscient, omnipotent, unchangeable, and eternal. Consequently, "Providence must exist, because the supreme good necessarily cares for and regulates all things."[26] If God did not care for all things, then his goodness would be in question; if God were not eternally aware of all things (past, present, and future), his wisdom, perfection, and true deity would be in jeopardy; and if God did not regulate literally everything, his power would be in question. Since God's goodness, power, and wisdom are beyond compromise or question, it follows that God must and does care for and govern everything in heaven and on earth, animate and inanimate, human and nonhuman.

Zwingli concludes: "Providence is the enduring and unchangeable rule over and direction of all things in the universe."[27] It "is, therefore, immovable, because the Deity is infallible and unerring, because His power is unwearying, because His goodness is uninterrupted."[28]

Zwingli argues that nothing can happen by chance. In a world loved and governed by a supremely good God, nothing can happen accidentally or occur fortuitously. Absolute determinism reigns. Nothing occurs randomly; no human thought or will is freely its own. "Freedom of action," "freedom of choice," and "cause-and-effect interaction" impose limits on divine power and goodness. They imply indifference on the part of God, which, in Zwingli's view, would compromise his wisdom, power, and goodness.

> For if anything were guided by its own power or insight, just so far would the wisdom and power of our Deity be deficient. And if this happened, the wisdom of the Deity would not be supreme, because it would not include and comprehend all things. Nor would his might be all powerful, because there would be a might independent of its powers and therefore different from it.[29]

Zwingli holds that secondary causes are not *causae* per se. Since God is in complete control of everything, "secondary causes are not properly called causes."[30] Zwingli asserts "that there is only one true cause of all

26. *On Providence,* 130.
27. Ibid., 136.
28. Ibid., 137.
29. Ibid.
30. Ibid., 138.

things"[31]—God. And he is the only effective force; "He alone can do and does do all things."[32] Hence, secondary causes are, at best, mere instruments through which God works directly. They are "but the agents and instruments with which the eternal mind works, and in which it manifests itself to be enjoyed."[33]

God is the power behind and in all things. In a statement clearly inspired by Stoic philosophy (he specifically cites Pliny and Seneca), Zwingli declares: "Through God's power all things exist, live, and act, nay all things are in Him, who is everywhere present, and of Him, who is the being, existence, and life of all things."[34]

Tillich finds this insight appealing, as it underlies his own concept of God as the ground of being. Tillich commends it and Zwingli's understanding of God "as the universal dynamic power of being in everything that is."[35]

Hence, Zwingli underscores again God's radical government of everything in the universe.

> In all these things, then, not less than of man, we discover the presence of the divine power by which they have their being, and live, and move. . . . By this we learn that even the things which we call fortuitous or accidental are not fortuitous or random happenings, but are all effected by the order and regulation of the Deity.[36]

Zwingli is well aware of the problem of evil which his position implies. Yet evil is reconcilable in a world determined by a supremely good God. Zwingli's stance is a mixture of rationalism, Greek anthropology, Augustinian theology, and Pauline insight.

Zwingli's theodicy, in keeping with the tone of his doctrine of providence, is dictated by the concept of God's goodness. Zwingli acknowledges that this theme is both Platonic and biblical.

Granted that God governs man in every aspect, Zwingli opens with the reminder that God created man that he might have fellowship with God both here and in the hereafter.[37] Man "was born to enjoy God."[38] To this end God created man as a combination of spirit and flesh—as spirit to

31. Ibid., 154.
32. Ibid., 155.
33. Ibid., 158.
34. Ibid., 148.
35. Tillich, *Complete History,* 258.
36. *On Providence,* 150.
37. Ibid., 160.
38. Ibid., 161.

enjoy God and other spiritual beings, and as body, "not to dishonor" its "worthy guest," the soul, but "softened and shaped" as is no other creature's, adapted with the potential for "gentleness, peace and friendship."[39]

Still, why did God create man this way? When God foresaw that human spirit and flesh would clash, why did God create man as he did? Above all, why did he provide him with a law against which God knew man would offend? "Why did He not rather suffer him to live without the law?"[40]

Zwingli's solution is complex and involved, but essentially contains three tenets.

First, God created man as he did because the "Deity willed to make him so, and for Him to have so willed it is enough."[41] This Ockhamistic reply, however, is softened by Platonic and Thomistic notes. As Zwingli explains, "nothing pleases [God] which is not good and holy and just."[42] Hence, God's will is always an expression of his goodness and justice.

Second, God provided the law to reveal his "constant will" and "nature," for God is "the nature of that which he shows us."[43] Hence, the law reveals God's love for his creatures and his love of justice. Nevertheless, God himself is always above the law, as he is his own law, and cannot be judged by the law. Since God is holy and just, he always acts ethically in whatever he chooses to do; yet God by his very nature enjoys an eternal suspension of the ethical—from a human point of view. Thus, God, the cause of all human actions and choices, cannot be faulted on ethical grounds, even when the brigand robs or the murderer kills. For God is without sin and cannot be judged by the law. Rather, God provided the law both to reveal his nature and love for man and to provide the human mind and spirit with fitting "inspiration," "light," and "knowledge of God."[44]

Third, God created man as he did, knowing he would fall, in order to reveal his own true nature as a righteous and merciful God. In Zwingli's estimation, God's supreme goodness could not have been grasped by mankind, if evil were not a possibility. Zwingli argues from an essentially Augustinian position: "For the good, therefore, of angels and men both were so fashioned that they could fall. . . . Thus by creating man so that he could fall, God manifested His goodness. For by the fall the splendor of the divine righteousness was made apparent."[45]

39. Ibid., 160f.
40. Ibid., 165.
41. Ibid.
42. Ibid., 164. .
43. Ibid., 166.
44. Ibid., 172–76.
45. Ibid., 177.

For Zwingli, predestination is the presupposition on which providence rests. Zwingli's argument is as follows: "God is all-knowing, all-powerful, and good. Hence nothing escapes His notice, nothing evades His orders and His sway, nothing which He does is anything but good."[46] Knowing that man would fall, God, on the basis of his justice and goodness, determined to elect some to salvation.

Zwingli defines election as "the free disposition of the divine will in regard to those that are to be blessed."[47] Election has to be completely the work of God, for if "predestination followed our decision," then salvation would be a matter of self-determination and, consequently, a matter outside of God's hands, which cannot be.

Moreover, election is based entirely on the will of God "as its principal cause."[48] Granted God's will is tempered by his goodness and wisdom, the final electing principle has to be "the work of will," not "of wisdom." Why? Because "wisdom" can be interpreted to imply the older patristic and later Thomistic position that God, foreseeing (i.e., "knowing") some action or attitude that we might take or espouse, elected us in the light of that "wisdom." Hence, will must be the highest criterion in God in order to safeguard his free decision and, ultimately, his grace toward humankind. Zwingli cites Exodus 33:19 and Romans 9:18 to confirm this position. He explains:

> So in destining men to salvation, the Divine Will is the first power, but attended by the handmaidens wisdom, goodness, righteousness, and the other attributes. Therefore it is attributed to will, not to wisdom, (otherwise God's gift and disposition would seem to depend upon our acts, as I indicated) not to righteousness. . . .[49]

Zwingli stops short, however, of advocating double predestination: "Election, therefore, is the free but not blind disposition of the Divine Will, as the principal cause, though not alone, but accompanied by majesty and authority, and applying to the blessed, not the damned."[50]

Having been elected, the blessed respond to God in faith, which is itself a gift of the Spirit, and believing in the gospel are justified. In time the elect will even come to realize their election by this possession of faith. Zwingli is confident of this: "Faith is the sign of the election by which we obtain real blessedness. If election as a blossom had not preceded, faith would never have followed."[51]

46. Ibid., 180.
47. Ibid., 184.
48. Ibid., 185.
49. Ibid., 186.
50. Ibid., 187.
51. Ibid., 201.

As for the damned, Zwingli prefers not to speculate about their condition or even its cause. To begin with, no one knows who they are. Zwingli does acknowledge that "him who has heard the doctrine of faith expounded and remains and dies in unbelief, we can perhaps count among the wretched."[52] But this is a mystery Zwingli prefers to leave to the will and wisdom of God.

Zwingli believes that the reality of God's electing mercy, known and experienced in the phenomenon of faith, and the reality of God's pervasive ordering of all of life ought to bring the highest joy to Christian hearts. Toward the close of his treatise, Zwingli reiterates a deterministic motif: "It follows that nothing is created by Divine Wisdom of which the end and all the attending circumstances to the end have not been foreseen and settled long before they take place. Life and activity, therefore, are just as much arranged by Divine providence for every man as are his birth and generation."[53]

This is a world, then, in which nothing whatsoever occurs by chance, nothing takes place which God has not foreseen and willed in his supreme goodness. It is a world in which divine knowledge of the sparrow's fall (Matt. 10:29) and the number of hairs on every head (Luke 12:7) witness to a Deity for whom "nothing . . . is of too little value for God's providence to have a care for it";[54] "nothing can be neglected by Him";[55] "nothing [is] trivial enough to be trivial in God's dispensation and activity."[56]

Therefore, whether one's lot is characterized by prosperity or adversity, one can bear all of life with either joy or equanimity. If one's lot is riches and honor, "what a sense of rest and also of responsibility is called forth in our hearts!" Or if one's days are marked with poverty and defeat, "what comfort [providence] brings us amid such hard lines! With what high spirit . . . such a man rises above the world and scorns what is below him!"[57]

For Zwingli, then, the providence of God is a singular and paramount doctrine of faith. It heralds the good news of God's supreme goodness, power, wisdom, and love, and attests to his guiding presence in every moment of life.

A Reformed theology can rightly marvel at Zwingli's treatise and draw inspiration from it. His doctrine fully vindicates the supremacy of God

---

52. Ibid., 200.
53. Ibid., 205f.
54. Ibid., 223.
55. Ibid., 226.
56. Ibid., 229.
57. Ibid.

over all things, the goodness of God in, under, behind, and through all things, and the will of God (molded by the eternal forms of divine love and holiness) as the formal and final cause of all things. Convinced that no event can be fortuitous, Zwingli assures us that God cares for and regulates all things, for all persons, at all times, in all places. Nothing can evade God, for he is everywhere in all things; and no one can fall outside the perimeters of God's wisdom and power, because his very being requires God to embrace everthing he has created and loves. Whatever the excesses of his position, Zwingli's emphasis on the scope and goodness of God's governance can certainly be appreciated by Reformed communities.

However, Zwingli's excesses must be acknowledged. Does his understanding of providence redound to God's wisdom, justice, and goodness in denying man any free choices? Does denying even fallen man a modicum of freedom imply God's indifference toward man or expose God to a kind of deficiency? Moreover, are God's omniscience, omnipotence, and goodness eroded by allowing the free interaction of cause-and-effect occurrences to be a way of ordering both man and nature? Does such an ordering prevent God from interacting with his creation as often, or as continuously, as he wills? Is not the moral character of the universe, as well as its wonder, preserved as fittingly in a system of moderate determinism or soft determinism, that allows for and elicits free interactions, as in a system which forbids all but the tightest kind of causal connection? Which vision of interaction truly witnesses to the God of revelation: an interaction in which God does it all, or one in which God, while governing it all, solicits his human creature's freest cries of "Abba, Father!"?

In addition, must not the modern Reformed reader recoil at the contradiction implied in Zwingli's insistence that, although the divine law displays the true nature of God, God is not bound by it? What does this mean? Certainly God is "above" the law. But if the law does not truly witness to God's justice and holiness, then to what does it witness? Zwingli seems to have been forced to create this caveat in order to justify his determinism motif in which God is the primary, indeed sole, cause of everything. Since God cannot be evil, then if God, as *causa,* lies behind the brigand's robbery and the murderer's killing, he would be culpable of sin, if judged by his own law. Hence, Zwingli suspends the ethical and places God under a "higher" law, the law of his own will.

However, the problem still remains: if the law reveals God's nature at all, then how can God remain God and contradict his own nature? One could answer that God "accommodates" himself, provided, of course, that some analogical unity is preserved between God in himself and God as revealed in the law. The other alternative is the Ockhamistic solution, which defines God as "arbitrary will." But even Zwingli rejects that approach. In the final analysis, Zwingli's solution simply fails to provide an ultimate resolution.

Finally, Zwingli's concept of man, even fallen man, turns him into an automaton. By denying man to be "guided by [his] own power or insight,"[58] does Zwingli not empty man of all that makes him human? Even fallen man becomes less than biblically fallen man in Zwingli's schema. For biblical man, at least, can be held accountable for his actions and choices and is led to believe that, in the common course of life, his free decisions, though tainted by pride and sin, or wooed and cleansed by the Holy Spirit, are still his to make or not make and have certain consequences. Obliterating this dimension of biblical man's nature, even fallen nature, and denigrating the role of secondary causes, serves neither to the greater glory of God nor to the minor glory of God's most cherished creation, man.

It is against the hard rock of this biblical note that all the ships of any deterministic fleet are bound to strike or so it would seem. It is of keen interest, therefore, to observe the way in which Calvin avoids this kind of danger.

John Calvin

In the 1559 edition of his *Institutes of the Christian Religion,* Calvin places his discussion of the providence of God at the end of book 1 (The Knowledge of God the Creator). Until this edition, he had discussed providence and predestination jointly, but with the 1559 edition he separates the two subjects.

Chapters 16–28 of book 1 of the *Institutes* contain Calvin's principal comments on providence. However, in a separate work, the *Treatise Against the Libertines* (1545), Calvin devotes a considerable portion of this polemic to problems posed by a pantheistic interpretation of the doctrine.

For Calvin, God is not merely the Creator of the universe but its Governor as well. In the broadest sense, God governs every aspect of the universe directly, immediately, knowingly, and willfully. In this regard, Calvin's position is very similar to Zwingli's, though his approach is more biblical.

In agreement with Zwingli, Calvin also holds that nothing can happen by chance: "The Providence of God, as taught in Scripture, is opposed

58. Ibid., 137.

to fortune or fortuitous causes"[59]; "all events whatsoever are governed by the secret counsel of God."[60] This pertains to all things, animate or inanimate, heavenly or earthly. Granted that each thing is endowed with its own unique properties, nothing functions of its own accord except "as directed by the immediate hand of God."[61]

Calvin offers two reasons for this. First, a biblical understanding of God's omnipotence requires his activity be understood as a dynamic phenomenon—"not the vain, indolent, slumbering omnipotence [of the Sophists], but *vigilant, efficacious, energetic,* and *ever active.*"[62] Note here that Calvin's terminology is not drawn from logic or the language of philosophical necessity or determinism. Instead his understanding of omnipotence underscores the dynamic character and quality of God's interaction with the world.

Second, Calvin rejects the mechanical and naturalistic concept of nature as something that unfolds in and of itself according to its own universal laws. More than "a perpetual law of nature" is at stake.[63] This is God's world, and it is his right, ability, and glory to govern it as he sees fit. Calvin sees this with amazing perspicuity and defends it with vigor: "Those . . . who confine the providence of God within narrow limits, as if he allowed all things to be borne along freely according to a perpetual law of nature, . . . defraud God of his glory [and] themselves of a most useful doctrine; . . ."[64]

In addition, Calvin warns that naturalistic views impair, if not eliminate, God's particular goodness toward individuals.[65] Hence, Calvin concludes: "There is no random power, or agency, or motion in the creatures, who are so governed by the secret counsel of God that nothing happens but what he has knowingly and willingly decreed."[66]

In this sense, then, all cause-and-effect interactions are interactions over which God is "vigilant" and in which he is "efficaciously" and "energetically" in control. To allow nature or man to be governed by universal laws offends Calvin's understanding of God's personal involvement in history and individual lives as depicted in Scripture. Hence, Calvin lifts

---

59. Unless otherwise indicated, all references to Calvin's *Institutes* in this section are to volume 1 of the Henry Beveridge translation (Grand Rapids: Wm. B. Eerdmans, 1957). See *Institutes,* 1.16.2.
60. Ibid.
61. Ibid.
62. Calvin, *Institutes,* 1.16.3.
63. Ibid; emphasis added.
64. Ibid.
65. Ibid.
66. Ibid.

the debate from the realm of the purely philosophical or rational, and even from the arena of historical cause-and-effect interaction, and sees it instead as a profound issue of faith in God as the ever-present Lord of all of life. It is for this reason that theologians have generally maintained that Calvin denied a "general providence."[67]

The question, then, for modern Reformed theologies is the extent to which Calvin's insight can be claimed, defended, and advanced, while allowing for a genuine "freedom" of interaction, such as Barth, Brunner, Tillich, and even Berkouwer want to espouse.

Certainly, Calvin's analysis clarifies the central issue and frees the doctrine, once and for all, from all attempts to reduce it to a kind of mechanical, philosophical, or formal determinism, which unfolds according to laws, even divine laws, of its own. This is precisely what biblical providence is not. It is not a system of theological or rational determinism but a doctrine of faith in the God of the universe who governs all things out of the profound personal depth of his wisdom, power, will, and love. As Calvin explains:

> For we do not with the Stoics imagine a necessity consisting of a perpetual chain of causes, and a kind of involved series contained in nature, but we hold that God is the disposer and ruler of all things,—that from the remotest eternity, according to his own wisdom, he decreed what he was to do, and now by his power executes what he decreed.[68]

Calvin maintains that God's will is the motivating and determining principle of his providential activity. In whatever God does, we must "account his will the best of all reasons."[69] Moreover, like Aquinas, Calvin argues that "the counsel of God" is always "in accordance with the highest reason."[70]

Hence, even for Calvin, we see that the divine will is defined in terms of "the highest reason," or the noblest ends, and is never to be conceived of as a raw, arbitrary phenomenon. Calvin explains: "When the tumultumous aspect of human affairs unfits us for judging, we should still hold that God, in the pure light of his justice and wisdom, keeps all these

---

67. See Gilkey, *Reaping the Whirlwind,* 179f.; Wilhelm Niesel, *The Theology of Calvin,* trans. by Harold Knight (Grand Rapids: Baker Book House, 1980), 72f.; Richard Stauffer, *Dieu, la création et la providence dans la prédication de Calvin* (Berne: Peter Lang, 1978) 264–66.

68. Calvin, *Institutes,* 1.16.8.

69. *Institutes,* 1.17.1.

70. Ibid.

commotions in due subordination, and conducts them to their proper end."[71]

Thus, God's will is to be understood in terms of his justice and wisdom and not in terms of blind, menacing power. Consequently, Calvin (like Zwingli) grounds God's will in his goodness; only the goodness in which God's will is grounded is not conceived philosophically (as in Plato) but is inferred from God's mighty acts and divine nature as attested to in Scripture.

Calvin acknowledges, however, that God's "incomprehensible counsel" does possess a quality of "hiddenness," which may be compared to "a great deep" or deep abyss (Deut. 29:29; Isa. 40:13–14; Rom. 11:33–34).[72] Still the "great deep" within God is never to be absolutized as a naked principle. As Calvin rightly perceives, the will in question is "not that absolute will, indeed, of which sophists prate, when by a profane and impious divorce, they separate his justice from his power, but that universal overruling Providence from which nothing flows that is not right, though the reasons thereof may be concealed."[73]

Consequently, in light of God's providential "overruling," founded on the highest and holiest of reasons, men and women are both accountable for their personal wickedness and expected to utilize wisdom and caution in all of life's interactions.

God cannot be blamed for human sin. The essence of God's overruling lies in the fact that he can take perversity and use it to his highest purposes. Hence, God commands none to act wickedly.

> This, assuredly, he does not command. Nay, rather we rush on, not thinking of what he wishes, but so inflamed by our own passionate lust, that with destined purpose, we strive against him. And in this way, while acting wickedly, we serve his righteous ordination, since in his boundless wisdom he will know how to use bad instruments for good purposes.[74]

In a similar manner, God's providential overruling excuses no one from acting wisely, cautiously, or energetically. Reflecting on the meaning of Proverbs 16:9, Calvin realizes that

> the eternal decrees of God by no means prevent us from proceeding under his will, to provide for ourselves, and arrange all our affairs. . . . For he who has fixed the boundaries of our life, has at the same time intrusted us with

71. Ibid.
72. *Institutes,* 1.17.2.
73. Ibid.
74. *Institutes,* 1.17.5.

care of it, provided us with the means of preserving it, forewarned us of the dangers to which we are exposed, and supplied cautions and remedies, that we may not be overwhelmed unawares.[75]

Calvin's doctrine, therefore, wisely balances God's rule with human accountability. In this way, Calvin avoids purely rationalistic theological reductionism.

Calvin takes secondary causes seriously. The importance of intermediate actions, choices, attitudes, and means must not be mitigated. Even though the Christian knows that God is "the principal cause of events," he will nonetheless pay "due regard to inferior causes in their own place."[76] This is a principle Calvin wisely maintains and astutely applies to the Christian life. In fact, it is noteworthy that Calvin's interest in the concept is not because of its philosophical or logical nuances, but because it serves to underscore human accountability—the true biblical concept of human dignity, even the dignity of fallen man, as he has been redeemed in Christ.

> At the same time, the Christian will not overlook inferior causes. For, while he regards those by whom he is benefited as ministers of the divine goodness, he will not, therefore, pass them by, as if their kindness deserved no gratitude, but feeling sincerely obliged to them, willingly confess the obligation, and endeavour, according to his ability, to return it. In fine, in the blessing in which he receives, he will revere and extol God as their principal author, but will also honour men . . . [with] kindness. If he sustains any loss through negligence or imprudence, he will, indeed, believe that it was the Lord's will it should so be, but at the same time, he will impute it to himself.[77]

In this connection, the *Treatise Against the Libertines* is highly relevant to Calvin's point. In it, he provides a penetrating outline for a responsible doctrine of the providence of God. He espouses a form of general providence, but denies all mechanical, fatalistic, or pantheistic interpretations of God's providence. Specifically, Calvin upholds the order of nature as an instrument of providence, argues for human accountability, and rejects the notion that God is the unqualified cause of all causes. Secondary causes, or the deeds and decisions of human beings, function in a manner that allows for and requires personal participation in its own right, and, thus, the possibility of incurring guilt.

Calvin insists that God works through the natural order: "There is a universal operation by which He guides all creatures according to the

75. *Institutes*, 1.17.4.
76. *Institutes*, 1.17.6.
77. *Institutes*, 1.17.9.

condition and propriety which He has given each at creation."[78] In addition, "this universal operation . . . does not prevent each creature, heavenly or earthly, from having and retaining its own quality and nature and from following its own inclination."[79]

Moreover, each of God's creatures, man especially, acts in its "own right." "For we must not suppose that God works in an iniquitous man as if he were a stone or a piece of wood, but he uses him as a thinking creature, according to the quality of his nature which He has given him."[80] In other words, even from God's side, there can be no mechanical or manipulative determination per se.

Hence, Calvin infers:

> We must observe that creatures here below do their works in accordance with their capacity, being judged good or evil based on whether they act in obedience to God or trespass against Him. Nonetheless, God is over all and directs things toward a good end and turns evil into good. Or at least He extracts good from what is evil, working according to His nature, that is, in [accordance with] justice and equity.[81]

Finally, Calvin, with Zwingli and Luther, extols the virtues of God's providence as a source of both comfort and courage, solace and hope.[82]

Far more could be written of Calvin's doctrine,[83] but suffice it to note that Calvin's attempt represents a serious and assiduous effort to do justice to both the *maior Dei gloria* and the *minor gloria creaturae*. Insofar as he succeeds, the deterministic aspects of Calvin's doctrine, which one must acknowledge, are to be measured against three constant factors: (1) his rejection of a mechanical or naturalistic governorship of the universe; (2) his insistence on God's wise, equitable, immediate, and dynamic guidance of all of life and history; and (3) his recognition that human beings are rational agents, who act in and through their own unique nature, with which God may sometimes concur, interfere, or redirect, ac-

---

78. See Calvin's *Against the Fantastic and Furious Sect of the Libertines Who are Called "Spirituals,"* in Calvin, *Treatises*, 242f.

79. Ibid., 243.

80. Ibid., 245.

81. Ibid., 247.

82. See *Institutes*, 1.17.10–11.

83. See Charles Brooks Partee, Jr., *Calvin and Classical Philosophy* (Leiden: E. J. Brill, 1977), esp. 126–45. Cf. Francois Wendel, *Calvin: The Origins and Development of His Religious Thought,* trans. by Philip Mairet (New York: Harper & Row, 1950), 177–84. See also John H. Leith, "A Study of John Calvin's Doctrine of the Christian Life," Ph.D. diss., Yale University 1949, esp. chap. 3, "The Christian Life in Relation to Providence and Predestination," 133–93.

cording to his hidden, holy, and ever just will. To minimize any of these factors, or to replace them with concepts of necessity and determinism, is to deny the biblical sources for constructing a doctrine of the providence of God. What Calvin spells out so clearly for all to see is that it is not necessity or determinism but divine guidance that lies at the heart of a biblical and Reformed understanding of God's providential overruling.

Chapter Seven

The Orthodox Period

IN THE VIEW OF MANY HISTORIANS, THE LATE SIXTEENTH AND SEVEN-teenth centuries saw a "hardening" of Calvin's theology and witnessed various controversies between Calvinists on major issues, particularly on "the decrees" and "predestination." It was a period in which theological methodology became formal and abstract, so much so as to be considered "scholastic." It was a time of winnowing down and defining Protestantism and, above all, Calvinism as precisely as theological language would allow.

Justo González expresses this view in his general summary of the orthodox period: "Whereas Calvin started from the concrete revelation of God, and always retained an awesome sense of the mystery of God's will, later Reformed theology tended more to proceed from the divine decrees down to particulars in a deductive fashion."[1]

Furthermore, it is sometimes held that orthodox theology was indifferent to the intellectual and scientific issues of the age. As John W. Beardslee, III has surmised, the theology of the seventeenth century "bears the stamp of the old and the dying. In intellectual history this theology often appears to be irrelevant even if not entirely obscurantist."[2] This view, however, is not shared by all; nor is it believed that seventeenth-century scholasticism was necessarily dry and useless, let alone "old and dying."[3]

---

1. Justo L. González, *A History of Christian Thought*, vol. 3 of *From the Protestant Reformation to the Twentieth Century* (Nashville: Abingdon, 1975), 244.

2. John W. Beardslee, III, ed. and trans., *Reformed Dogmatics: Seventeenth-Century Reformed Theology Through the Writings of Wollebius, Voetius, and Turretin* (Grand Rapids: Baker Book House, 1965), 4.

3. See Richard A. Muller, "Giving Direction to Theology: The Scholastic Dimension," *Journal of the Evangelical Theological Society* (June 1985), 183–93.

It would certainly continue to influence both Reformed and Protestant thought well into the nineteenth century.

Nevertheless, the placement of the divine decrees at the head of theology and the deductive exposition of theological insight are developments that characterize the orthodox perspective of the seventeenth century. Furthermore, they delineate the emerging Reformed understanding of the providence of God. But this need not be seen as either obscurantist or irrelevant.

As indicated in the preceding chapter, Calvin separated providence from predestination and addressed providence first. Even Aquinas had done as much, defining providence in terms of God's eternal planned disposition of all things and predestination in terms of salvation. As we have seen, however, Calvin does not make providence an extension of God's nature; rather, he infers it from the biblical account of God's interaction with the world.

Calvin also rejects the temptation to base predestination on God's divine nature. It too must be founded on Scripture wherein God is disclosed as electing a chosen people as well as certain persons to faith (as indicated particularly in the books of Romans and Galatians).[4]

According to Calvin's now classical definition:

> By predestination we mean the eternal decree of God, by which he determined with himself whatever he wished to happen with regard to every man. All are not created on equal terms, but some are preordained to eternal life, others to eternal damnation and, accordingly, as each has been created for one or the other of these ends, we say that he has been predestinated to life or to death.[5]

Calvin understands God's predestinating to rest on his "hidden counsel" (inscrutable will), and emphasizes the doctrine's practical application to faith as a means of encouragement and solace. As a doctrine of edification, it is not meant to be explored speculatively, that is, beyond the bounds of Scripture. Admittedly, this does become a temptation in the century following Calvin, but when that century's work is reviewed objectively, such tendencies are often found in an infralapsarian context, thus softening their effect.

The Orthodox Confessional Statements

A reading of the major creeds of the latter sixteenth century is helpful and demonstrates that no "hardening" of the Reformed perspective had

4. See Calvin, *Institutes*, 3.21.2–7.
5. *Institutes*, 3.21.5.

yet occurred. If one surveys this period chronologically, moving from Calvin to the Palatinate, and from the Palatinate to Switzerland, a remarkably personal, warm, pietistic, and practical doctrine of the providence of God is evident.

The French Confession of Faith (1559)

The *Confessio Fidei Gallicana* represents the collaboration of Calvin and his French pupil, De Chandieu. It was approved by the Synod of Paris in 1559 and was adopted by the Synod of La Rochelle in 1571.

In this confession, the paragraph on providence (par. 8) is preceded by statements about God, Scripture, the Trinity, and the creation of angels. It reflects Calvin's position succinctly and eloquently. As early as the second paragraph, the confession emphasizes God's work of creation, preservation, and control.[6]

In summary, the paragraph on providence affirms that God "governs and directs" all things; that he "disposes" and "ordains" according to his "sovereign will" (Fr., *sa volonte*); that no higher criterion than his will exists; that he is neither the author of evil nor the cause of its associated guilt; that "he can turn to good the evil" sinners do, and, hence, that Christians ought "humbly bow before the secrets which are hidden . . . , without questioning what is above . . . understanding," and therein find "peace and safety."[7]

Predestination is not specifically discussed. Paragraph 12 simply acknowledges that "God, according to his eternal and immutable counsel, calleth those whom he hath chosen by his goodness and mercy alone in our Lord Jesus Christ . . . ; leaving the rest in this same corruption and condemnation to show in them his justice."[8]

The Belgic Confession (1561)

The *Confessio Belgica* was written by Guy de Bres in 1561. In 1571 it was adopted by a Reformed synod at Emden and later, in 1619, by the National Synod of Dort.[9] Its statements on providence are similar to those in the *Gallic Confession*.

Here, too, in the second article, reference is made to the "creation,

6. See Philip Schaff, *The Evangelical Protestant Creeds, with Translations,* vol. 3 of *The Creeds of Christendom* (New York: Harper & Bros., 1877), 360.

7. Ibid., 364.

8. Ibid., 366–67.

9. See Schaff's introduction to the *Confessio Belgica, Creeds,* 3:383.

preservation, and government of the universe"—those clear motifs of *preservatio* and *gubernatio*. Articles on Scripture, the Trinity, and creation follow. Article 12 focuses on God's work of *conservatio*. Not only does God provide "being, shape, form, and several offices" to all created entities, but he "doth also still uphold and govern them by his eternal providence and infinite power for the service of mankind."[10]

Finally, article 13 is devoted specifically to God's providence. As with Calvin, emphasis is placed on God's immediate, direct, and present governance of all things; fortune or chance is denied and God's "holy will" is affirmed as the single motivating criterion ("nothing happens in this world without his appointment"); God is not the author of evil but uses it to his ends; his ways simply surpass "human understanding" and must be accepted with "humility and reverence." Hence, the "doctrine affords . . . unspeakable consolation" and acknowledges "that nothing can befall us by chance, but by the direction of our most gracious . . . Father, who watches over us with a paternal care. . . ."[11]

Also following Calvin, the confession separates eternal election from providence and does not present it until Article 16. The key theological concept is God's eternal and unchangeable council, by which he elects to deliver some and justly leaves others in that perdition "wherein they have involved themselves."[12]

The Heidelberg Catechism (1563)

In John T. McNeill's estimation, no document of this period is "more remarkable . . . both for its content and for the extent of its circulation" than Zacharias Ursinus and Caspar Olevianus's *Heidelberg Catechism*.[13] They composed it in 1562, and the following year, Frederick III, Elector of the Palatinate, adopted it as the official confession for all his territories. Williston Walker has called it "the most sweet-spirited and experiential of the expositions of Calvinism."[14]

Ursinus and Olevianus discuss the providence of God in Questions 27 and 28 and allude to predestination in Question 54, which is the article on the Holy Spirit and, in particular, is the question pertaining to the church:

10. Ibid., 395.
11. Ibid., 396–97.
12. Ibid., 401.
13. See John T. McNeill, *The History and Character of Calvinism* (New York: Oxford University Press, 1954), 270.
14. Williston Walker et al., *A History of the Christian Church,* 4th ed. (New York: Charles Scribner's Sons, 1985), 528.

Question 27. What dost thou understand by the Providence of God? *Answer.* The almighty and every where present power of God, whereby, as it were by his hand, he still upholds heaven and earth, with all creatures, and so governs them that herbs and grass, rain and drought, fruitful and barren years, meat and drink, health and sickness, riches and poverty, yea, all things, come not by chance, but by his fatherly hand.[15]

Question 28. What does it profit us to know that God has created, and by his providence still upholds all things? *Answer.* That we may be patient in adversity, thankful in prosperity, and for what is future have good confidence in our faithful God and Father that no creature shall separate us from his love, since all creatures are so in his hand that without his will they can not so much as move.[16]

Question 54. What dost thou believe concerning the *Holy Catholic Church? Answer.* That out of the whole human race, from the beginning to the end of the world, the Son of God, by his Spirit and Word, gathers, defends, and preserves for himself unto everlasting life, a chosen communion in the unity of the true faith; and that I am, and forever shall remain, a living member of the same.[17]

The Second Helvetic Confession (1556)

Heinrich Bullinger, whom Calvin greatly admired and with whom he frequently corresponded, originally wrote this confession in 1562 as a personal expression of his faith. Soon afterward, Frederick III became aware of its existence, and by 1566 it was being adopted by Reformed churches throughout the Swiss cantons.

Bullinger opens his confession with chapters on Scripture, the Trinity, idols, and worship (the last two chapters reflecting Zurich's continuing polemic with Catholicism). Then Bullinger discusses, in order, providence (chap. 5), Creation (chap. 7), free will (chap. 9), and predestination

15. See Schaff, *Creeds,* 3:316.
16. Ibid.
17. Ibid., 324. Ursinus came to the University of Heidelberg in 1561. In 1562 he was promoted to the degree of Doctor of Divinity and lectured at the university until 1577. One of his duties was an annual review of the *Catechism* with his students. Student notes, taken on these lectures, were later published after Ursinus's death. In these lectures, Ursinus devotes a full section to the providence of God. He defends it, defines it, and lists those headings which properly belong to the doctrine. His definition: "Providence is the eternal, most free, immutable, wise, just and good counsel of God, according to which he effects all good things in his creatures; permits also evil things to be done, and directs all, both good and evil, to his own glory and the salvation of his people." For specifics, see *The Commentary of Dr. Zacharias Ursinus on The Heidelberg Catechism,* trans. by G. W. Williard (Columbus: Scott & Bascom, 1851), 147–64.

(chap. 10). His position, in spirit, is similar to Calvin's, while incorporating echoes of Zwingli.

Bullinger asserts that everything is governed by the providence of God: "We believe that all things in heaven and on earth, and in all creatures, are preserved and governed by the providence of this wise, eternal and almighty God."[18]

He condemns any Epicurean view that would deny the existence or scope of providence and, with Calvin, acknowledges the importance of secondary causes: "We do not spurn as useless the means by which divine providence works, but we teach that we are to adapt ourselves to them in so far as they are recommended to us in the Word of God."[19]

Bullinger rejects the popular (if not Libertine) view "that if all things are managed by the providence of God, then our efforts and endeavors are in vain."[20] He also denies that anything occurs because of blind fortune or uncertain chance. "For God, who has appointed to everything its end, has ordained the beginning and the means by which it reaches its goal."[21]

As one can see, these are broad tenets and, in the limited scope and intent of Bullinger's purpose, are neither defended philosophically nor elaborated at any length.

Chapter 10, "On Predestination," is highly christological and emphasizes the Son's role, the need to preach the gospel, and the importance of the believer's response of faith. Bullinger warns that the doctrine ought not be so interpreted as to frighten off the unchurched. Still, salvation proceeds from election, and the elect are those who "from eternity God has freely, and of his mere grace, without any respect to men, predestinated or elected . . . to save in Christ." He prefers not to speculate about the reprobate and concurs, with Zwingli, "that if you believe and are in Christ, you are elected."[22]

In none of these orthodox confessions do we detect any "hardening" of the Reformed position. However, within the next century, the eternal decrees and predestination will be considered before the doctrine of the providence of God and his governance of the world.[23] But, from a Reformed perspective, neither of these developments is improper or unbib-

---

18. See *The Second Helvetic Confession,* in Arthur C. Cochrane, *Reformed Confessions of the 16th Century* (Philadelphia: Westminster, 1966), 232.

19. Ibid., 233.

20. Ibid.

21. Ibid.

22. Ibid., 240–41.

23. See Gonzáles, *History of Christian Thought,* 242–62; Beardslee, *Reformed Dogmatics,* 3–25.

lical. If anything, they ground God's providential activity in his mysterious but always merciful and just will, by virtue of which he acts redemptively toward all humankind.

From Jerome Zanchi to Francis Turretin

Jerome Zanchi

Perhaps the best place to begin this section is with Jerome Zanchi (1516–1590) and his *The Doctrine of Absolute Predestination Stated and Asserted.*[24]

Zanchi was a disciple of Peter Martyr Vermigli. Forced to leave Italy in 1550, he visited Geneva briefly, and in 1553, became professor of theology at Strasbourg. He remained in Strasbourg until 1568, at which time, following Ursinus's death, he accepted the professorship of theology at the University of Heidelberg. He later moved to Newstadt, where he also taught and preached. Throughout his professorships, he enjoyed the support and protection of Frederick III and Prince John Casimir.

A. M. Toplady, Zanchi's English translator, adequately summarizes the Italian's position in his own analysis of Zanchi's system: "*God's sovereign will* is the first link, His *unalterable decree* is the second, and His all-active *providence* the third in the great chain of causes. What His will determined, that His decree established, and His providence, either mediately or immediately, effects."[25]

Zanchi's doctrine of the providence of God is articulated in his *Absolute Predestination*. It is interesting to note that, throughout this work, Zanchi appeals to Luther's *On the Bondage of the Will* and Augustine's *On the Gift of Perseverance* to corroborate his own position.

For Zanchi, neither predestination nor providence can be understood apart from God's attributes, or God's very nature. With Zwingli, thus, more so than with Calvin, Zanchi holds that God's electing and providential activity flows, of necessity, from what is deducible from his being.

Zanchi opens with a definition of God's wisdom and foreknowledge, then proceeds to examine God's will, unchangeableness, decrees, omnipotence, justice, and mercy. For Zanchi, everything that can occur has already been foreseen and predetermined by God's hidden purposes and counsel and can never be averted or thwarted. In this scheme, providence

---

24. See *The Doctrine of Absolute Predestination Stated and Asserted,* trans. by Augustus Montague Toplady (London: Sovereign Grace Union, 1930).
25. Ibid., 23; emphasis added.

is largely the manner in which God's predetermining counsel of all things unfolds in secondary causes.

Zanchi stresses that God never intended to save all men (a direct echo of Calvin), only a few; he then provides both biblical and intellectual justification for this recondite theme, and offers both solace and challenge to the elect.

> I. With respect to The Divine Wisdom and Foreknowledge, I shall lay down the following positions:
>
> Position 1.—God is, and always was so perfectly wise, that nothing ever did, or does, or can elude His knowledge. He knew, from all eternity, not only what He Himself intended to do, but also what He would incline and permit others to do. . . .
>
> Position 2.—Consequently, God knows nothing now, nor will know anything hereafter, which He did not know and foresee from everlasting, . . .
>
> Position 3.— . . . , so that whatever He foreknows to be future shall necessarily and undoubtedly come to pass. . . .[26]
>
> II. [With respect to the Will of God]
>
> Position 5.—God's hidden will is peremptory and absolute, and therefore cannot be hindered from taking effect. . . .
>
> Position 6.—Whatever comes to pass, comes to pass by virtue of this absolute omnipotent will of God, which is the primary and supreme cause of all things. . . .
>
> Position 8.— . . . God never did, nor does He now, will that every individual of mankind should be saved. . . .[27]
>
> III. [With respect to the Unchangeableness of God and His Decrees]
>
> Position 1.—God is essentially unchangeable in Himself. . . .
>
> Position 2.—God is likewise absolutely unchangeable with regard to His purposes and promises. . . .
>
> By the purpose of decree of God, we mean His determinate counsel, whereby he did from all eternity preordain whatever He should do, or would permit to be done, in time . . . so that whatsoever God hath determined, concerning every individual person or thing, shall surely and infallibly be accomplished in and upon them.[28]

Certainly, Zanchi's emphasis stands out in such words as *necessarily, undoubtedly, absolute omnipotence, essentially unchangeable, determined, preordain, determined,* and *surely.* In his system, everything that can and will take place *in* time has been fixed *before* time. On this basis, one could

26. Ibid., 44–45.
27. Ibid., 49–52.
28. Ibid., 59–60.

argue that Zanchi presents a hard determinism that overshadows grace. But Zanchi makes a strong distinction between positive divine willing and divine permission: God knew, from eternity, not only what he himself intended to do, but also what he would incline and permit others to do. Furthermore, one must remember the context of Zanchi's statements. The intent of his doctrine is to defend God's total governance of the world, so that true believers might take courage in the midst of life's demands and exigencies.

Theodore Beza

Theodore Beza (1519–1605) succeeded Calvin at Geneva. Although his theology is less deductively inferred than Zanchi's, it is carried out, like Zanchi's, wherever possible in dialogue with Scripture.

Of especial note is where Beza places the doctrine of the providence of God. In his *La Confession De Foi Du Chrétien,*[29] Beza presents the doctrine in part 1, chapter 1, article 3. He entitles the article *"La Providence Éternelle De Dieu"* and defines it accordingly:

Nothing happens by chance and without the singular just decree of God (Eph. 1:11; Matt. 10:29; Prov. 16:4). Nonetheless, God is neither the author of nor culpable of an evil which is committed. For, his power and goodness are so incomprehensible, that although he acts through the wiles of the devil or the wicked, he punishes [them] lawfully, and neither fails to ordain nor govern well and justly his holy work (Acts 2:23; 4:28; Rom. 9:19–20).[30]

Beza underscores God's work of creation and preservation:

It is he [the Triune God] who, when it seemed good to him, created everything out of nothing (Gen. 1:1; Heb. 1:2; 11:3; John 1:3), which he did by his eternal Word, that is, through his Son working with the Father. He arranged and ordained everything, and he likewise sustains and governs everything according to his eternal providence, by means of his infinite and co-essential power, being the Holy Spirit, who proceeds from the Father and the Son.[31]

29. All references to Beza's *Confession* are to the edition reprinted in *La Revue Reformée,* entitled *La Confession De Foi Du Chrétien* par Théodore de Beze, Introduction, préface, texte modernisé et notes de Michel Réveillaud, in No. 23-1955/3, Tome 6. All translations are the author's.
30. Ibid., 16.
31. Ibid., 17.

In part 3, entitled "Jesus Christ, God's Unique Son," Beza discusses election and providence. He maintains that "God is immutable in his decisions. He cannot be wrong in them, or ever impeded in any manner in executing them (Num. 23:19; Mal. 3:6). Hence, whatever happens to men has been eternally decreed by him (Eph. 1:11; Matt. 10:29), in accordance with what we have said regarding providence."[32]

From an objective point of view, a note of determinism does creep into these paragraphs ("whatever happens to men has been eternally decreed"). But, if one reads Beza's text with discernment, it is clear that he seeks to distinguish between what God has "ordained" by his "singular just decree" versus its execution in time and history, which "he [now] likewise sustains and governs." In addition, Beza is careful to note that God "is neither the author of nor culpable of any evil which is committed." For the most part, these themes simply represent development of Calvin's own principles.[33]

Johannes Wollebius

Johannes Wollebius (1586–1629) became a pastor in 1611 and in 1618 became professor of Old Testament at the university in Basel. His doctrine of the providence of God is found in his *Compendium Theologiae Christianae*,[34] a work that was reprinted many times in Latin and was translated into both Dutch and English—all during the seventeenth century.

Wollebius's work reflects the Reformed consensus in that the decrees of God and predestination are posited as the accepted presuppositions of divine providence. When one considers that his theology was developed during the peak of the predestination controversies between the Arminians and the framers of the Synod of Dort, Wollebius's doctrine reveals an incredibly irenic spirit and amazing flexibility.

The order in which Wollebius discusses his subjects displays the seventeenth century's fascination with God's decrees as both an organizational principle and a hermeneutical device. With regard to the providence of God, Wollebius places it within the following schema:

Book I. The Knowledge of God
Chapter I. The Essence of God
II. The Persons of the Godhead
III. The Works of God and the Divine Decrees

---

32. Ibid., 19.

33. For further elaboration of Beza's position, see book 1 of *Questionum et responsionum christianarum libellus* (Ann Arbor, Mich.: University Microfilms International).

34. All references to Wollebius's *Compendium Theologiae Christianae* are to the Beardslee edition.

IV. Predestination
V. Creation
VI. The Actual Providence of God

Wollebius emphasizes that the Trinity is involved in the works of God—
thus softening a purely rationalistic definition of God.[35]

He defines a decree of God as "an internal act of the divine will, by
which he determines, from eternity, freely, with absolute certainty, those
matters which shall happen in time."[36] The decrees may also be called
"eternal providence." to distinguish them from "actual providence,"
"which is nothing other than the execution of the decrees of God."[37]

However, once Wollebius makes this distinction, he emphasizes, not so
much the necessity of God's decrees, but the vital and free role rational
creatures are invited to exercise. Hence, Wollebius favors a principle of
"permission," by means of which God controls what he has decreed,
while allowing freedom for mankind.

Wollebius observes that many things can be contrary to what God
wants; however, they still conform to the divine plan. For example, "God
did not will man's sin. . . . Nevertheless, at the same time he decreed it
according to his will, as a means of revealing his glory."[38] Hence, "good
and evil . . . result from the decree and will of God: the former he causes,
and the latter he *permits.*"[39] Again, "evils are decreed not effectively, but
permissively."[40] Consequently, the inevitability of God's decrees neither
destroys freedom in creatures nor contingency in secondary causes. For
"the necessity is not a necessity of coercion," and the evil men do only
witnesses to God's glory and justice. For "the purpose of the divine decrees is the glory of God."[41]

Wollebius further distinguishes between God's general and special decrees. The former has to do with God's work of creation and preservation,
the latter with predestination. The general decree reveals God's "power,
wisdom, and glory," while the special decree witnesses to his "grace,
mercy, and justice."[42]

As for predestination, it means "that out of the human race which [God]
created in his own image, but which fell into sin through its own act, God
has determined to save some eternally through Christ, but to condemn

35. Ibid., 45.
36. Ibid., 47.
37. Ibid.
38. Ibid., 48.
39. Ibid.; emphasis added.
40. Ibid.; emphasis added.
41. Ibid., 49.
42. Ibid., 50.

the remainder eternally, leaving them in their own misery, in order to reveal the glory of his mercy and justice."[43]

Wollebius now defines "actual providence" (in distinction from "eternal providence") as "that work by which God not only preserves his creatures, but governs all things with unlimited wisdom, goodness, power, justice, and mercy." It is a "governance of all things, from the greatest to the least," but a governance which "upholds" secondary causes.[44]

At the same time, providence does not bind God in a net of secondary causes (as does Stoicism). With Calvin, Wollebius denies that God's providence is little more than the cause-and-effect interactions of the natural order, or that God's operations are limited to such interactions. Rather, "Christian [teaching] subordinates secondary causes to the absolute free will of God, which employs them freely, not of necessity, not because he needs them, but because he wants them."[45]

Finally, both good and evil are controlled by God's providence. "Good deeds are controlled by his effective act, under which heading belong the divine prevenience [*praecursus*], concurrence [*concursus*], and support [*succursus*]." "Evil deeds are controlled by realized permission, and hence by allowing, limiting, and directing them . . . toward a good result."[46]

Here, then, is a "softened" Reformed Calvinism. Wollebius's conception of the providence of God is one in which any principles of determinism fade into the background in favor of the broad decrees of God. These decrees function as types of Platonic forms, by means of which God actively and actually, wisely and graciously, governs his present universe.

To that extent, Wollebius's doctrine provides Reformed theology with an intriguing view. It is possible that Barth and Brunner's positions represent a type of modern Wollebian theology, in which the divine decrees become the presupposition for God's loving and redemptive governance of all creation and of mankind's historical pilgrimage.

The Synod of Dort

As noted above, the seventeenth century erupted with debate among Calvinists regarding the order of the decrees and the nature of predestination. While Wollebius was refining his system in relative calm in Basel, the Netherlands witnessed the rise of Arminian resistance to the form of Calvinism that would triumph at Dort. Although the Synod of Dort did

43. Ibid.
44. Ibid., 58–59.
45. Ibid., 59.
46. Ibid.

not adopt the supralapsarian views of some of its delegates, it did affirm unconditional election, limited atonement, the total depravity of natural man, irresistible grace, and the perserverance of the elect.

Equally as important as these themes, however, is the language and philosophical tenor of Dort's affirmations. They are more evangelistic than abstract, more positive than negative, more biblical than deductive. To be certain, Dort's first head of doctrine is predestination. That is due to the context of the debate. In addition, God's predestinating is based on his eternal decrees, governed by his "good pleasure" and "unchangeable, omniscient, and omnipotent" essence. Nevertheless, what is repeatedly stressed is the dynamic appropriation of one's election and not its deterministic character.

Nowhere is this better spelled out than in articles 26–27 on the "Third and Fourth Heads of Doctrine." As Dort insists: "This grace of regeneration does not treat men as senseless stocks and blocks, nor take away their will and its properties, . . ."[47] Or again:

> The almighty operation of God, whereby he prolongs and supports this our natural life, does not exclude, but requires the use of means, by which God of his infinite mercy and goodness hath chosen to exert his influence, . . . For grace is conferred by means of admonitions; and the more readily we perform our duty, the more eminent usually is this blessing of God working in us, and the more directly is his work advanced.[48]

If there is any "hardening," it is not in the language or in the content of the theology. Rather, Dort establishes the decrees and predestination as indispensable principles of theological interpretation.

The Westminster Confession of Faith

The consensus of Dort was united with Cocceius's covenant theology in the mid-seventeenth century and is evidenced particularly in the *Westminster Confession of Faith's* understanding of God's providence and its proper place among theological subjects. This confession is often regarded as the culmination of the "hardening" process, in its ordering of subjects as well as in its famous definitions:

Chapter I. Of the Holy Scripture
  II. Of God, and of the Holy Trinity
  III. Of God's Eternal Decree (Predestination)

---

47. See *The Canons of the Synod of Dort*, A.D. 1619, in Schaff, *Creeds*, 3:591.
48. Ibid., 592.

IV. Of Creation
V. Of Providence

More objectively, however, what Westminster represents is the perfecting of a way of doing theology in the light of the seventeenth century's understanding of the decrees.

The chapter on God's eternal decree is admittedly deterministic in language and tone. "God from all eternity did . . . ordain whatsoever comes to pass"; "angels and men, thus predestined and foreordained, are particularly and unchangeably designed; and their number is so certain and definite that it can not be either increased or diminished."[49] At the same time, however, this chapter insists, with both Calvin and Augustine, that God is not the author of sin, "nor is violence offered to the will of the creatures, nor is the liberty or contingency of second causes taken away. . . ."[50]

As for the chapter on providence, all the essential nuances of Calvin's position are restated here, but via the long journey of their transmission. Again, God directly governs everything by means of his "free and immutable counsel"; all things come to pass "immutably and infallibly"; yet they occur "according to the nature of secondary causes," over which God "is free to work without, above, and against them at his pleasure"; nonetheless, sin is of human doing, though never beyond God's control; nor is sin a matter of "bare permission."[51] God is always in command.

Hence, Westminster affirms key Reformed ideas without elaborating them in a biblical context. For this, one must turn to the Scripture, or to Calvin, who constantly seeks to subordinate his theology and language to Scripture and who finds there the dynamic God, that ever active One, who encounters mankind in history.

Francis Turretin

Francis Turretin's (1623–1687) most important work is his *Institutio Theologiae Elencticae.*[52] It contains a brilliant summary of Reformed thought concerning the providence of God and represents a masterful, positive commentary on Dortian theology. With respect to the eternal decrees, Turretin adopts an infralapsarian position, which he rigorously and logically develops in propositional style. He is thematically obedient to Scripture, but dogmatic in his presentation. Furthermore, Turretin freely uses

---

49. See *The Westminster Confession of Faith,* A.D. 1647, in Schaff, *Creeds,* 3:608.
50. Ibid.
51. Ibid., 612–13.
52. See *Institutio Theologiae Elencticae,* vol. 1 (Edinburgh: John D. Lowe, 1847).

the Aristotelian concepts of actuality versus potentiality, the supremacy of the universal over the particular, and the causation schema, in which God is ultimately the complete *causa* of all. Yet he emphasizes that God is the noncoercive and just director of every event, which he guides toward the highest good, according to his inscrutable "good pleasure."

In line with accepted orthodox practice, Turretin presents the following order for the major heads of theology (i.e., through the subject of providence):

Locus I. On Theology
Locus II. On Holy Scripture
Locus III. On the One and Triune God
Locus IV. On the Decrees of God in General, and Predestination in Particular
Locus V. On Creation
Locus VI. On the Actual Providence of God

After considerable discussion, Turretin suggests the following infralapsarian order with respect to the logical sequence of the decrees: (1) the creation of man; (2) the permission for the fall; (3) the election of some to salvation; (4) the sending of Christ as mediator and advocate for the elect; and (5) the effectual calling of the elect to salvation through the gospel by the grace of the Holy Spirit.[53]

As for providence, the Creator acts as a "constant provider, cherishing and sustaining his own work by his continual influx, and taking perpetual care of it."[54] This is a providential ordering in which "all things without exception are under divine providence, whether heavenly or sublunary, great or small, necessary and natural or free and contingent, so that nothing in the nature of things can be granted or happen, which does not depend upon it."[55]

At the same time, it is a providential ordering which respects the contingent nature and liberty of secondary causes—especially the will of man. "For God, who works all in all, so governs and rules second causes as not to take away their nature and condition, but rather keeps and conserves and permits them also to exercise and act out their own motions."[56]

Thus God directs all while doing so contingently. Yet, for Turretin, the biblical point is always that God controls (immediately, specifically, and

53. Ibid. 381.
54. The reference here is to loc. 6, ques. 1, art. 5. The translation is that of G. M. Giger in "*The Theological Institutes* of Francis Turretin" (unpublished ms., Princeton Theological Seminary Library).
55. Ibid., loc. 6, ques. 3, art. 1.
56. Ibid. art. 10.

effectively) even this contingent world of give-and-take, down to the very will of man.

Drawing upon Thomistic and Aristotelian principles to defend what he believes to be the scriptural view Turretin argues:

> Because as man depends upon God as to essence and life, so he must depend upon him as to the actions and movements of his soul, the better part of man. For to pretend that man is independent in will and action, is to make him independent in being, because whatever he is in acting such is he in being. Finally, if free actions do not depend upon God and are not governed by him, they would be performed, God being either ignorant and unconscious, or neglecting or unwilling, which cannot be said and thought without impiety.[57]

Following this statement, Turretin next devotes his attention to the principle of *concursus*. One can argue that Turretin's discussion ushers him into the "danger-zone." But that is not the issue. The issue is whether God does more than merely permit humankind to decide its own fate; the issue is the extent to which God actually controls and directs both the choices and interactions of men and the consequent course of world events. Turretin maintains that, if one is to be true to the Bible, *concursus* must be defended as a way of acknowledging God's directing hand in, as well as previous and subsequent to, the interactions of human beings in history.[58]

Once again, Turretin argues along Aristotelian and Thomistic lines. But he supports his conclusion with numerous references to biblical passages in which God works in, through, with, and in spite of the Israelites and the universal human condition of a fallen world. In so doing, God always orders and directs all things so as to effect the highest good, in accordance with his own "good pleasure."

Throughout his work, Turretin's presentation ripples with the best of the classical world's philosophical assumptions, the theology of Paul's doctrine of predestination, the evocative rumblings of Augustine's emphasis on grace, and the ever present shadow of Dort.

From a negative point of view, it can be argued that during the orthodox period Calvin's understanding of God's dynamic overruling is often overshadowed by a deterministic motif and a way of perceiving God in static, metaphysical terms. Yet the orthodox period contributes important and positive elements to the doctrine of providence.

57. Ibid., art. 11.
58. See loc. 6, ques. 4, art. 1–6.

From a positive viewpoint, the divine decrees and predestination are recognized as valid and necessary presuppositions for any responsible biblical doctrine of the providence of God. For God's providential ordering of the world grows out of his will to create a world in which his goodness and glory are revealed as well as his justice and righteousness. To this extent, orthodoxy was being obedient to Pauline and Augustinian motifs, deeply believed by all Calvinists.

Furthermore, the orthodox emphasis on *concursus* should not be minimized. It too represents the undeniable biblical conviction that God directly oversees everything. God's governance can neither be reduced to "bare permission" nor identified with the natural order alone. More is ultimately at stake, and it is this "more" that *concursus* seeks to explore, define, defend, and, where possible, explain.

Chapter Eight

Scientific and Philosophical Perspectives of the Modern Era

As noted in the preceding chapter, historians have sometimes charged that theological reflection during the late sixteenth and early to mid-seventeenth centuries often occurred in isolation from the scientific and intellectual stirrings of the day. The scientific discoveries, attitudes, and methodologies that would come to characterize the modern period offered new possibilities for accounting for nature and its order, as well as God's place in that order; they often powerfully intimidated orthodox views. That many of these scientists were Christian or avowed theists does not minimize the profound significance their findings had for a non-theistic interpretation of nature or of God's place in it.

The Greeks perceived nature and the natural order in terms of the logos. Chrysippus and Cicero saw nature as the manifestation of the logos and the result of all its cause-and-effect occurrences. Aristotle maintained that the world order was a harmony of eternal entities responding out of eros to a perfect *summum bonum* that motivated them to complete their final purposes. In accordance with Platonic and neo-Platonic principles, the world order was viewed as the result of first a descent from perfection to imperfection and then ascent again, through the chain of being, to that eternal realm of perfection. That the Christian church during its patristic, medieval, and Reformation periods drew upon these classical perceptions to enhance its understanding of God's providential activity in the world is beyond dispute.

The scientific revolution, however, that began with Copernicus and continues unabated today has made reassessment of the church's understanding of God's interaction with the world an ongoing theological necessity. At the same time, the scientific revolution has produced a variety of philosophical reassessments of the world which have both challenged and contributed to the Christian position.

Certainly, Reformed doctrines of the providence of God cannot be insensitive or indifferent to these views. The truth of the matter is, Reformed theologies (broadly defined) have appropriated many nuances of these modern perceptions into their own systematics in an effort to address today's world precisely in the name of the triune God and Father of biblical faith.

This claim does not mean that a Reformed doctrine of the providence of God is impossible apart from the endorsement of a particular scientific view of the world. If anything, the liberal theological movement of the nineteenth century, that aligned itself with theories of historical progress, and the orthodox theological movement of the same period, that set itself against the Enlightenment and scientific solutions, have shown us the folly of this kind of approach. The world's self-assessment, from its own scientific and philosophical perspectives, provides the Reformed tradition with a major source for relevant theologizing as it attempts to address its own particular time and place in God's vast ordering of the whole.

With this thought in mind, it is helpful to review something of the modern era's scientific and philosophical understanding of our world and of God's interaction with it.

From Copernicus to Newton

Copernicus, Kepler, Boyle, and Newton did not believe that their scientific discoveries were opposed to faith in God or his governance of the system. Their readings of the book of nature were not intended to desacralize the world; rather, they wanted to discover, define, and clarify its laws of continuity and harmony. Their readings, however, did result in a perception of the nature of reality that conflicted sharply with the orthodox picture of reality based on a literal interpretation of Scripture.[1]

1. See John Dillenberger, *Protestant Thought and Natural Science: A Historical Interpretation* (Garden City: Doubleday, 1960), 21. For excellent studies of the modern period, see also E. A. Burtt, *The Metaphysical Foundations of Modern Physical Science*, rev. ed. (New York: Humanities Press, 1951); Herbert Butterfield, *The Origins of Modern Science* (New York: Macmillan, 1953); Ernst Cassirer, *The Philosophy of the Enlightenment* (Princeton: Princeton University Press, 1951); and Frederick Copleston, *A History of Philosophy*, vol. 5 (Garden City: Image Books, 1962).

Nicolaus Copernicus

Nicolaus Copernicus (1473–1543) describes something of his own frustration and joy with regard to his work in astronomy as he realized the need for a fresh breakthrough concerning a mathematical comprehension of nature:

> Accordingly, when I meditated upon this lack of certitude . . . concerning the composition of movements of the spheres of the world, I began to be annoyed that the philosophers . . . had discovered no sure scheme for the movements of the machinery of the world, which has been built for us by the *Best and Most Orderly Workman* of all. . . .
>
> And so, having laid down the movements which I attribute to the Earth farther on in the work, I finally discovered by the help of long and numerous observations that if the movements of the other wandering stars are correlated with the circular movement of the Earth, . . . this correlation binds together so closely the order and magnitudes of all the planets . . . and the heavens themselves that nothing can be shifted around in any part of them without disrupting the remaining parts and the universe as a whole.[2]

Copernicus's theory was received hesitantly at first, but the implications of his views became increasingly apparent as the modern era progressed. As John Dillenberger explains: "For those schooled in the Aristotelian Christian tradition, this new conception had drastic consequences."[3] The earth, which had heretofore occupied a unique place in God's creation and which was the scene of God's redemptive activity, appeared to have lost its "special spatial setting." As a result, the world's "identity of purpose and place was called into question," and it was this identity that was the central issue "attending the dislodging of the earth from the center of things."[4]

Furthermore, as Dillenberger points out, Copernicus's theory implied that "the stars of the eighth sphere were so distant as to border on infinity with the consequence that the closely knit and compact universe was gone, and man was exposed to the dread of infinity in spatial terms."[5]

It is this "anxiety engendered by infinity"[6] that unnerved the church and still gnaws at the modern consciousness. It is this anxiety to which

2. Nicolaus Copernicus, *On the Revolutions of the Heavenly Spheres,* vol. 16 of Great Books of the Western World (Chicago: Encyclopedia Britannica, 1952), 508; emphasis added.
3. Dillenberger, *Protestant Thought,* 25.
4. Ibid., 26.
5. Ibid.
6. Ibid.

orthodox theology had to speak then and to which Reformed theology must speak today, if its doctrine of the providence of God is to be respected.

Johann Kepler

Johann Kepler (1571–1630) was a Lutheran. Building on Tycho Brahe's expansions of Copernicus's observations, Kepler believed that God's ordering of the universe could be explained by "certain simple mathematical harmonies"[7] which God enables mankind to grasp through reason. Kepler explains:

> May God make it come to pass that my delightful speculation (the *Mysterium Cosmographicum*) have everywhere among reasonable men fully the effect which I strove to obtain in the publication, namely that the belief in the creation of the world be fortified through this external support, that thought of the creator be recognized in its nature, and that his inexhaustible wisdom shine forth daily more brightly. Then man will at least measure the power of his mind on the true scale, and will realize that God, who founded everything in the world according to the norm of quantity, also has endowed man with a mind which can comprehend these norms.[8]

Kepler's scientific theories, however, were wed with Pythagorean mysticism and philosophical speculations. These elements tainted both his theological and astronomical perceptions of the world. Kepler concludes that the sun was the center of the universe and the dwelling place of God. But more importantly, Kepler believes strongly in the rational structure of the universe and the power of reason to comprehend that structure; in fact, he interprets that structure as revealing the very thought of the creator. It remained only for Galileo to bring the painful awareness of the meaning of the Copernican system to his time.

Robert Boyle

Robert Boyle (1627–1691), English physicist and chemist, disagreed with Thomas Hobbes who favored scientific exploration at the expense of theological consideration. Boyle believed that the order of the universe argued for intelligent design and purpose:

7. See Jones, *History of Western Philosophy,* 617.
8. Quoted from G. Holton, "Johannes Kepler's Universe: Its Physics and Metaphysics," *American Journal of Physics* 24 (May 1956): 349–50; cited by Dillenberger, *Protestant Thought,* 82 n. 7.

That Divine providence had several Ends, in making the World, and the several creatures that compose it . . . is evident, some being made for the manifestation of the Glory of God, others the usefulness of man, or the maintenance of the System of the world, with respect to particular Creatures or the propagation of their kinds.[9]

However, Boyle was not convinced that astronomy offered the kind of defensible argument for the world's design that biology did.[10] Like the Stoics, Boyle believed that the eye was the masterpiece of creation that attested to an intelligent designer's presence. He also favored the metaphor of the clock as a fitting symbol of the world's dependable orderliness.

Dillenberger maintains that Boyle was a deeply pious scientist who accepted both nature and Scripture as "two impressive orders of knowledge."[11] But as Dillenberger acknowledges, "at no point did theology dictate the form of a scientific question or the content of the answer. His religious views entered only as he opposed philosophical assumptions which were not necessarily inherent in the new science and which appeared antithetical to a Christian understanding of the world."[12]

In Copleston's view, Boyle is noteworthy because he "regarded his . . . work in science as a service of God." He "spoke frequently of the divine conservation of the world and of God's 'concurrence' with all its operations." Furthermore, he "insisted that God is by no means bound to His ordinary and general concurrence," and that miracles "are possible and have occurred."[13]

Isaac Newton

Isaac Newton (1642–1727) best exemplifies the desire of early scientists to shed light on the order of nature as well as God's possible interaction with it.

With regard to the order of nature, Newton offers a thoroughly scientific explanation. Newton admits "no more causes of natural things than such as are both true and sufficient to explain their appearances."[14] Hence, science need only proceed by subjecting the phenomena of nature to the

9. See *The Theological Works of the Honourable Robert Boyle,* ed. by Richard Boulton (London, 1715), 2:131; cited by Dillenberger, *Protestant Thought,* 115.

10. Boyle, *Theological Works,* 220.

11. Dillenberger, *Protestant Thought,* 117.

12. Ibid.

13. See Copleston, *History of Philosophy,* 5.1:157.

14. Isaac Newton, *Mathematical Principles of Natural Philosophy,* vol. 34 of Great Books of the Western World (Chicago: Encyclopedia Britannica, 1952), 270–71.

laws of mathematics and then proceed "from the phenomena of motions to investigate the forces of nature, and then from these forces to demonstrate the other phenomena."[15]

Newton was uninterested in metaphysical solutions. Consequently, his theories favored a mechanical interpretation of the universe, allowing for implications that Newton himself would no doubt have rejected. In E. A. Burtt's opinion, Newton's work gave eminent authority to the view that the cosmos is such that man, at best, is "a puny irrelevant spectator . . . of [a] vast mathematical system whose regular motions according to mechanical principles constituted the world of nature."[16]

Newton, however, was a Christian, and for him the natural world was still a world open and present to God. In *Mathematical Principles of Natural Philosophy* he writes:

> From his true dominion it follows that the true God is a living, intelligent, and powerful Being; and, from his other perfections, that he is supreme, or most perfect. He is eternal and infinite, omnipotent and omniscient; that is, his duration reaches from eternity to eternity; his presence from infinity to infinity; he governs all things, and knows all things that are or can be done. He is not eternity and infinity, but eternal and infinite; he is not duration or space, but he endures and is present. He endures forever, and is everywhere present; and, by existing always and everywhere, he constitutes duration and space. . . .[17]

Copleston's assessment of this specific passage is especially pertinent. He observes that Newton "was convinced that the cosmic order provides evidence for the existence of God" and believed that "God does not simply conserve His creation in a general sense of the word, but He also actively intervenes to keep the machine going."[18]

More could be said of Newton's theology; however, what historians of science deem significant are his view of nature and its implications for man's understanding both of his world and of God's place in it. As Burtt explains:

> The world that people had thought themselves living in—a world rich with colour and sound, redolent with fragrance, filled with gladness, love and beauty, speaking everywhere of purposive harmony and creative ideals—was crowded now into minute corners in the brains of scattered organic beings.

15. Ibid., 1.
16. See Burtt, *Metaphysical Foundations*, 236.
17. Newton, *Mathematical Principles*, 370f.
18. Copleston, *History of Philosophy*, 5.1:165.

The really important world outside was a world hard, cold, colourless, silent, and dead; a world of quantity, a world of mathematically computable motions in mechanical regularity.[19]

Burtt's description of the "mechanical" universe is perhaps overstated, but the problems such a world poses for the providence of God are obvious.

From Descartes to Schleiermacher

How the philosophical mind of the West both responded and contributed to new scientific perceptions constitutes a major period in the long history of Western philosophy. From a Reformed viewpoint, much of that history is an attempt to edge God out of his own universe or requires that Christianity account for his providential activity in radically new ways, many of which are either incompatible with Scripture or demand an inordinate amount of accommodation to modern assumptions.

Rene Descartes

Rene Descartes' (1590–1650) significance is multifaceted, but at least two aspects of his thought demand our attention.

First, his division of nature into two substances—thought and extension—inevitably contributes to the successful rise of the mechanically conceived universe. In Descartes' system, body, mass, or extended phenomena conform to mechanical and mathematical laws. Mind, heart, soul, and will belong to thought and conform to laws that govern mental processes. In man these two do unite and interact. But Descartes' analysis of the two as separate phenomena added authority to the emerging school that favored a mechanically ordered universe.[20]

In a Tillichian sense, finite and infinite are kept separate; the finite belongs to the categories of extension, while thought alone can grasp the infinite. But from a Reformed point of view, one of Calvin's central tenets is that nature does not sustain itself according to some perpetual law of nature alone; rather, God preserves nature energetically and efficaciously beyond its own powers to propagate itself.

Second, Descartes' method of "radical doubt" requires the suspension of traditional authority until a carefully calculated rational solution, that

---

19. Burtt, *Metaphysical Foundations,* 236f.

20. For Descartes' view of the mind-body division, see his *Meditations on First Philosophy,* in *Descartes: Philosophical Writings* (New York: Modern Library, 1958).

leads to an *indubitandum,* can be attained.[21] Thus the Cartesian method gave impetus to a scientific spirit that, if it chose, could ignore theological issues; it also emphasized the importance of unaided reason as a principle of knowledge.

Although Descartes retained belief in God, argued for God's existence, and remained faithful to the Catholic Church, the implications of his *Meditations* are unavoidable. A world of nature, operational strictly on its own terms, and a human world, potentially comprehensible in terms of reason alone, result in a world view that directly challenges the Calvinist notion of a universe governed by a God who foresees, predetermines, and guides all phenomena and persons toward the attainment of his hidden purposes, according to his own good pleasure. After Descartes, that picture of the world increasingly conflicts with the nature of the world as described scientifically and reflected upon philosophically.

Baruch Spinoza

Baruch Spinoza (1632–1677), who read Descartes and Hobbes with avid interest, provides a remarkable conception of God and the world: in essence, he identifies God with the universe.

His formula is *Deus sive Natura* ("God or nature"); each is interchangeable with the other. For Spinoza, it is not so much God's relation with the world that is at issue, but God's unity with the world:[22] "Whatever is, is in God, and nothing can either be or be conceived without God."[23]

For Spinoza, all of reality is a single phenomenon, and God is inextricably bound up with that phenomenon. Spinoza begins with a clear set of definitions:

III. By *substance* I understand that which is in itself and is conceived through itself. . . .
IV. By *attribute* I understand that which the intellect perceives of substance as constituting its essence.
V. By *mode* I understand the modifications of substance. . . .
VI. By *God* I understand Being absolutely infinite, that is to say, substance

21. See Descartes, *Discourse on the Method of Rightly Conducting the Reason and Seeking for Truth in the Sciences,* in *The Philosophical Works of Descartes* (Cambridge: Cambridge University Press, 1911).

22. See Samuel E. Stumpf's discussion of Spinoza in *Socrates to Sartre: A History of Philosophy,* 2d ed. (New York: McGraw-Hill, 1975), 258ff.

23. See Spinoza's *Ethics Demonstrated in Geometrical Order,* in *The European Philosophers: From Descartes to Nietzsche,* ed. by M. C. Beardsley (New York: Modern Library, 1960), 149.

consisting of infinite attributes, each one of which expresses eternal and infinite essence.[24]

The bottom line of these definitions [Descartes's *indubitandum*] is that "besides God no substance can be nor can be conceived."[25] Hence, "in Nature there is but one substance" (i.e., God); from which it follows "that the thing *extended* and the thing *thinking* are either attributes of God or modifications of the attributes of God."[26]

Spinoza proceeds to infer other corollaries and propositions, their significance being that all things are what they are because God is *immanently* involved in all extension and thinking. Spinoza writes: "God is the efficient cause of all things which can fall under the infinite intellect"; "God is cause through Himself, and not through that which is contingent";[27] "God is the immanent . . . cause of all things."[28] Hence, "in Nature . . . all things are determined from the necessity of the divine nature to exist and act in a certain manner."[29] Thus, "things could have been produced by God in no other manner and in no other order than that in which they have been produced."[30]

For Spinoza, "it clearly follows that things have been produced by God in the highest degree of perfection, since they have necessarily followed from the existence of a most perfect nature. Nor does this doctrine accuse God of any imperfection, but, on the contrary, His perfection has compelled us to affirm it."[31] Thus, "all things have been predetermined by Him, not indeed from freedom of will or from absolute good pleasure, but from His absolute nature or infinite power."[32]

Spinoza rejects all teleological explanations of the universe and God's role in it: "It is commonly supposed that all things in Nature, like men, work to some end; and, indeed, it is thought to be certain that God Himself directs all things to some sure end, for it is said that God has made all things for man and man that he may worship God."[33] But all this is "falsity." The thought that God should aim toward some end im-

24. Ibid., 140.
25. Ibid., 149.
26. Ibid; emphasis added.
27. Ibid., 153.
28. Ibid., 156.
29. Ibid., 158.
30. Ibid., 160.
31. Ibid., 161.
32. Ibid., 164.
33. Ibid.

plies that God "necessarily seeks something of which He stands in need,"[34] thus obliterating his perfection.

Since, however, the mind and body of man "express the nature of God [only] in a certain and determinate manner,"[35] there is always room for man to deceive himself and settle for less than he can become. Hence, man's only hope lies in the gradual recognition of God as the sole substance of all, his acceptance of the modes or modifications of God's twin eternal attributes (extension and thinking), and his acknowledgement of the knowledge of God as the highest happiness of all.[36]

Spinoza's pragmatic conclusions have remarkable affinities with the practical admonitions of both Calvin and Zwingli:

> 1. [This doctrine] . . . teaches us that we do everything by the will of God alone, and that we are partakers of the divine nature in proportion as our actions become more and more perfect and we more and more understand God. . . .
> 2. It is of service to us in so far as it teaches us how we ought to behave with regard to things of fortune, . . . to wait for and bear each form of fortune because we know that all things follow from the eternal decree of God. . . .
> 3. [It] . . . teaches us to hate no one, to despise no one, to mock no one. . . . It teaches every one . . . to be content with his own, and to be helpful to his neighbor, . . . by the guidance of reason alone. . . .
> 4. [And it] . . . teaches us by what means citizens are to be governed and led, . . . that they may freely do those things which are best.[37]

Spinoza views the world as thoroughly mechanistic yet filled with the immanent presence of God. His doctrine of providence represents a pantheistic reinterpretation of the Reformers' positions as well as a modern restatement of the Stoic position. Because of its pantheism, as well as its naturalistic determinism, it cannot be endorsed by a biblically informed Reformed theology.

Gottfried Wilhelm von Leibniz

Along with Descartes and Spinoza, Gottfried Wilhelm von Leibniz (1654–1716) also accepted a mechanical world. Leibniz, however, made important alterations in Spinoza's single-substance theory which allowed him to emphasize the uniqueness of persons rather than their unity with

34. Ibid., 166.
35. Ibid., 171.
36. Ibid., 186.
37. Ibid., 186–87.

the divine. He also argued for God's transcendence and for a world in which freedom (self-development) may be realized.[38]

For Leibniz, the world is comprised of many monads which act in harmony with each other because God has preestablished that harmony. Yet, each monad acts on its own, insofar as each fulfills its potentiality; or, in the case of individuals, persons fulfill their preestablished destinies as each individual realizes his unique purpose predetermined by God.

For Leibniz, therefore, this is the best of all possible worlds. For if it would have been possible for God to have created and arranged a better world, then God, being perfect, omnipotent, and omniscient, would have done so. Furthermore, evil is a reconcilable part of this world. Leibniz claims that his own views represent nothing more than a restatement of Augustinian theology which recognizes that the possibility (not necessity) of evil is a requisite for greater good.

In the summary of his *Theodicy,* Leibniz writes:

> I have proved this is in . . . detail . . . , that an imperfection in the part may be required for a greater perfection in the whole. I have followed therein the opinion of St. Augustine, who said a hundred times that God permitted evil in order to derive from it a good, that is to say, a greater good.[39]

Leibniz articulates a more Christian rationalization of a mechanical world than does Spinoza.

David Hume

David Hume (1711–1776) was the first great spoiler of the grand system that Descartes, Spinoza, and Leibniz had advanced and sought to show that none of the unity, causality, and divine involvement that his predecessors assumed to be present was actually so.

Hume argues that causation is little more than the habitual observance of entities related by time in sequence; that the so-called unique "soul" or "self" is little more than a bundle of fleeting mental perceptions; and that the universe need hardly have been created by a single, omnipotent, omniscient, and beneficent God. The principle of accounting for similar effects on the grounds of similar causes only requires that the universe

38. For general introductions to Leibniz's thought, see Jones, *History of Western Philosophy,* 706–18; Stumpf, *Socrates to Sartre,* 263–71; and Copleston, *History of Philosophy,* 4:270–336.

39 See Leibniz, *Theodicy,* trans. by E. M. Huggard (London: Routledge & Kegan Paul, 1951); quoted by Johnson, *Introduction to Philosophy,* 355.

and man, as we currently know them, be thought of in terms of "growing" like a plant.[40]

For Hume, the mechanically certain world of the sciences was an unproven if not unprovable assumption, and the certainty of theologians that the book of nature could be read in such a way as to corroborate its divine design and purposiveness was equally a misjudgment on the part of a proud rational age.

Blaise Pascal

Blaise Pascal (1632–1662) gained no sense of certainty from either the metaphysics of the past or from arguments purportedly derived from the order of nature. Neither reassured him of the existence of God or of God's activity in the world.

> This is what I see, and what troubles me. I look on all sides, and see nothing but obscurity; nature offers me but matter for doubt. . . . I see too much to deny [the marks of a Creator], and too little to affirm; so my state is pitiful. . . .
>
> The metaphysical proofs of God are so far apart from man's reason . . . that they are but little striking. . . . [They are too weak] to convince hardened atheists. All who seek God in nature find no light to satisfy them. They fall either into atheism or into deism, two things which the Christian religion equally abhors.[41]

When Pascal looks toward the heavens, he concludes: "I feel engulfed in the infinite immensity of spaces whereof I know nothing, and which know nothing of me, I am terrified. The eternal silence of these infinite spaces alarms me."[42] But when he contemplates the minute structures that comprise the material world, he is compelled to marvel how paradoxical human life is.

> Not from space must I see my dignity. . . . Man is but a reed, weakest in nature, but a reed which thinks. . . . It needs not that the whole universe should arm to crush him. A vapor, a drop of water is enough to kill him. But were the universe to kill him, man would still be more noble than that which has slain him, because he knows that he dies, and that the universe has the better of him. The universe knows nothing of this.

40. See specifically Hume's *An Enquiry Concerning Human Understanding* and *Dialogues Concerning Natural Religion,* in *The English Philosophers: From Bacon to Mill,* ed. by E. A. Burtt (New York: Modern Library, 1939).

41. See Pascal, *Pensées,* in Castell, *Introduction to Modern Philosophy,* 182.

42. Ibid., 184.

> Know then, proud Man, how great a paradox thou art to thyself. Bow down thyself, impotent reason; be silent, thou foolish human nature. Learn that man is altogether incomprehensible by man.[43]

Thus his very nature requires man to look beyond himself in order to comprehend himself and his place in the universe. Hence, Pascal is driven to esteem the Scriptures, where he encounters anew the truth that "men are in darkness and estranged from God" and that "God has hidden Himself from their knowledge," that God himself awaits man there as the *Deus absconditus,* who alone redeems mankind and the world.[44]

A Reformed theology can appreciate, if not stand in awe, of Pascal's honest reflection on that "pitiful" state of anxiety the infinite spaces caused him to feel. Above all, it can rightly applaud his return to Scripture and "leap of faith," or "wager" as he preferred to call it. But in the final analysis, Pascal's solution cannot be entirely embraced by a Reformed doctrine of the providence of God.

From Calvin's perspective as well as Scripture's, the natural order witnesses to the majesty and power of God, and, even more, its operations and laws witness to the creative power and presence of God in his universe. No matter how estranged from God or self modern man may become, the Reformed heritage reminds us that God did create the world and that he created it "good." Reformed theologies cannot take as their starting point a view of the world that assumes "the infinite immensity of spaces" to be cold, silent, or devoid of God. It cannot accept the Cartesian dichotomy which divides the universe in such a way as to "locate" God only in the mind or soul of a "thinking thing." To that extent, therefore, the piety and theology of Isaac Watts (1674–1748) comes closer to the truth:

I sing the mighty power of God,
That made the mountains rise;
That spread the flowing seas abroad,
And built the lofty skies.

I sing the Wisdom that ordained
The sun to rule the day;
The moon shines full at His command,
And all the stars obey.

There's not a plant or flower below,
But makes Thy glories known;

43. Ibid., 185.
44. See *Pensées,* no. 194, in Beardsley, *European Philosophers,* 109.

And clouds arise, and tempests blow,
By order from Thy throne;

While all that borrows life from Thee
Is ever in Thy care,
And everywhere that man can be,
Thou, God, art present there.[45]

Immanuel Kant

Immanuel Kant's (1724–1804) importance is far-reaching and has profound significance for the Reformed doctrine of the providence of God. Kant confesses that it was while he was pondering Hume that he was aroused from his "dogmatic slumber."[46]

For Kant, Hume was correct to question our facile assumptions regarding the self, nature, and God. Kant's epistemology, therefore, rules out the possibility of establishing the reality of God based on mere human knowledge of the phenomenal world. As human beings, we can know only what sensory data permit us to know as our sensory perceptors respond to those data. Those data, in turn, are shaped by the a priori manner in which our minds function. Thus, we can only know the world as it appears to us. We cannot know the world in and of itself. Since God is not a sensory datum, we cannot know God or his providential operations in this manner.

Yet mankind has come to entertain such ideas as "the self," "nature," and "God." How are these to be accounted for? Kant answers that they are "transcendental ideas," "postulates" of human reason. The mind strives to get behind the bits and pieces that comprise its field of awareness in order to discover their essential unity. Hence, the mind postulates the self as the unifying entity behind its experiences of fleeting mental perceptions; it infers nature as the unifying phenomenon embracing our knowledge of cosmic bits and pieces; and it postulates God as the highest being logically prior to all concepts of unity, being, and perfection.[47]

Furthermore, Kant's ethical studies and theories permit him to defend the concepts of freedom, immortality, and the existence of God.[48] Based

45. Quoted from *The Hymnbook* (Philadelphia: Presbyterian Church in the United States et al., 1955), 80.

46. See Kant's *Prolegomena to Every Future Metaphysics That May Be Presented as a Science*, in *The Philosophy of Kant*, ed. by Carl J. Friedrich (New York: Modern Library, 1949), 45.

47. For a general introduction to Kant's epistemology, see Copleston, *History of Philosophy*, 6.2:7–100.

48. Ibid., 101–40.

on mankind's common rational awareness of a sense of obligation, Kant
argues: (1) if that sense of obligation is to be satisfied, then man must be
"free" to elect to pursue it; (2) to fully attain that goal requires "immortality," or a sufficient duration of time for its fulfillment; and (3) the only
guarantor of (1) and (2) must be a reality which is itself moral, rational,
and eternal. Hence, man's very awareness of his moral and rational nature
compels him to understand himself as belonging to a moral and rational
system, sustained and sponsored by the highest moral and rational Being
of all—God.

Kant joins his emphasis on the moral and rational with his view of
nature and the meaning of history, insofar as both God and man are
involved.

From a religious perspective, God has provided man with an exemplar
and archetype in the person of Christ. Thus, a "practical faith in this Son
of God" as one whom God has sent down from heaven awakens in man
a "moral disposition" to become as Christ-like as possible.[49]

From the point of view of nature and history, a different struggle is
taking place, although it is not unrelated to the religious one. Kant sees
a clear pattern emerging in nature that gives meaning and purpose to
human life. This meaning and purpose is inseparable from nature, because
"human actions are determined by general laws of nature like any other
event of nature." "History is concerned with telling about these events."[50]

What, then, is the pattern this history unveils? Kant discusses it in his
essay, "Idea for a Universal History with Cosmopolitan Intent" (1784).[51]
Kant defines this pattern using a series of propositions:

1. Any creature developed by nature has the potential to realize its final purpose.
2. In man, the highest aim will be developed in the species only, not in every
   individual.
3. By the use of reason, man transcends mere human existence and creates on
   his own a happiness for himself.
4. Social antagonisms help man develop his endowed potential. "The means
   which nature employs to accomplish the development of all faculties is the
   antagonism of men in society, since this antagonism becomes, in the end,
   the cause of a lawful order of this society."[52]
5. Man's greatest problem is the establishment of a civil society that adminis-
   ters law.

49. See Kant's *Religion Within the Limits of Reason Alone,* trans. by T. M. Greene (New
York: Harper, 1960), 54–57, 108–9.
50. See Kant's *Idea for a Universal History with Cosmopolitan Intent,* in *Philosophy of
Kant,* 116–31.
51. Ibid.
52. Ibid., 120.

6. While this problem is the most difficult, it is also the one that man solves last.

7. It can only be solved insofar as man creates an international society based on law.

8. Thus the history of mankind lies in the "realization of a hidden plan of nature," by means of which man's rational nature is fully developed.[53]

Hence, the meaning of human history becomes a natural, rational, and human problem, to be solved by men in accordance with natural law and by the use of their own reason. God can never be more than a postulate of human reason, and his Son never more than an archetype of what each human being can become.

What is one to make of Kant? Tillich observes that Kant's greatness lies in the fact that "he understands man's creaturely finitude."[54] He truly grasps that "the finite mind is not able to reach the infinite,"[55] that "the only thing we can do is to accept our finitude."[56] Hence, Kant "is the philosopher who saw most clearly and sharply the finitude of man and man's inability of breaking through the limits of his finitude to that which transcends it, namely, to the infinite."[57]

But, as Tillich notes, Kant also saw more. For Kant's moral imperative points man beyond his impasse. Tillich writes: "He showed one thing, that in the finite structure of our being there is a point of unconditional validity. This point is the moral imperative and the experience of its unconditional character."[58]

Thus, there looms on the one hand Spinoza, in whom the finite and the infinite are identified, and on the other hand, Kant, in whom the two are divided. And it is this problem, Tillich claims, that "the whole continental philosophy" and the modern theological era have inherited.[59]

Where Reformed theology takes post-Kantian philosophical and theological movements seriously, then it too has to address this problem. What the Reformed position allows, however, is that both nature and history are guided by and are under divine care; neither unfolds outside God's holy and gracious will.

To that extent, let Kant be praised for reminding us of our finitude and

53. Ibid., 120–29.
54. Paul Tillich, *Perspectives on 19th and 20th Century Protestant Theology,* ed. by Carl E. Braaten (New York: Harper & Row, 1967), 70.
55. Ibid., 64.
56. Ibid., 66.
57. Ibid.
58. Ibid., 66f.
59. Ibid., 74.

for causing us to ponder afresh the meaning of an unconditioned element of our humanness. In the final analysis, Kant himself says it best: "Two things fill the mind with ever new and increasing awe and admiration the more frequently and continuously reflection is occupied with them; the starred heaven above me and the moral law within me."[60]

Friedrich Schleiermacher

We shall bypass German idealism (Fichte, Schelling, and Hegel), which advanced its own solution for unifying the finite and the infinite, or for understanding God and his place in his universe, and shall focus instead on Friedrich Schleiermacher (1768–1834) and his resolution of the problem.

The key concept for Schleiermacher is man's "feeling of absolute dependence" upon his Creator. Richard R. Niebuhr summarizes Schleiermacher's view:

> True humanity emerges only where the God-consciousness so informs the total Self-consciousness that all particular relations to the world or in the world, whether they express free action or passive determination, . . . are taken up into the God-consciousness without being annulled and are transformed into occasions for the further expression of and enjoyment of the self's utter dependence on its creator.[61]

Schleiermacher specifically discusses the providence of God in the first section of the "First Part of the System of Doctrine" in *The Christian Faith.*

Schleiermacher views creation and preservation as two propositions that express the identical truth—"that the totality of finite being exists only in dependence upon the creator." Creation is the proposition "that the world was created by God," and preservation is the claim "that God sustains the world."[62] But for Schleiermacher the distinction is superfluous, as what the two propositions declare is that "no point of space and no point of time, should be exempted from the Divine All-Sovereignty."[63] Both propositions witness to "the absolute feeling of dependence." Still, Schleiermacher examines each separately.

Creation refers to the "universal condition of all finite being" and means

60. See Kant's conclusion to his *Critique of Pure Practical Reason,* in *Philosophy of Kant,* 261.

61. See Friedrich Schleiermacher, *The Christian Faith,* ed. by H. Mackintosh and J. Stewart (New York: Harper Torchbooks, 1963), 1:xviii.

62. Ibid., 142.

63. Ibid., 144.

that nothing in it is or ever has been independent of God.[64] Hence, "the origin of the world must, indeed, be traced entirely to the divine activity."[65] Schleiermacher is convinced that science best understands this origin and how it occurred and that this "how" need not conflict with the principle of absolute dependence that underlies the meaning of the biblical stories of creation.

Preservation, or conservation, means that human life is not only dependent upon God but, at the same time, is conditioned and determined by the interdependence of nature. The two are one. Schleiermacher states: "The religious self-consciousness, by means of which we place all that affects or influences us in absolute dependence on God, coincides entirely with the view that all such things are conditioned and determined by the interdependence of Nature."[66] In other words, the providence of God manifests itself in the fact that every individual's destiny is determined by the complex interdependent occurrences of nature and history. Thus our feeling of absolute dependence upon God is one and the same as our recognition that we are governed by the universality of the nature-system.

Schleiermacher rejects the notion that either claim denies the other:

It is said that the more clearly we conceive anything to be entirely conditioned by the interdependence of nature, the less can we arrive at the feeling of its absolute dependence upon God; and, conversely, the more vivid this latter feeling is the more indefinitely must we leave its interrelatedness with nature an open question. But . . . we cannot admit such a contradiction between the two ideas.[67]

Or, as he states it again: "*Divine preservation,* as the absolute dependence of all events and changes on God, and *natural causation,* as the complete determination of all events by the universal nexus, are one and the same thing simply from different points of view."[68] Hence, Schleiermacher explains that if the idea of divine government means that nothing can happen except as God has "originally willed and always wills" for it to happen, "by means of the powers distributed and preserved in the world"—then that concept of government is already included in his.[69]

Schleiermacher rejects miracles (understood as the intervention of the supernatural). The omnipotence of God cannot mean that he suspends

64. Ibid., 151.
65. Ibid., 152.
66. Ibid., 170.
67. Ibid., 171.
68. Ibid., 174; emphasis added.
69. Ibid., 177.

the interdependence of nature. He does not alter its "original immutable course." "If such an interference be postulated as one of the privileges of the Supreme Being, it would . . . have to be assumed that there is something not ordained by Him which could offer Him resistance and thus invade Him and His work; and such an idea would entirely destroy our fundamental feeling."[70]

Evil also has its place within Schleiermacher's principle of absolute dependence. Evil is of two kinds: natural and social. Natural evil is "determined by the total forces of nature"; social evil is determined "by the collective conditions of human activity."[71] Evil as such is not ordained by God, but arises in nature and human society as a definite possibility and "comes within the absolute dependence on God."[72] Schleiermacher also incorporates the twofold Augustinian theme that evil, as a possibility, can serve a higher good and that it "has its grounds in a mere defect."[73]

Our consciousness of ourselves as free moral agents is a consciousness "which is received and is gradually developed in a universal system."[74] Hence, our freedom and activity are inseparable from this universal system and are both determined by and determinants within its complex natural and social interplay (i.e., a form of soft determinism). Thus we are free as well as determined while ever dependent upon God.

Schleiermacher's doctrine is candid and appealing. A modern Reformed position can appreciate his insistence that theology ought not tinker with the forces and interdependence of nature. To want a system of nature that can be interfered with, rescinded, or nullified by either divine whim or human pleading is hardly a universe worthy of a wise, holy, omnipotent, and beneficent God. It would be chaos, not cosmos, a violation of Genesis 1:1–2:3 as well as Proverbs 8.

A biblical and Reformed doctrine of the providence of God must take nature and its orders seriously. To want to be exempt from the "universal nature-mechanism," as Schleiermacher refers to it, is tantamount to denying our creatureliness. Nature cannot be bypassed. In the Calvinist tradition, no providence of God can spurn secondary causes. They are part of the divine plan.

A Reformed position, however, may rightfully take issue with Schleiermacher's implied subordination of God to that very chain of natural causation which Calvin insists God governs directly and dynamically, and not simply mechanically or naturalistically. Calvin warns that if God's will is

70. Ibid., 179.
71. Ibid., 185.
72. Ibid., 188.
73. Ibid.
74. Ibid., 190.

identified totally with natural law and natural occurrences, then God cannot show his goodness to individuals.[75] Nevertheless, this is not the crucial problem Schleiermacher's system poses for Reformed thought.

Rather, what should concern a Reformed understanding of the providence of God is Schleiermacher's philosophical starting point. His defining principle, though contained in Scripture, is not the central focus of Scripture. Schleiermacher's principle is an abstract and popular concept derived from his era that exalts an aspect of our humanness ignored by Kant and the rationalism of the Enlightenment, namely, the subjective feeling of the finite in all its dependence upon the infinite. While such a feeling constitutes a legitimate element of religious experience, that is not how Scripture describes the providence of God.

One example should suffice to demonstrate this point. What makes Abraham's life unique? His subjective feeling of absolute dependence upon the infinite? Although that aspect is present, it is actually God's election of and steadfast loyalty to Abraham that make the saga unique and of historical and religious value. Then comes Abraham's awareness of his absolute dependence upon God in the form of a human response, itself solicited and made possible by God, that is, his faith.

It is this focus on God's initiative, call, and provision that a Reformed doctrine of the providence of God must preserve and declare as central. Otherwise, we are overwhelmed by subjectivism, and, eventually, self-doubt and despair.

Darwin's Impact

In retrospect, if Reformed and orthodox theologies had been able to acknowledge that our humanness cannot exist apart from an interdependence of nature (Schleiermacher), and that God's divine activity occurs in, through, and by means of secondary causes (Calvin), then Darwin would not have become the great threat he did. However, Darwin's theories of evolution and natural selection seemed to compromise, if not obviate, God's providential activity in nature and, above all, in the realm of human development. Man was perceived as a product of blind, random forces, that possessed neither purpose nor design. Hence, one can understand why orthodox Protestantism resisted a view of nature whose origins and future, as well as whose creatures and inhabitants, were deemed the result of godless forces.

Charles Hodge acknowledged that Darwin stood "in the first rank of

75. *Institutes*, 1.16.3.

naturalists," but was concerned by the fact that Darwin's account of the origin of man relied on the principle of "unintelligent physical causes."[76] Hodge readily concedes that a theistic interpretation of Darwin's theory is possible, but he charges that, although the naturalist acknowledges the existence of God, his "theory is that hundreds or thousands of millions of years ago God called a living germ . . . into existence, and that since that time God has no more to do with the universe than if He did not exist."[77]

Although many contemporary theologians and probably most modern scientists accept evolution as a fact, many evangelical Reformed theologians do not hesitate to call attention to the spirit of Hodge's objection. In this sense, Bernard Ramm's critical evaluation of fundamentalism's reaction to Darwin and his own search for an intellectually honest yet biblical solution to the problem is a study worthy of Reformed reflection today. This is true even if one espouses a more thorough form of "progressive creation" than Ramm does.[78] Ramm is willing to accept evolution in its broadest sense, but not an evolution that is not controlled by the power of the Holy Spirit at every moment of its development.[79]

Beyond Darwin

Since Darwin, nontheistic philosophical interpretations of the world and the meaning of human existence have become part of our contemporary legacy. One thinks of Nietzsche and his "death of God" philosophy, with its emphasis on the "will-to-power" and the *Übermensch*. Or, more recently, one's thoughts turn to Sartre and Camus and to their existential humanism, with its emphasis upon the "absurd man," who wants to find out if it is "possible to live *without appeal*"; or who asks, in the words of one of Camus' characters, "Can one be a saint without God?"[80]

In reply, one cannot help but think of Pascal's insight that we are utterly "incomprehensible" to ourselves apart from faith in God. Or again one thinks of Bertrand Russell, or of Ernst Nagel, or of Rudolph Carnap and

76. Hodge, *Systematic Theology,* 2:13–15.

77. Ibid., 16.

78. See Bernard Ramm, *The Christian View of Science and Scripture* (Grand Rapids: Wm. B. Eerdmans, 1955), 112–16.

79. Ibid., 105–12. See esp. Ramm's section on the limitations of evolutionary theory, 273–80.

80. See Albert Camus, *The Plague,* trans. by Stuart Gilbert (New York: Alfred A. Knopf, 1948); quoted by R. Gill and E. Sherman in *The Fabric of Existentialism* (Englewood Cliffs: Prentice-Hall, 1973), 554; emphasis added.

the Vienna Circle and its "principle of verification," which has absorbed such a preponderant amount of contemporary philosophical reflection on the problem of language and its possible usages and meanings. In response to this latter passion, how strangely relevant the tower of Babel becomes, where mankind's language is confused and its people, who would have reached the very heavens, scattered!

At the same time, contemporary science no longer offers unifying world views, or perhaps even believes that a single theory, if it did exist, could tie all our experiences together. The quantum physics of the modern age, Heisenberg's principle of indeterminacy, and Einstein's theory of relativity have made the old Newtonian world quaint. Indeed, from a philosophical point of view, they imply that the universe is far more open and far less determined than previously thought by either scientists or theologians.

Theology is not equipped to provide us with scientific solutions. It is concerned, however, with views which imply that either God is nonexistent or unable to act effectively within his own creation.[81] Therefore, based on revelation, theology readily witnesses to God's presence in his universe and to our human need to respond in faith and with reformed lives to the mystery of his grace and redemptive activity on our behalf. Hence, what our theologies can do is to draw upon the biblical understanding of creation, redemption, and history, and, in the light of that knowledge, provide us with an interpretation of the meaning and purpose of human life. In the light of that revelation, it can allow God to speak to and direct us in the midst of the complex natural and sociohistorical occurrences that embrace us both individually and collectively.

81. See Holmes Rolston, III, *Science and Religion: A Critical Survey* (New York: Random House, 1987). Esp. relevant are chaps. 6 and 7. See also *The Caring God: Perspectives on Providence,* ed. by Carl S. Meyer and Herbert T. Mayer (St. Louis: Concordia, 1973), esp. chaps. 4–8, which explore psychological, sociological, and biological challenges to providential thought.

Chapter Nine

Twentieth-Century Theological Positions, Questions, and Insights

THE DOCTRINE OF THE PROVIDENCE OF GOD HAS CONTINUED TO ATTRACT theological reflection. Barth's *Church Dogmatics, III, The Doctrine of Creation, Part 3,* cited in the first two chapters, is certainly one of the more rigorous volumes dedicated to the doctrine in modern time. However, as we shall see, it is hardly the only major study of the subject.

Issues surrounding theological and scientific questions have persisted and sparked lively discussion, especially among evangelical Reformed theologians. This discussion has been largely concerned with the physical, biological, and anthropological dimensions of God's interaction with nature. One thinks in particular of Bernard Ramm's *The Christian View of Science and Scripture* or more recently of Carl Henry's *Horizons of Science.*

Yet the twentieth century has also seen considerable interest in problems related to history and God's activity therein. Certainly, among theologians who have made their "peace with science," so to speak, or have abandoned nature, an interest in God's acting and action in history has dominated their thought.

An interest in God's interaction in history is nothing new. It is as old as the biblical witnesses to God's providential action in Israel's history. To that extent, in the same genre belong the New Testament's eschatological view of history, the early church's struggle against Gnostic interpretations of nature and history, and Augustine's *The City of God.*

Nonetheless, since the Enlightenment, and especially since Kant, Hegel, and Marx, interpretations of history and the search for the factors governing the historical nexus have inspired numerous philosophical and theological explorations of God's providence. Thus, in this chapter, we shall examine a selection of theological positions that explore specifically the historical dimensions of God's providential operation, while also briefly examining contemporary reflection on the classical tradition of the first cause–secondary cause solution.

God's Activity in History

Much contemporary discussion concerning God's providential activity in history has focused on problems involved in the interpretation and analysis of history; its nexus, events, and actions; and the extent to which God directs or guides any of these processes. Specific foci include:

1. Philosophical interests in history and the meaning of "historical events"
2. Phenomenological, psychological, sociological, anthropological, and especially theological analyses of history
3. Assessment of the biblical story using a "history-of-religions" approach, along with a rejection of this methodology and its implied hermeneutic (e.g., Bultmann and Barth)

Perhaps the best summary and analysis of both classical and contemporary attempts to interpret God's action in history and its meaning for a doctrine of providence is Langdon Gilkey's *Reaping the Whirlwind*.[1] Also helpful is Owen C. Thomas's *God's Activity in the World*,[2] in which he abridges the comments of twelve contemporary writers who explore the problem of God's acting in history. In this section, we shall examine the positions of three twentieth-century theologians who particularly merit our attention.

George Ernest Wright

G. Ernest Wright's position is clearly articulated in both *God Who Acts* and *The Book of the Acts of God*.[3] Wright's point of departure is history

---

1. Gilkey's work will be evaluated in the following chapter.
2. See Owen C. Thomas, *God's Activity in the World: The Contemporary Problem* (Chico, Calif.: Scholars Press, 1983).
3. See *God Who Acts: Biblical Theology as Recital* (London: SCM, 1952), and *The Book of the Acts of God: Contemporary Scholarship Interprets the Bible* (Garden City: Anchor Books, 1960).

as "the arena of God's activity."[4] By this Wright means at least four things.

First, God's activity occurs as an objective event in time. His mighty acts are precisely that—acts, events, objective occurrences. Hence, God's providence unfolds in the historical nexus; it is never simply a postulate of subjective mysticism.[5]

Second, God's actions in history are always grasped by inference. "Inference" is one of Wright's favorite terms. God's actions are the deductions of faith.[6] They cannot be proven to be events in the way that secular historians treat events. Hence, they are confessional, interpretative, and "recital" in form.

Wright never tires of blending the two themes of history and inference: "The knowledge of God was an inference from what actually had happened in human history."[7] Consequently, Wright identifies three elements that are critical to biblical faith and relevant to a doctrine of providence. First, there is "the peculiar attention to history . . . as the primary sphere in which God reveals himself."[8] Hence, the "objectivity of God's historical acts" becomes the focus of study. Second, "the chief inference from this view of history . . . was the mediate nature of God's action in history: that is, his election. . . ."[9] The third is the event of the covenant and all its implications.[10] For Wright, these are not abstract or propositional elements; rather, they are "based on historical events and the inferences drawn from them."[11]

Third, these events are always redemptive in character and culminate in the coming of the Christ and in the historical reality of his cross. Hence, all of history—both prior and subsequent to the cross—is to be interpreted in the light of God's redemptive activity in Christ.[12]

Fourth, accordingly, history itself cannot and must not be understood as an independent phenomenon. It is never simply the sum total of naturalistic occurrences and sociohistorical developments, guided solely by the interplay of cause-and-effect forces. In a manner which echoes Calvin, Wright concludes:

> Biblical man . . . was aware that events were not really understood except
> as they were searched for the revelation they contained of what God was

4. *God Who Acts*, 38.
5. Ibid., 44.
6. Ibid., 57–58.
7. Ibid., 44.
8. Ibid., 55.
9. Ibid.
10. Ibid., 56.
11. Ibid.
12. Ibid., 56–57, 80–81.

doing and what he willed. History thus could not be conceived as a secular, naturalistic, cause-and-effect process in which events are to be explained solely by the interplay of environment and geography on individual and social organisms. Happenings become history when they are recognized as integral parts of a God-planned and God-directed working, extending from creation to eschaton.[13]

Certainly, Reformed doctrines of the providence of God can appreciate Wright's emphasis on the historical character of God's revelatory interaction and of God's redemptive presence in the midst of historical and political events. All this is "God-planned" and "God-directed." It can also appreciate Wright's christological emphasis (Brunner's "foreground") and his insistence on the incompleteness of secular interpretations of history.

But having said that, one can understand why some Reformed communities hesitate to embrace Wright's position (the biblical theology movement). Its hermeneutic, which emphasizes the role of inference, is problematic. The focus suddenly shifts from God's sovereignty and omnipresent guidance to a human understanding of what might or might not be occurring in the historical milieu in the name of divine activity. A sharper normative principle is required than the criterion of an unqualified inference. Such a criterion is simply too broad. On the basis of this hermeneutic, one can never know whether the biblical writers, and the traditions that they preserve and interpret, infer too much or too little about God's interaction in history.

Owen C. Thomas offers his own criticism: "There is considerable obscurity about the relation between observable historical events, the interpretation of these events by faith, and the divine action."[14] Thomas asks, "Is God's action located in the event or in the faithful interpretation? Is God active in all events whether or not they are seen by faith?" Moreover, how "is God's action related to the finite causal nexus?"[15] In Thomas's opinion, Wright and the biblical theology movement of the 1960s is unable to resolve these dilemmas.

Rudolf Bultmann

Rudolf Bultmann's demythologization and his existential interpretation of God's acting in history represents, perhaps, one of the most commanding modern attempts to explore the nature of God's providential activity.

Bultmann's discussion of providence is found primarily in his *Jesus*

---

13. Ibid., 81–82.
14. Thomas, *God's Activity*, 4.
15. Ibid.

Christ and Mythology.[16] He opens his discussion first, however, with an explanation of demythologization.

For Bultmann, the mythological form in which the New Testament message has been preserved can never be divorced from that message. We must simply accept the mythological form and reinterpret its meaning for our time. Part of this mythological framework is the eschatological view that the kingdom of God is about to come upon mankind and bring an end to the powers of this age. This kingdom of God is not immanent in history, nor is it a product of the natural and historical nexus; instead, it transcends the historical order and will only come "through the supernatural action of God."[17]

Bultmann explains that this perception is mythological, for modern science does not believe that nature can be interrupted in this way, nor does the modern study of history accept such an outside invasion of "the course of history."[18] Hence, "modern men take it for granted that the course of nature and of history, like their own inner life and their practical life, is nowhere interrupted by the intervention of supernatural powers."[19]

What, then, is the meaning of the New Testament's message and its preaching of Jesus, if we cannot accept a *sacrificium intellectus* to its mythological framework? Do we retain the ethical teachings and abandon the eschatological features? No, Bultmann replies. We must "recover the deeper meaning behind the mythological conceptions."[20]

What is this deeper meaning? Bultmann maintains that "mythology expresses a certain understanding of human existence" — "the knowledge that man is not master of the world and of his life."[21] It knows that he is dependent upon a transcendence which can enlighten and make glad his life. It also knows that there is a tremendous evil power which enslaves existence. This is the deeper meaning of the mythological framework that can be retained.

The eschatological dimension, too, can be demythologized and its deeper meaning explored. The present time must be viewed "in the light of the future and it says to me that this present world, the world of nature and history, the world in which we live our lives and make our plans is not the only world; that this world is . . . ultimately empty and unreal in the face of eternity."[22] It means the possibility of freedom, "the freedom of

16. *Jesus Christ and Mythology* (New York: Charles Scribner's Sons, 1958).
17. Ibid., 12.
18. Ibid., 15.
19. Ibid., 16.
20. Ibid., 18.
21. Ibid., 19–21.
22. Ibid., 23.

man to be himself"[23] and "to be open to God's future which is really imminent for every one of us."[24]

Bultmann insists that all this can be retained while rejecting the obsolete ancient world view of Scripture. The demythologized Word of God calls men away from "subjective freedom," from the belief that science and technology can make men masters of themselves and the world, and it calls them to genuine freedom in God.

In none of this does God perform "in an irrational manner something that interrupts the natural course of events."[25] God does not work as some kind of *causa* among other *causae*. Rather, in the proclamation of his Word, God encounters us as the gracious and mysterious God who sets mankind free to be itself.

Bultmann next addresses how an existential philosophy is part of a program of reinterpretation and why it is inseparable from his hermeneutic. He believes that the primary question and presupposition that the modern age must bring to the Scriptures is this: *"How is man's existence understood in the Bible?"*[26]

Bultmann argues that since every interpreter is dependent on conceptions that he has inherited, and since every set of conceptions is dependent on some philosophy, the question becomes, "What philosophy best sheds light on the question of existence and hence best serves to interpret the biblical understanding of man's existence?" Bultmann then identifies existentialist philosophy as the key to his hermeneutic, "because in this philosophical school human existence is directly the object of attention."[27]

An existentialist philosophy claims that "you must exist," that "every man has his own history," and that every man's existence can be realized only in his own unique moments of the "here and now." It makes "personal existence my own personal responsibility, and by doing so it helps to make me open to the word of the Bible."[28] Bultmann concludes:

> If it is true that the revelation of God is realized only in the concrete events of life here and now, and that the analysis of existence is confined to man's temporal life with its series of here and now, then this analysis unveils a sphere which faith alone can understand as the sphere of the relation between man and God.[29]

23. Ibid., 29.
24. Ibid., 31.
25. Ibid., 44.
26. Ibid., 53.
27. Ibid., 55.
28. Ibid., 56.
29. Ibid., 58.

Bultmann is now ready to address the question of what it means to say that God acts. He does so by attempting to reply to a number of objections.

Objection #1

It is not mythological to speak of God as "acting"? Yes, Bultmann replies, but God's "action" can still be protected. It is mythological to think of God's action as an intervention between the natural and the historical, or as the psychological course of events, in which those events are broken and then relinked. In this conception, "divine causality is inserted as a link in the chain of the events which follow one another according to the causal nexus."[30] If this were true, then God's action would be viewed "in the same way as secular actions or events are conceived."[31] But this is not how God works in history.

God's action is not something that happens *between* worldly events; rather, it is an action that occurs *within* them: "The close connection between natural and historical events remains intact as it presents itself to the observer. The action of God is hidden from every eye except the eye of faith. . . . It is within [events] that God's hidden action is taking place."[32]

The Reformers themselves acknowledge that God's action is often hidden to our understanding. However, they differ from Bultmann in that he refuses to accept the natural and historical course of events as necessarily reflecting the activity of God, and instead locates God's action secretly within events. The Reformers tend to identify the events of history and nature as outwardly manifesting either the active or permissive hidden will of God. In Bultmann, then, we have God's hidden *action* which need not be identified with a historical event; in the Reformers we have God's hidden *will* which tends to justify the historical event or to treat it as the event's cause.

As for the preposition *within,* several questions come to mind. Does God's action *within* history make any real difference on history? Is God actually doing anything? If so, what is it? That is, does God's action *within* history influence history in any way? If it does, how? What Bultmann seems to mean by his use of the preposition is that God is immanent in his world; God is never absent; the world is never devoid of God. The preposition *between* suggests that God comes into his world from outside, which might imply that the world is quite able to run on its own, except now and then when it needs God, for whatever reason. But a Reformed

30. Ibid., 61.
31. Ibid.
32. Ibid., 61–62.

reader will lament that Bultmann does not press *within* satisfactorily enough to dispel such equivocations.

Objection #2

If God's hidden action occurs within the chain of secular events, then what prohibits a "pantheistic piety"? Bultmann replies that it is precisely because faith does not identify God's action with worldly events that no pantheism results. Rather, what Christian faith must say is: " 'I trust that God is working here and there, but His action is hidden, or it is not directly identical with the visible event. What it is that He is doing I do not yet know, . . . but faithfully I trust that it is important for my personal existence. . . .' "[33]

The bottom line of all this for Bultmann is the concept of paradox. Our lives are determined by the natural and historical course of events; yet, the eye of faith recognizes that our existence is nevertheless pardoxically determined by the God of grace who, in the preaching of his Word, meets us in the here and now and keeps us open to the future. "This is the paradox of faith, that faith 'nevertheless' understands as God's action here and now an event which is completely intelligible in the natural or historical connection of events."[34]

Objection #3

If God's action is hidden, then how can theology make positive statements about it? Are not all our statements automatically negative? Bultmann replies that the fact that it is hidden does prevent us from making *general* statements about God's action. But this does not detract from the existentialist hermeneutic that allows one to speak of what God does here and now with the individual.[35]

Objection #4

If this is true, then what does it mean when we claim that God acts? It means that our speech about God's action is analogous. For Bultmann, "to speak of God as acting involves the events of personal existence."[36] Man lives within the limits of space and time, and hence his speech about God's action can only be speech about the here and now. Thus, since God acts in ways that are analogous to personal actions, our speech about his acting is limited to analogy.

33. Ibid., 64.
34. Ibid., 65.
35. Ibid., 66.
36. Ibid., 68.

Accordingly, Bultmann draws two important conclusions. First, the only legitimate statements about God's acting are statements that express "the existential relation between God and man."[37] One cannot speak of God's actions as cosmic events. Second, statements about "God as acting are legitimate only if they mean that God is a personal being acting on persons."[38] Conceptions of God as acting politically and juridically are not permissible.

Objection #5

If this is so, then what is to prevent the reduction of God's action to a purely psychological inner experience of the soul? Does not analogous speech rob God's action of all its objective reality? For Bultmann, that "God cannot be seen or apprehended apart from faith does not mean that He does not exist apart from faith."[39] His hiddenness is actually faith's strength. Hence, it is "enough to say that faith grows out of the encounter with the Holy Scriptures as the Word of God."[40] Indeed, "God's Word is hidden in the Scriptures as each action of God is hidden everywhere."[41]

Objection #6

What becomes then of God's revelation and its power? Does not an emphasis on self-understanding eclipse an emphasis on God's revelation? No, Bultmann argues. For an existentialist self-understanding requires a daily here-and-now reanalysis, that happens only as the self responds to the Word of God.

Objection #7

Finally, what becomes of the biblical "once for all" of God's action on behalf of the whole world? "Are we not in danger of relegating the divine dispensation, the history of salvation, to the dimension of timelessness?"[42] No. For God meets us in the concrete word of the "preaching instituted in Jesus Christ." This Word of God is never an invention "by the human spirit and by human sagacity; it rises up in history."[43] For this event is Jesus Christ, whose work and destiny happen within the nexus of history and display him paradoxically as the eschatological event that frees man from the past and opens his existence to the future.

37. Ibid., 69.
38. Ibid., 70.
39. Ibid., 72.
40. Ibid., 71.
41. Ibid.
42. Ibid., 78.
43. Ibid., 79.

In conclusion, Bultmann explains that the very nature of faith is inseparable from God's hiddenness. God is a hidden God; he cannot be observed empirically. "The invisibility of God excludes every myth which tries to make God and His action visible. . . . We can believe in God only in spite of experience."[44] Yet "the world is God's world and the sphere of God as acting."[45]

How do we assess Bultmann? In all candor, there are commendable features in his theology.

To begin with, the Scriptures do depict God's action as a phenomenon hidden within history, grasped principally by the eyes of faith. The plagues in Egypt parallel the natural occurrences of the annual flooding of the Nile and can be understood as the results of such. Faith sees them as signs and wonders. The conquest of the Promised Land meshes perfectly with the political upheavals that occurred in Canaan between the fourteenth and eleventh centuries B.C. Only faith sees the conquest as the fulfillment of God's promise to Abraham. Even the words and deeds of Jesus are rejected and resisted, except by those who have eyes to see and ears to hear what the Spirit is saying and doing.

But, of course, far more than the hiddenness of God's action is at issue in the Bible. For Scripture goes beyond Bultmann to claim that both God's Word and God's acting are no longer shrouded in total mystery. Yes, God's ineffability remains; his wholly-otherness can never be penetrated by us. Nevertheless, God has chosen to act in history and to enable the prophet, the historian, the poet, the evangelist, and the apostle to see enough of what he is doing in the universe so as not to leave man the victim of his own scientific and intellectual speculations. Hence, the Scriptures provide critical criteria by means of which we are lifted out of subjectivism, doubt, and despair into the light of divine truth and action.

There is also merit in Bultmann's insight that we do not have to identify the occurrences of the natural-historical nexus with either the final will or overt action of God. [Note that Bultmann is diametrically opposed to Schleiermacher here.] Rather, God acts within those occurrences in ways that are hidden to our understanding.

Bultmann's christological focus and his emphasis on the "here and now" of God's acting, with all its existential import, are worthy themes for any Reformed theology to sound. It is one thing to reflect philosophically about God's work of *creatio, sustentatio, concursus,* and *gubernatio.* It is quite another to be grasped existentially by the God of the universe and to trust him totally in the "here and now."

44. Ibid., 83f.
45. Ibid., 85.

Yet, there are questions we are forced to raise and there is, in particular, the one-sidedness of Bultmann's existentialist hermeneutic.

Schubert Ogden discusses this "one-sidedly existentialist character" of Bultmann's solution and subjects it to a twofold criticism.[46] First, Bultmann tends to reduce all statements about God to statements about man and vice versa, which of course is unacceptable and extreme. His insistence upon the categories of personal encounter results in a fragmentary understanding of analogy, that leads in turn to a fragmentary understanding of God and his action.[47] Furthermore Bultmann fails to be consistent in his program of demythologization and thereby weakens his own position.[48]

Thomas offers some additional criticisms. In Bultmann's theory, God's action cannot be understood as a cosmic action. Hence, Thomas asks, "Does God in fact act in the world, or is it only that faith sees the world *as if* God were acting?"[49] Bultmann's obscure appeal to the "paradoxical" dimension of faith and to God's "hiddenness" leaves many questions still unanswered. Again, we are swamped by subjectivism, short of the inner testimony of the Holy Spirit and a divinely provided criterion that enables us to distinguish between the true acts of God and their meaning and our own voices of inner consciousness and conflict.

Furthermore, Thomas wonders how we can "conceive of an act of God which is real and yet which does not have any objective effect on the finite causal nexus."[50] If God's acting has no influence on the causal nexus, then who or what is in charge of that nexus? What is God's relationship to this nexus? Is it purely an analogous one, or only a psychological one, insofar as humankind is concerned? Bultmann denies even the latter, as there can be no interruption of the course of history, not even of the "psychological course of events." Yet, in the preaching of the Word of God, this is precisely what God does, insofar as he awakens human lives to authentic existence in him. Either God is doing something that influences the nexus or he is not.

Bultmann also denies that God's action influences cosmic, political, or juridical events, since we can speak of God's action only in personal terms. Yet Scripture presents God precisely as the One who commands the heavens and the earth, who is nature's Creator and Sustainer, and who governs history's great and inscrutable course.

---

46. See Schubert M. Ogden, *The Reality of God and Other Essays* (London: SCM, 1967), 170.
47. Ibid., 171–72.
48. Ibid., 173.
49. Thomas, *God's Activity,* 7.
50. Ibid.

Bultmann would dismiss this as mythological speech. Yet the Scriptures affirm that God's action and acting influence the sociohistorical nexus in objective ways. In the events of the exodus, a nation of enslaved people is set free. Sargon II, Nebuchadezzar, and Cyrus II become instruments of God's judgment and grace. Man is both a political and social being. Not even the stranger at Israel's gates is without rights. God is as concerned for humankind's political and social well-being as he is for mankind's spiritual and inner existential wholeness. Indeed, "the coastlands wait for his law" (Isa. 42:4). In sum, God's action does bear upon political and juridical events.

In the final analysis, perhaps, it is not so much that Bultmann is wrong, but, as Ogden suggests, it is rather that his hermeneutic is too one-sided. We are simply forced to draw the line in favor of a more comprehensive hermeneutic for understanding God's work and providential activity in the world.

Gordon D. Kaufman

In *God the Problem,* Gordon Kaufman acknowledges that the concept of a God who "continuously performs deliberate acts in and upon his world, and in and through man's history," has become highly problematical for a modern age.[51] Modern man simply views all of life—nature and history—as subject to natural causes that lead to natural effects.[52] If there is any mystery left, it is in the cosmic process; it is not a mystery that points to God. Hence, talk about God has become "hollow and abstract" and "uncomfortable and difficult" for many contemporary theologians.[53]

In Kaufman's view, proposals that abandon nature to an "autonomous and self-contained" system, but see history as "the realm of freedom and purpose" in which God operates, are decidedly "shallow." There is simply no sharp demarcation between nature and history. History has never been "a realm of freedom" separate from the causal forces of nature. Not even the "biblical perspective is . . . characterized by such nonsense."[54] Moreover, "referring acts of God to historical events really helps little to resolve the fundamental problem," since modern historians analyze history without ever having to "invoke a transcendent agent."[55]

What, then, is theology to do? It must examine and interpret afresh its

51. *God the Problem* (Cambridge: Harvard University Press, 1972), 120.
52. Ibid.
53. Ibid., 121.
54. Ibid., 122.
55. Ibid., 123.

understanding of an "act of God" as well as its understanding of a God who is "a supreme Actor or Agent."[56]

Kaufman identifies three alternatives: (1) grant that "God is dead"; (2) reinterpret "the notion of God in such a manner that the conception of agent is no longer implied" (which he believes Tillich does); or (3) reinterpret the notion of "act" to see if it is possible "to reinterpret the conception of 'God's act(s)' " in a manner that is consistent with its traditional usage "but . . . theologically significant and philosophically intelligible."[57] Kaufman adopts the third alternative.

He begins by defining *act* and *agent*. An act is "something done" for an intended purpose; it requires an agent and involves creativity. An agent formulates intentions to be realized and must be capable "of working through time . . . to realize . . . goals."[58] In turn, acts may be broken down into subacts—steps within the agent's total act that he intends to accomplish. Thus an Aristotelian Unmoved Mover would not qualify as an agent nor would the teleological capacity of an acorn to become an oak constitute an act. Hence, an act of God "would be a deed performed by God, an event that did not simply 'happen,' but that was what it was because God did it."[59] At least, Kaufman argues, this is what Scripture means by the notion. Moreover, it is in the light of this definition that Kaufman believes the problem of how God acts in nature and history can be resolved.

First, however, there is the acknowledged problem that the modern age poses. It does not conceive of events as planned steps but "presupposes the interrelation and interconnection of all events in an unbroken web."[60] This means that it is simply "no longer possible for us to think . . . of individual or particular events somehow by themselves. . . ."[61] We simply cannot conceive of events that do not have finite antecedents. Thus, an "act of God" in this context is "literally inconceivable."[62]

Nevertheless, Kaufman believes that his analysis of "act," "agent," and "subact" illumines as well as helps to resolve the problem. Subacts are parts of a "master act," and it is this "master act . . . that renders any given piece of activity intelligible."[63]

Hence, an "act of God" refers to "the *master act* in which God is

---

56. Ibid., 124.
57. Ibid., 124–25.
58. Ibid., 126–27.
59. Ibid., 128.
60. Ibid., 133.
61. Ibid.
62. Ibid., 135.
63. Ibid., 136.

engaged. . . . [It] is *the whole course of history* . . . that should be conceived as God's act in the primary sense."[64] God is the one who has
planned it all, who makes known the end from the beginning (Isa. 46:10),
to the coming of Jesus Christ and the consummation of his kingdom (Matt.
25:34; 1 Peter 1:20). This is the "single all-encompassing act of God."[65]
"Thus, to conceive the whole cosmic movement as comprehended within
a single 'act' through which God is achieving some ultimate purpose is
consistent with the modern understanding of nature as in process of evolutionary development."[66] Unless this is done, states Kaufman, then all
speech about God "providentially guiding history . . . is hollow and
empty."[67]

Kaufman next reexamines the more traditional meaning of an act of
God as an "unusual" or "special" event. Theoretically, he argues, one
can only make sense of particular acts insofar as they occur in a certain
structural context. Hence, God's activity in the "fundamental order"
must precede his activity in "particular events"[68] (a clearly Aristotelian
principle). Thus particular events are not impulsive, arbitrary, or contradictory acts, but are subacts or "subordinate steps" toward God's master
goal.

Finally, Kaufman attempts to identify what some of God's subordinate
acts might be. Among them he includes the creation of the solar system,
the evolution of man, "the crucial phases of the actual movement of
human history, and the emergence of *Heilsgeschichte* within that history."[69]

Kaufman warns, however, that not every event in the natural and historical nexus has to be viewed as a "distinct subact of God." They are
simply part of the general order that God has set in motion in his goal to
complete his master plan.[70] Hence, Kaufman allows for a general versus
a special providence. Only those events, however, that "directly advance
God's ultimate purposes" should be viewed as "acts of God" in the true
sense.[71]

Kaufman concludes: "It must be admitted that the doctrine of providence here entailed is more austere than the pietistic views often found
in Christian circles. God's subordinate acts here are governed largely by

64. Ibid., 137.
65. Ibid.
66. Ibid., 139.
67. Ibid., 140.
68. Ibid., 142.
69. Ibid., 143.
70. Ibid., 144.
71. Ibid., 145.

his overarching purposes and ultimate objectives, not simply by the immediate needs or the prayerful pleas of his children."[72]

Kaufman's proposal to reexamine an "act of God" under the rubric of "act," "agent," and "subact" certainly has its merits. Kaufman seriously attempts to do justice to the biblical understanding of God as a genuine agent whose actions impinge on history and whose intent guides history toward an ultimate goal that God himself has determined. Surely Calvin, Bullinger, Wollebius, and Turretin would applaud Kaufman for seeing God's subacts as secondary causes by means of which he accomplishes his primary will.

Kaufman's study is helpful, if we understand his rubric of subacts to refer to genuine actions that God himself not only intends but performs. Furthermore, that God performs these within the nexus of history is in keeping with a Reformed emphasis on secondary causes.

Kaufman's proposal also represents an attempt to work within a modern framework in which an empirical understanding of nature and history is an accepted assumption about the universe. For theologians who accept evolution as a "fact," Kaufman's solution is both welcome and helpful.

Furthermore, Kaufman's criticisms of those who would divide nature and history are well taken. One cannot abandon the former to hide "within" the latter.

Aspects, however, of Kaufman's position do raise questions. Because of the emphasis that he places on the unbrokenness of the historical and natural nexus, once the process is begun, one wonders just how free God is to "act" within it. Does he actually do anything following an initial act? Simply to divide one continuous act into subacts does not clarify God's specific involvement in or with each subact. If anything, God seems to come across more as the *Master Planner* than as the *Master Actor*.

A similar set of questions is applicable to man. Because of the unbrokenness of the natural-historical nexus, how free is man? In Kaufman's proposal, are not both God and man subject to a degree of determinism that makes it difficult for either party to "transcend" the nexus? Yet it is precisely man's capacity to transcend and reflect on his time and place in history that makes him human and underlies the meaningfulness of all his actions and choices. Indeed, it is his very capacity to transcend himself which allows him to act differently than he might have. If such transcendence is ascribed to man, then surely it must also be ascribed to God. God too must be as free to act within the nexus as is man, although God's actions would not represent changes of his original will but effective actions within the scope of his will and purposes.

72. Ibid., 146.

Calvin was right. Once nature and history are abandoned to inexorable laws, or to an unbroken web of natural-historical causation, then God is excluded from his own universe and cannot effect special events for individuals. Yet, that is precisely what God was doing in Joseph's life. He was working in, under, and through the historical nexus to turn Joseph's life into a blessing, for both Joseph and Israel's sake (Gen. 45:5–8; 50:19–20).

What the Reformed tradition wishes to preserve is not that God exempts us from the course of the natural-historial nexus (he certainly did not exempt Joseph), but is at work sustaining, preserving, and guiding each of us in a manner at least equivalent to the extent that he is sustaining, accompanying, and guiding the universe. For the universe is God's, and it is filled with his continuous acts and subacts, not just one undifferentiated act.

Divine Action and the Activity of Created Agents

As the previous section demonstrates, it is extremely difficult for theology to explain empirically how God acts in or within the historical nexus. What each of the preceding theological positions displays, however, is that every Christian theology worthy of its name, and every biblical theology, regardless of its hermeneutic, is compelled to affirm God's providential activity. Hence, throughout its history the church has addressed this problem with seriousness and ingenuity.

That an attempt to analyze "history," "historical event," "act(s)," "action," and "analogous speech" should fail either to prove conclusively that God does act in history or to demonstrate beyond objection how God acts in history should neither surprise nor erode Christian faith. After all, the psalmist experienced this: "Such knowledge is too wonderful for me; it is high, I cannot attain it" (Ps. 139:6). And Paul echoes this wonder and finitude in a similar acknowledgement: "O the depth of the riches and wisdom and knowledge of God! How unsearchable are his judgments and how inscrutable his ways!" (Rom. 11:33).

Hence it is not surprising to find that contemporary theology has occasionally reexamined the adequacy of the first cause–secondary cause tradition, in which God is viewed as the total cause but not the coercive cause of contingent effects. This tradition was embraced by the Reformers as well as by seventeenth-century orthodoxy. For many, it is still philosophically appealing.

In *The Christian Philosophy of St. Thomas Aquinas,*[73] Gilson reassesses

---

73. See Etienne Gilson, *The Christian Philosophy of St. Thomas Aquinas,* trans. by L. K. Shook (London: Victor Gollancz, 1961).

this classical tradition and finds it convincingly relevant.[74] He explains that the genius of Aquinas's system, in which God "does whatever creatures do" and yet creatures themselves do whatever they do"[75] lies in Aquinas's desire to avoid two unacceptable extremes.

The first extreme is derived from Platonism, and Gilson holds that it solves the problematic relationship between divine and created agents by positing a basic "extrinsicism." By "extrinsicism" Gilson means the erroneous belief that God acts as an "extrinsic agent" upon physical operations, as an outside agent influencing "the cognitive operation of the reason," or as an "exterior cause" operating upon the moral will. In other words, change comes from outside the world. Consequently, this position denies the efficacy of secondary causes.[76]

The second extreme Aquinas wished to reject may be called "Anaxagorism." Gilson describes this error as one of a basic "intrinsicism."[77] All change and operation are said to be derived from within created agents. Everything is explained as a realization of "seminal reasons," "innate ideas," or "natural virtues." Thus in extrinsicism God does it all, and secondary causes "receive . . . everything from outside," whereas in intrinsicism, God does little or nothing.[78]

Even Calvin rejects such extremes. Rather, he advocates the efficacy of secondary causes and their right to operate according to their own natures; while, at the same time, he rejects the notion that either nature or man is governed by any sort of perpetual natural law.

Gilson's restatement of Aquinas's position underscores the fact that God is intimately present in all *esse* and efficaciously active in all operations while upholding the integrity of each created *esse* to act on its own and for itself. His argument may be summarized as follows.

Since all existing things have *esse* in common, and God is the cause of this *esse,* God's causality extends necessarily to everything.[79] Granted that everything exists for God, "a being cannot exist for God unless it also exists for itself and for its own good."[80] Since God has created everything's form and matter, or everything's "substantial unity" and "ultimate good," then God is intimately present in everything's substance and operations.

74. Cf. Austin Farrer, *Faith and Speculation: An Essay in Philosophical Theology* (New York: New York University Press, 1967), 52–67, 142–55.

75. Gilson, *Aquinas,* 182.

76. Ibid., 185.

77. Ibid.

78. Ibid.

79. Ibid., 176.

80. Ibid.

Nevertheless, God's intimacy with his created beings "leaves their efficacy absolutely intact."[81] Things still operate according to their unique substantial unity and the purpose which God has assigned them.

Hence, this is the "first effect of the Providence of God."[82] This is his means of governing things, through their concreated form, matter, and ultimate end, by means of which they serve and glorify him. It is also the means by which he "assures their conservation" and displays that his "divine efficacy extends totally to the being of creatures."[83]

Yet God's presence in each created being's *esse* does more than assure its conservation. In the same way that a created being's *esse* is possible only because of God's *esse,* so the capacity of a created being to act is a capacity conferred upon it by God alone. Thus "every operation presupposes God as its cause"[84]; "it is God who is the principal cause of all actions performed by His creatures."[85] Thus God as the "supreme Act-of-Being" is "everywhere present and acting by His efficacy."[86] Hence, Aquinas denies the validity of any intrinsicism.

Only divine goodness prevents created beings from being swallowed up by a divine "extrinsicism." "When God imparts existence to things, He confers upon them at the same time their form, their movement and their efficacy. Nevertheless, it is to them that this efficacy belongs from the moment they receive it. Hence it is they who perform their operations."[87]

Calvin adopts a similar position. This is particularly true in his *Treatise Against the Libertines,* in which he maintains that God has given everything its own "quality and nature" and its own "inclination."[88] Insofar as God has given each agent this capacity, it performs its own operations and is accountable for them. Although God always remains the unquestioned primary cause, man is responsible for his own actions.

Gilson concludes, then, that "he must hold firmly to two apparently contradictory truths. God does whatever creatures do; and yet creatures themselves do whatever they do."[89] Every effect then has two different causes: "God and the natural agent which produces it."[90] The fact that God has willed the existence of secondary causes in no way compromises

81. Ibid., 178.
82. Ibid., 179.
83. Ibid.
84. Ibid., 180.
85. Ibid.
86. Ibid.
87. Ibid., 182.
88. See Calvin, *Treatises,* 243.
89. Gilson, *Aquinas,* 182.
90. Ibid.

his power or encroaches upon his divine privilege. On the contrary, it only displays God's "infinite goodness." Hence, the highest glory of human beings is to become "coadjutors of God through the causality we wield."

As we have seen, contemporary efforts to fathom God's relationship with the world have generated considerable interest in the meaning of God as an agent who acts in history. Although the theologies we have surveyed are open to criticism, none is to be deprecated for its attempt to understand the problem. Each attests to the seriousness and magnificence of the doctrine of providence and to the exacting patience required of all who would reflect on it.

It is not necessary to reiterate the distinctive contributions of Wright, Bultmann, Kaufman, or Gilson. Nor is it necessary to repeat our objections to their views. What needs to be emphasized is their plea that all who would contemplate the doctrine of the providence of God rethink their own positions if they are tempted to isolate God from his creation and view him essentially as an outsider. Neither Wright, Bultmann, nor Kaufman commits the error of extrinsicism.

It can equally be argued that none of them are guilty of intrinsicism. To be certain, they zealously champion theories of history that espouse the unbrokenness of the historical web. Still, for each, God is the undeniable objective reality who meets mankind "in" and "within" the historical nexus as Creator, Judge, and Redeemer. They all endorse a general providence of God. It is when we push them for more than this that they become uneasy and cause the traditional Christian uneasiness as well. But their principal insight is well taken. God must never be viewed as one whose operations are from the outside, as one who interrupts, or has to force or break his way into his universe or the realm of human activity. God is already everywhere present, as Lord of his universe, in all that we do and in all that we think; yet God is never to be confused with our own operations or thought, or with any historical processes or occurrences.

Chapter Ten

The Challenge of Process Theology

IN RECENT YEARS, NO THEOLOGICAL SYSTEM HAS OPPOSED TRADITIONAL
Christianity as forcefully as process theology. Because it rejects so much
of what is considered central to a traditional interpretation of biblical
Christianity, it is essential for us to review the school's basic tenets, its
precise objections to traditional doctrines of the providence of God, and
its own solution to the problem.

Philosophical Underpinnings

Process theology represents a serious contemporary effort to refor-
mulate Christian doctrine in the light of philosophical principles espoused
by Alfred North Whitehead and Charles Hartshorne.[1] William Temple,
Teilhard de Chardin, and Norman Pittenger all drew their inspiration from
Whiteheadian motifs. More recently Schubert Ogden, John B. Cobb, Jr.,
and David Griffin have contributed to its popularity in America.

1. The primary sources of process theology are Alfred North Whitehead's *Process &
Reality: An Essay in Cosmology* (New York: Macmillan, 1957 [1929]) and *Adventures of Ideas*
(New York: Macmillan, 1937); Charles Hartshorne, *Anselm's Discovery: A Re-Examination
of the Ontological Proof for God's Existence* (La Salle, Ill.: Open Court, 1965), *The Divine
Relativity: A Social Conception of God* (New Haven: Yale University Press, 1948), *Reality as
Social Process: Studies in Metaphysics and Religion* (Boston: Beacon, 1953), *Man's Vision
of God and the Logic of Theism* (Hamden, Conn.: Archon Books, 1964), and *Omnipotence
and Other Theological Mistakes* (Albany: State University of New York, 1984).

What are the philosophical underpinnings of process theology? In *Process Theology: An Introductory Exposition,* John B. Cobb, Jr. and David Griffin identify eight principles.

First, process is fundamental: "To be actual is to be a process."[2] The world as we experience it is characterized by becoming, change, and process. Hence, what is fully real cannot be beyond change or process. The temporal process itself is "a 'transition' from one actual entity to another" in which entities come into being and pass away. "True individuals" or "actual occasions"—to borrow Whiteheadian language—are characterized as "momentary experiences" or "occasions of experience." In fact, real individual occasions are themselves processes. Whitehead called this process of becoming "concrescence," which means that individual occasions of experience are acts of becoming concrete.[3]

These two process themes—transition and concrescence—open new levels of religious understanding. In Griffin's view, they undergird the reality of time and the uniqueness of the historical while making the concept of the "eternal now" intelligible. Every moment of time becomes a "now" that is unique and unrepeatable and in that sense is "timeless."

Second, enjoyment is primary. All units of process "enjoy" their coming into being; they experience "subjective immediacy." This means that every unit of experience possesses "intrinsic value" or "an inner reality in and for itself." Hence all experience is a form of enjoyment and precedes the phenomenon of consciousness. Consciousness increases the enjoyment of experience, but consciousness is not the only form of experience. Hence, "every level of actuality enjoys experience" and has its meaningful place in the scheme of the universe.[4]

Third, relatedness is essential. All occasions of experience are related to previous experiences. Occasions of experience are individual and distinct, but they are never independent of or separable from other units of process. Every momentary experience "feels" or "prehends"—in Whiteheadian terms—previous occasions of experience. Thus every "present occasion is nothing but its process of unifying the particular prehensions with which it begins."[5] As Griffin explains: "Whiteheadian process thought gives primacy to interdependence as an ideal over independence."[6]

Fourth, incarnation is a fact of process. The processes of enjoyment are related to each other incarnationally. This means that "past experi-

2. See John B. Cobb, Jr. and David Ray Griffin, *Process Theology: An Introductory Exposition* (Philadelphia: Westminster, 1976), 14.

3. Ibid., 15.

4. Ibid., 16–18.

5. Ibid., 20.

6. Ibid., 21.

ences are incorporated into the present experience."[7] Griffin acknowledges, however, two qualifications: (1) the past is incorporated only selectively and limitedly; (2) the past is present "as *having been* an experience, as an experience that *was* enjoyed."[8] This means that the past is present only as an object of the present subject's experience. It lives on, but not subjectively, that is, in the sense of still being experienced. Whitehead referred to this phenomenon of the presence of the past in the present as "objective immortality."

Griffin notes that objective immortality has a twofold religious significance. First, "the past is the totality of that which influences the present, and the future is the totality of that which will be influenced by the present." This implies "that our activities will make a difference throughout the future" and that the future "will necessarily prehend us."[9] Second, efficient causation occurs incarnationally. Process thought rejects the notion that cause is completely external to an effect; instead, "we influence each other by entering into each other."[10]

Fifth, occasions of experience are partially self-determined. Each occasion of experience begins in debt to and in relationship to countless past experiences, yet each present actuality determines how it will use that past. Hence each actuality is "partially self-creative." It builds on the giveness of its environment, but in its own process of becoming it shapes its unique existence or concrescence. Hence, we can say that we are "totally determined and yet . . . free."[11]

Sixth, creative self-expression is universal. Occasions of experience aim not only at self-creation but equally at self-expression. True actualities are not only partially self-determined but also desire to "pervade the environment" and shape the future. No occasion of experience aims solely at its own private enjoyment; it contributes also to the enjoyment of other entities.[12]

Seventh, novelty is life's highest aim. The process of becoming allows for the actualization of innumerable heretofore unrealized possibilities. Griffin explains that one way of interpreting the divine function is to see God as the source of these possibilities, that is, as the "primordial envisagement of the pure possibilities"; "the divine reality is understood to be the ground of novelty."[13] Hence, the possibility of novelty increases the

7. Ibid., 22.
8. Ibid.
9. Ibid., 23
10. Ibid.
11. Ibid., 25.
12. Ibid., 26f.
13. Ibid., 28.

enjoyment of experience as well as its intensity and makes for meaningful existence.

Finally, everything is God-related. Insofar as anything is, it is God-related. Indeed, our prehension of God is "an essential part of all experience."[14] For without God, there would be nothing but repetition and chaos. It is God who makes our freedom and self-creation possible by confronting us with unrealized opportunities and continual creative transformation.

Objections to Traditional Perceptions of God and His Providence

Process theology denies the existence of the God of traditional theism. In particular it denies the following perceptions of God, along with their implications for his providence.[15]

God as Cosmic Moralist

Process theology denies that God is the divine Lawgiver and Judge who keeps records and punishes sinners. It denies that his fundamental concern is the development of moral attitudes. It must be acknowledged, however, that even the best patristic, medieval, and Reformed theologians deny such a purely Hesiodic, Pelagian, or deistic God. However, they all would affirm the righteousness and goodness of God. Process theology is at odds with a principal motif in Scripture, or at least with the traditional way in which the righteousness of God has been interpreted. Process theology subsumes it under "enjoyment," which, in turn, radically influences its understanding of God and his activity in the world.

God as the Unchanging and Passionless Absolute

Process theology considers the absolute God of patristic and Reformed orthodoxy to be a product of Greek thought. The Greek concept of perfection, with its emphasis on immutability and impassibility, implies that God is independent of and unaffected by the world. This makes God purely external to the world and means that the world, in turn, contributes nothing to God. It further implies that God foresees and determines all

14. Ibid., 29.
15. Ibid., 8–10.

future events. But process theology cannot accept this God, since the God of process thought cannot foresee all future, self-determined possibilities until they are actualized.

Again, however, it must be acknowledged that Calvin is careful to build his doctrine of God on biblical language and denies that God is an arbitrary power or absolute principle in the sophistic sense of a pure *deus potestas*. Brunner and Barth lament this tendency in the older theologies (in which God is defined along abstract lines) while remaining committed to Reformed principles.

God as Controlling Power

Process theology also rejects the God who controls the cosmos, because this implies that he determines every effect in and aspect of the world. As we have seen, Zwingli certainly stressed the deterministic manner in which God exercises his providential activity—a logical corollary inferred from the God of immutable attributes. Process theology denies the existence of such a God. But then even Calvin denies that God is the unqualified cause of all causes, while nevertheless affirming that God is still in control. In Reformed theology, God controls the process; in process theology, however, God and man are both subject to the phenomenon of process. This may seem like an oversimplification, but it is a crucial distinction.

God as Sanctioner
of the Status Quo

Process theology denies that God has willed the present order of the universe, that there is an order to be upheld, or that God is even interested primarily in order. God is the God who welcomes change, novelty, and process. The divine never champions or defends a static order to be realized by every human.

God as Male

Finally, process theology denies perceptions of God that emphasize an unresponsive, inflexible, and independent attitude in God, which it charges traditional theism has tended to promulgate in its doctrine of the trinity and in other sexist emphases.

God and His Relationship
to the World

How is God to be perceived, and what precisely is his relationship to the world?

Essentially, God is the agency that mediates between the purely abstract possibilities of becoming and the definite possibilities that are concretized by every occasion of experience. Process theologians argue that since definiteness cannot be imposed by the past, and since it can be derived only from the sphere of possibility (which is purely abstract), an agency is required to mediate between these pure possibilities and the actual world. God is this agency and "lures the world toward new forms of realization."[16]

Griffin explains that process theism is essentially "dipolar theism" in contrast to traditional theism which emphasizes divine simplicity. In a system of divine simplicity, God is always what his attributes declare him to be: omniscient, omnipotent, eternal, immutable, and so on. But process theism—following Hartshorne's lead—acknowledges two poles or aspects of God.

Hartshorne distinguishes between God's "abstract essence" and his "concrete actuality."[17] God's abstract essence is "eternal, absolute, independent, unchangeable." It includes all those "abstract attributes of deity which characterize the divine essence at every moment." But God's "concrete actuality is temporal, relative, dependent, and constantly changing"; "in each moment of God's life, there are new, unforeseen happenings in the world which only then have become knowable." Hence both God's knowledge and emotional state are dependent on the world. Or as Griffin explains it, "God enjoys our enjoyments, and suffers with our sufferings. This is the kind of responsiveness which is truly divine and belongs to the very nature of perfection."[18]

In light of these distinctions, process theology defines God in the following way.

First, God is creative love. Central to the Bible is the view that God is active in history overcoming evil and creating new possibilities. It is precisely how this should be interpreted that has become problematic for theology. In the view of process theology, traditional theism has gone astray whenever it has emphasized God as the total or primary cause of

16. Ibid., 43.
17. See especially Hartshorne, *Anselm's Discovery*, 38, 41–43, 92, 106, 116, 122; and *Divine Relativity*,, 62f., 80, 83, 95, 100, 144.
18. See Cobb and Griffin, *Process Theology*, 48.

all events, whether they are mediated by natural antecedents or secondary causes (i.e., as in Aquinas, Calvin, Zanchi, Turretin, and much of orthodoxy). In particular, traditional theism has erred wherever it understands "miracles" as directly caused divine events.

There are two reasons why this older approach is problematic. First, it is incompatible with the concept of God as love. For the older approach implies that God is the total cause of every event; hence the problem of evil has to be explained, insofar as God, as the total cause, is implicitly responsible for any event. Second, since the time of the Renaissance, it has become axiomatic that no event occurs without natural causes; hence, where does God fit in as a casual factor? Thus, in the view of process thought, the notion of God as the total cause must be abandoned for a less problematic understanding of God and divine activity, which the concept of love favors.

In fact, in Griffin's opinion, neither Barth, Bultmann, Bonhoeffer, nor Tillich has provided an "intelligible means" of explaining God's activity in the world. In Griffin's estimation, this is due to the fact that twentieth-century theologians lack "the conceptuality for consistently explicating this doctrine."[19]

Second, God's love is persuasive. In lieu of God as the all-controlling power who foresees immutably all events and their outcomes, process theology prefers to see God as the agent which persuades occasions toward the best possibilities suitable to them.

Process theology finds much in the Bible that suggests that God is not the all-determining power of the world. Although God is responsive to the world, he is not wholly in control of it. Since actualities are partially self-determined, their futures are still undetermined; hence, God cannot perfectly know their futures nor cause them to occur. The most God does is to provide each actuality with an "initial aim." Each actual occasion is responsible for responding to this aim and is free to actualize it or not. But God "cannot control the finite occasion's self-actualization."[20] Hence, when evil comes upon any actual occasion, the evil is not God's doing, nor is it incompatible with God's highest hope for each actuality.

Third, God as creative love promotes enjoyment. Process theology charges that traditional Christianity has espoused the notions of God as cosmic moralist and God as controlling power in order to solve the dilemma of the problem of evil. By championing man's long-range moral goodness over his creaturely enjoyment or intrinsic goodness, God could be spared the charges of malevolence or powerlessness. Thus a world that

19. Ibid., 48–52.
20. Ibid., 53.

contributes to "soul-making" could tolerate, if not require, the possibility of both natural and moral evils (the old Greek character-building motif). Hence God could still be viewed as being in control of the world while willing the possibility of evil.

Process theology avoids this dilemma by maintaining that God's fundamental aim is to promote every creature's intrinsic goodness. For process thought, "enjoyment" is more universal than "morality." Only mankind can be moral. God loves all his creatures, all occasions of experience. Hence God wishes for each experience to enjoy its appropriate level of intrinsic goodness.[21]

Fourth, divine love is adventurous. Since God neither controls the world nor determines any creature's future, but only acts persuasively to lure creatures toward the actualization of their intrinsic good, God's creative activity is "a love that takes risks."[22] In process thought, God never knows what the end result will be. His aim is to maximize the "intensity" of enjoyment that novelty provides.

Consequently, God must not be viewed as a sanctioner of the status quo. Order is important, insofar as it contributes to each creature's intrinsic good or maximization of enjoyment, but beyond that, order can inhibit enjoyment. Or in the existentialist sense, order in the form of a heteronomous requirement can lead to inauthenticity. Hence, change, novelty, and process best represent God's intention both in and for the world.

Furthermore, since God does not control the world coercively, "the existence of a given state of affairs does not imply that God willed it."[23] Hence, there is no need to justify the present world order or to explain how any given event (e.g., the tragic death of a child) reflects either the hidden will of God (Calvin) or the hidden activity of God (Bultmann). In fact, there is no fixed order or aim that represents any absolute goal that God always aims to achieve. As Griffin explains, "since God encourages the actualization of novel possibilities as a means to maximizing creaturely enjoyment, continuation of a state of affairs that originally resulted from a high degree of conformity to God's aims may not express God's present will."[24]

Finally, God's own life is an adventure and God's own being is interdependent on the novelties actualized by all his creatures. God, too, is dependent on his creatures, as well as on the process that governs them.

21. Ibid., 54–57.
22. Ibid., 57.
23. Ibid., 60.
24. Ibid.

Hence, God feels both the harmonious and discordant experiences that comprise the occasions of concrescence of every creature.[25]

God, Nature, and Evil

Process theology does not hesitate to embrace the evolutionary process. There are two reasons for this. First, it denies the God of the *actus purus* concept, and thereby the God who has already actualized all possible values and who stands independent of the world. Second, since it equally denies the God who creates out of nothing, it can embrace the God who lures the discordant occasions of the universe toward greater harmony and complexity.[26]

In the view of process theology, both the Old Testament and Plato suggest that God created out of chaos rather than nothing.[27] From protons, electrons, and neutrons, creation gradually emerged into a stage of atoms and molecules. The movement was always from chaos and disharmony, or triviality, toward intensity and greater harmony, or enjoyment. From simplicity to complexity (Teilhard's "complexity-consciousness" motif[28]), the universe has slowly built up to what it is today.

The point is that the evolutionary process is not incompatible with God's character and purpose: "This creatively and responsively loving God is incarnately active in the present, bringing about immediate good on the basis of activity in the past, and with the purpose to bring about greater good in the future—a greater good that will involve a fuller incarnation of the divine reality itself."[29]

Of course, how God does this, other than by providing for the initial aim of every creature and by serving as the mediating agent for unactualized possibilities, is not explained. Indeed, how God "works" as cosmic, creative, responsive love, or exactly what God "does" in this capacity, is not less problematic than trying to explain how the God of history "acts" within or in the historical-natural nexus.

Finally, the question of evil is posed. Process theology charges that traditional theism (Augustine, Aquinas, Calvin, and Schleiermacher), by perceiving God as the all-controlling power, makes God responsible for evil while not indictable. This it does by arguing that evil is only apparent,

25. Ibid., 60–61.
26. Ibid., 63–65.
27. Ibid., 64.
28. See in particular Pierre Teilhard de Chardin, *The Phenomenon of Man* (New York: Harper & Bros., 1959).
29. *Process Theology*, 68.

insofar as evil serves the greater moral good of God and man. Griffin explains that process theology is also willing to make God responsible but not indictable for evil, but, unlike traditional theism, it denies that evil is only apparent. Evil is genuine, but God is not blameworthy. Griffin explains that there are three justifications for this position.

First, God's power is persuasive, never coercive. Since actualities can fail to achieve their inner aims, evil or "deviation" can occur. Deviation proper is not necessary to the world, but its possibility is necessary. Hence evil can be present, while not making God indictable.[30]

Second, a twofold evil is to be avoided: "triviality" and "discord."[31] Discord is always evil. But a "trivial enjoyment," Griffin explains, "is not evil in itself."[32] If an experience could have been more intense than it was, then evil occurs. So the challenge is to minimize discord and "unnecessary triviality."

In process thought, some discord always exists in a universe undergoing transition and process. Hence, God's sole concern can never have been to eliminate all discord or suffering. Rather God's aim has been to eliminate "unnecessary triviality while avoiding as much discord as possible."[33] Thus God's goal is the perfection of experience, or "the maximal harmonious intensity" for any experience, not the elimination of discord itself. Consequently the presence of evil in the form of discord does not make God blameworthy.

Third, the necessity of the possibility of evil can be justified on the basis of an intricate correlation between the following dimensions of experience: "(1) the capacity for intrinsic good; (2) the capacity for intrinsic evil; (3) the capacity for instrumental good; (4) the capacity for instrumental evil; (5) the power for self-determination."[34] If any of these dimensions increases, the others increase proportionately. That is, "the increased complexity that makes greater enjoyment possible also makes greater suffering possible."[35] God is responsible for having lured and for luring the world in this direction, for without such "luring," nothing positive could be risked. But God is not indictable for the evil that occurs.

Reformed Objections and Considerations

A Reformed perspective may justifiably question process theology's understanding of God and his providential activity. Certainly, the following objections arise.

30. Ibid., 69.
31. Ibid., 70.
32. Ibid.
33. Ibid., 71
34. Ibid.
35. Ibid., 72.

First, its hermeneutic represents a principle derived from a philosophical reflection on scientific data and scientific theory that exalts an abstract concept (i.e., "process") in place of the divine reality (God). That principle is made the supposition for all hermeneutical exploration of the Scriptures, as well as the principle of organization and interpretation for all theological understanding of God. A Reformed perspective, committed to *sola scripture* and *sola gratia* as the principal norms of theological reflection, is reluctant to abandon the Scriptures to mediating concepts, however appealing they might be.

Second, process theology's understanding of God and of his activity necessarily makes God subservient to "process." Such reductionism issues in the finitization of God, or the creation of an awkward dualism: God and process. This means that God is set in juxtaposition to a rival: a rival that he cannot control, but which can and does control him; it is a rival that God cannot limit, but which surely limits him; it is a rival that drives toward an unknown *telos* which God can neither fully foresee nor hope to command.

Third, process theology is a strikingly modern version of Aristotelianism, insofar as its deity, which is principally a nonpersonal agent, lures the entities of the universe toward the realization of their individual entelechies (God as final cause). Beyond this, however, process theology's other affinities with Aristotelianism become problematic. Indeed, it represents a form of inconsistent Aristotelianism, insofar as God, the agent of novelty, who must be prior to all potential actualities, turns out to be imperfect or not totally actualized himself. How can this be? Must not such a God require an agent to envision his own full potential?

More specifically, God, as the agent which envisions all future possibilities, must be viewed as the *actus primus* of the universe, for insofar as any potentiality requires an actuality to precede it, God must be posited as both logically and ontologically prior to, and the embodiment of, all potential actualities or contingent possibilities. Consequently, God, necessarily, must both contain (as the locus of these potential forms) and comprehend all future possibilities. However, in process thought, God does not comprehend these possibilities perfectly. This means that God's own actuality is incomplete and must be preenvisioned by some logically prior agent for God to have a future or to fulfill his own beingness. At this point, then, process thought becomes inconsistent, for insofar as process thought must of necessity argue for God as *actus primus*, can it deny, at the same time, God as *actus purus* without undermining God's essential aseity as *actus primus*?

E. L. Mascall has rightly challenged Whiteheadian cosmology with his observation that there is a critical difference between God as "the *ens maximum,* the greatest being that exist," and God as the "*maxime ens,* that which completely is."[36] Traditional Christianity has sided with the latter rather than deny God's aseity in any form and thereby create for itself a host of philosophical inconsistencies.[37]

Fourth, the finitization of God, or the inability of God to control destiny and the future, no more resolves the problem of evil than defining God as "luring love" explains how God operates within history or nature. Evil still remains evil, and diminishing the power of God, or subsuming his goodness under the notions of novelty and enjoyment, hardly seems to do justice to either God's deity or his accountability toward the universe.

There are many other problems that critics of process theology have identified,[38] but they need not be presented here. It is enough for a Reformed perspective to refuse to be drawn aside by process theology's reformulations of Christian doctrine in the name of "process."

Nevertheless, having said this, other assessments are possible; some aspects of process criticism are even notable. For example, Reformed theology has tended to define God along lines derived from Greek influence. This tendency certainly possesses the possibility of eroding the principle of *sola scriptura*. Calvin himself sought to control and moderate this tendency, although Zanchi, Turretin, and Westminster are closer to classical thought.

Has Reformed theology wed itself too closely to the classical world's concepts of God's perfection, omnipotence, omniscience, and immutability in its attempts to witness to the God of Scripture? To be certain, such concepts have their place in guiding the church's reflection on the biblical God of providential activity. They enable the church to avoid the pitfalls of defining God in ways that make him subservient to other factors in the universe; they call the church's attention to glaring inconsistencies in its assertions about deity. But they need not "control" our understanding of God's interaction with his world. At best, at least traditionally speaking, their proper role has been that of serving as "handmaidens" of theology.

In particular, Langdon Gilkey's *Reaping the Whirlwind* provides a com-

---

36. See E. L. Mascall, *He Who Is* (London: Libra, 1943), 13.

37. An outstanding contemporary discussion of this problem may be found in Stephen T. Davis's *Logic and the Nature of God* (Grand Rapids: Wm. B. Eerdmans, 1983). Davis defends the traditional Christian understanding of God but frequently favors a reinterpretation of God's "timelessness," "omniscience," and "omnipotence."

38. See Mascall, *He Who Is,* 150–60; Stephen L. Ely, *The Religious Availability of Whitehead's God: A Critical Analysis* (Madison: University of Wisconsin Press, 1942); Edward H. Madden and Peter H. Hare, *Evil and the Concept of God* (Springfield, Ill.: Charles C. Thomas, 1968), chap. 6; and John H. Hick, *Philosophy of Religion,* 3d ed. (Englewood Cliffs: Prentice-Hall, 1983), 49–56.

mendable assessment and utilization of process insight. Gilkey is both critical and appreciative of the movement.

Gilkey argues that the "destiny"/"freedom" polarity refers to ontological entities that are inseparable from our understanding of existence. By "destiny" Gilkey means all that we have inherited from the historical and natural nexus and all that has power to determine and shape our existence. By "freedom" he means the "free" yet limited human capacity we possess to act on that past and participation in shaping our own futures."[39] To that extent, he draws on both Whiteheadian and Tillichian themes.

But Gilkey is highly critical of any attempt to compromise the sovereignty of God, which he maintains process thought requires. Gilkey argues that Scripture makes it clear that we owe both our existence and freedom to God. We may well be "partially self-determined," but we are never "partially indebted to God."[40] We are totally indebted to God for both our destiny and freedom, our past and future.

Gilkey also refuses to make God subservient to process. Whatever process exists is because of God. God is always the ground of all process, history, and hope.[41]

Gilkey is likewise critical of the notion of God as the luring agent that draws humankind toward higher novel actualizations and levels of enjoyment. Such a concept fails to take sin seriously. It fails to realize the extent to which mankind requires "redemption."[42] Gilkey properly insists that God sits in judgment on the distortions of destiny which human beings create in their acts of freedom.[43] Hence, one of the ways in which God acts providentially is not only as Creator, but also as Judge of all human use and misuse of destiny and freedom.[44] Thus Gilkey emphasizes that a true understanding of the providence of God requires acceptance of the Christian doctrines of the incarnation, atonement, and eschatology.[45]

At the same time, Gilkey is willing to accept key process concepts. Granted that theology must never subsume God under process, Gilkey believes that a responsible Christian interpretation of history and providence can adopt the principle of the self-limitation of God, the view that God experiences temporal passage, and the perception of God as one who undergoes change.

Gilkey believes that all arises from God, but God is not the sole shaper

39. Gilkey, *Reaping the Whirlwind,* 43, 121f., 125.
40. Ibid., 114, 248–49.
41. Ibid., 307–11.
42. Ibid., 114ff.
43. Ibid., 258, 264.
44. Ibid., 264.
45. Ibid., 266.

of the historical-natural nexus. This limitation of God must always be understood as a "self-limitation . . . in creating and preserving a finitude characterized by freedom and so by self-actualization."[46] Hence, the human capacity to be partially self-determined is given to man by God, not by the dictates of process itself.

By the temporality of God, Gilkey means that God is the ground of all process, a participant in all process, the condition for each of its moments, and thus "transcendent to its moving moments." Yet, God only knows the future as possibility and never as actuality.[47]

Finally, God may be said to be subject to change insofar as he "is related to actuality *as* actuality and to possibility *as* possibility. Consequently, as possibility *becomes* actuality, . . . God's creative and providential relations to process themselves change, and God's 'experience' and 'knowledge' of his world change."[48] Nonetheless, for Gilkey, God's aseity, transcendence, and eternity are never compromised by any of his temporality or changeability.[49]

On the one hand, then, there are biblical and philosophical objections that Reformed theologians might well choose to cite in rejection of process concepts; however, on the other hand, as Gilkey illustrates, it is possible for a traditional Christian perspective to endorse many process affirmations—so long as God's sovereignty is not compromised. Which direction Reformed communities take will probably depend as much on their hermeneutic as it will on their respective confessional symbols and heritage.

46. Ibid., 307.
47. Ibid., 308–9.
48. Ibid., 309.
49. Ibid., 314.

Chapter Eleven

The Quintessential Features of a Reformed Perspective:
The Triumph of God's Sovereignty, Goodness, and Purposes

Summary

As we have noted, the Reformed doctrine of the providence of God emphasizes that the triune God, in his goodness and power, preserves, accompanies, and directs the universe. This work of preservation, accompaniment, and direction pertains to the entire universe—physical and human—and excludes no facet of God's work.

The doctrine of providence constitutes a central tenet of Reformed theology and belongs to the essence of the biblical message. To that extent, it is held and expounded as a doctrine of the church's faith, based on divine revelation, and must be energetically preached as part of God's Word.

Furthermore, it is derived theologically from an exploration of the biblical text in a manner that always seeks to make the church's hermeneutical principles subservient to Scripture first, guided specifically by the Old Testament, Pauline, Augustinian, and Calvinist awareness of the primacy of election in God's relationship with his world. For this reason, modern proponents of a Reformed perspective (e.g., Brunner and Barth) have rightly argued that the older orthodox interest in the divine decrees and predestination plays an important hermeneutical role in enlarging our understanding of the providence of God. This is seen in the realization that, ultimately, providence is a function of divine election that in turn constitutes the presupposition on which providence rests (chap. 1).

In accordance with Reformed practice, the doctrine of the providence of God has traditionally been treated under three headings: *conservatio, concursus,* and *gubernatio.*

First, God's providential activity in the world may be understood as a work of *conservatio, sustentatio,* or *preservatio.* God continues to see that creation is maintained, that order prevails, that life is sustained through, in, and above the species' divinely bestowed powers of self-propagation and survival. In particular, God may be said to directly preserve the physical universe and all its creatures, mankind, and his covenant people in particular. For Berkhof this not only means that all created things owe their full powers to God, but, also, that they possess real efficiency as secondary causes. For Brunner *preservatio* means that God has given the world of nature its constancy and order, through which God continues to reveal himself as "Creator-Spirit." Hence, nature can never stand as an independent phenomenon apart from God.

Second, closely associated with God's work of *conservatio* is his *concursus.* As we saw, Berkhof defines *concursus* as "the co-operation of the divine power with all subordinate powers, according to the preestablished laws of their operation, causing them to act and to act precisely as they do."[1] *Concursus,* states Berkhof, reminds us that although the powers of nature do not work by themselves (echoes of Calvin), yet secondary causes are real.[2] We also saw that Brunner prefers not to pursue *concursus* and labels it off limits, as the "danger-zone" of theological investigation. Yet, Barth praises the doctrine for its attempt to deal justly with "the problem of a co-existence and antithesis of the divine and creaturely action which everywhere abounds in Scripture."[3] Consequently, Barth develops his doctrine of *concursus* in a manner similar to Aquinas's concept of God as total cause.

Third, God's providential activity includes his work of guiding and steering mankind and history toward a *telos* God himself both wills and controls. This means that the natural-historical nexus of occurrence cannot be understood in itself (Brunner).[4] In the words of Barth, "God has an aim for the creature when He preserves and accompanies it . . . and . . . as Ruler guides it towards this *telos*"[5] (chap. 2).

Following the introduction, we saw how classical literature and philosophy addressed the phenomenon of fate and fortune. The Graeco-Roman

1. Berkhof, *Systematic Theology,* 171.
2. Ibid.
3. Barth, *Church Dogmatics,* 3.3:96.
4. Brunner, *Dogmatics,* 2:176.
5. Barth, *Church Dogmatics,* 3.3:155.

world developed a number of views regarding necessity and freedom, or doctrines of "providence," as its philosophers referred to the matter.

The classical world's concept of God, or the logos, and the relationship of this logos to the world, tended to take three distinct forms. According to Stoic principles, nature was the manifestation of the logos and, hence, nature and history were interpreted as results of the sequential cause-and-effect occurrences of the logos within the natural-historical nexus (as illustrated by Chrysippus and Cicero). Based on Aristotelian principles, the divine-world order was perceived as a harmony of eternal entities responding in eros to a *primus actus* which motivated all entities toward their respective realizations. In accordance with Platonic and neo-Platonic principles, the world order was viewed as the result of a descent or emanation from the realm of perfection to imperfection or nonbeing and ascent again to perfection (chap. 3 and sects. of chaps. 4 and 5).

In addition, we traced the development of the idea of the providence of God through the patristic period, noting how the church fathers either modified, rejected, or incorporated aspects of the classical understanding of providence. This was true even of Augustine, whose overall doctrine is most compatible with a Reformed perspective (chap. 4).

We noted further how the scholastic era continued to build on neo-Platonism (Proclus, Dionysius, Boethius, Erigena, and Anselm) until the rediscovery of Aristotle and the medieval philosophy of Aquinas, Scotus, and Ockham. Attention was especially directed to Aquinas's and Ockham's attempts to articulate a clearer doctrine of *concursus* in which God acts as total cause while not acting coercively on secondary causes (chap. 5).

The positions of Luther, Zwingli, and Calvin were presented next. Both Luther and Zwingli adopted classical concepts of immutability, tending to interject elements of determinism into their doctrines of God's providence. In contrast, Calvin's approach saves him from so binding a reductionism and allows him to argue for God's dynamic accompaniment and guidance of all creatures, while at the same time permitting him to preserve the reality and efficiency of secondary causes (chap. 6).

We saw further how during the orthodox period Reformed positions tended both to incorporate varying degrees of determinism (Zanchi, Beza, Turretin, and Westminster) and to emphasize the role of secondary causes and their freedom to act as such (Bullinger, Zanchi, Beza, Wollebius, Dort, and again, Turretin). Throughout this period we noted how the divine decrees were inched forward as a hermeneutical principle, thus acknowledging grace (or predestination and election) as an essential presupposition for an understanding of divine activity (chap. 7).

Overlapping the period of orthodoxy, we observed how a fledgling scientific and philosophical world view began to replace Calvin's sense of God's dynamic guidance of creation with a mechanical view of the universe and with increasing skepticism about God's reality or presence in that universe (chap. 8).

We then reviewed the attempts of certain contemporary theologians to explain the realm of history as the arena within which God operates as an active agent. We noted, in particular, the modern era's insistence that nature and history form an "unbroken web" in which all cause-and-effect occurrences are tightly interconnected. We further acknowledged the claim that God's providential activity must not be viewed as an activity that comes into history from without, as if God were an alien force in his own universe and its natural-historical nexus. We also reviewed Gilson's reinterpretation of Aquinas's concept of God as total cause and saw how that view supports a Reformed allegiance to *concursus* and the efficiency of secondary causes (chap. 9).

Finally, we examined the claims of process theology. We critiqued the idea of process, as well as aspects of Whiteheadian cosmology, and observed how Gilkey both rejects and uses major process ideas.

Penultimate Considerations

Before drawing any final conclusions, there are appropriate penultimate statements to be made. These have to do with the wider boundaries within which the doctrine of the providence of God is set, as well as with the doctrine's purpose.

First, our knowledge of God ultimately depends on what God chooses to disclose of himself. Our understanding of both God and his relationship with the world hinges on what God decides is most proper for us to know. Calvin referred to this as "accommodation." It is how God spoke to Job out of the whirlwind (Job 38–41).

Because God is ineffable—"for my thoughts are not your thoughts, neither are your ways my ways" (Isa. 55:8)—both his aseity and *modus operandi* are for God alone to know and enjoy. Thus we can only respond to him insofar as he gives himself to us to be known and insofar as he provides us with the means for knowing him. This he has done: (1) by creating us in his image and endowing us with rationality, accountability, and an awareness of his existence; (2) in his self-disclosures to the central figures of the *Heilsgeschichte* story; and (3) through his gracious election that is behind all calling to effectual faith.

His ineffability remains. Nevertheless, the triune God's self-revelation and love for the world—expressed especially in the life, death, and resurrection of Jesus Christ—more than assures his people that they can live with his ineffability.

Second, the problem of verifying the divine presence and fathoming its *modus operandi* is inseparable from God's aseity and the mystery of faith itself. The fact that mankind can never penetrate the how of God's operation within his universe—other than through the phenomena of secondary causes—in no way detracts from the reality of God or from the realization that God has done marvelously or was "in Christ . . . reconciling the world to himself" (2 Cor. 5:19).

Science and modern philosophy emphasize the necessity of verification. This is absolutely essential, for if statements are to be valued as meaningful, then data must be cited in support of their claims. However, the whole phenomenon of faith transcends this data-hungry preoccupation of our time, and so too does the aseity of God. This is not to say that religious experience and revelation do not constitute forms of data. The matter, however, is more complex.

If God were not ineffable, if he were entirely knowable as an object, a thing, or a datum, then he would not be the God of Scripture. For that God refuses to be identified with any "fact" of creation, other than as its Creator. Indeed, faith itself is only possible because God refuses to identify himself with any "object" per se. To do so would be to rob man of completing his own joy, save in the response of faith, which God himself elicits and makes possible. The only exception to this identification is the mystery of the God-Man: the logos becomes flesh, and yet in such a way as both to require and invite faith.

Scripture abounds with divinely called servants of God who witness that God *has* acted and *is* acting in the natural-historical nexus. In general, God grants them to see that he acts as Creator, Judge, and Redeemer within the human arena. *How* he so acts often escapes them; *that* he acts in these ways they cannot deny. Nonetheless, the "thatness" of God's providential activity can be theologically and philosophically pursued, defended, and explored, as the history of Christian thought and Western philosophy amply illustrates—from Paul's admiration of "his invisible nature" (Rom. 1:20) to Hartshorne's reflections on God's "dipolar modes" and activity of "making things make themselves" out of the profundity of divine love.[6]

Third, the providence of God requires history to look beyond its nexuses for ultimate meaning. In the final analysis, the purpose of the doctrine of providence, as it is derived from revelation, is both to remind and assure us that the meaning of history is incomplete apart from the will

---

6. See Hartshorne, *Theological Mistakes,* 46, 73.

and goal of God. History rests in God's hands. And so does the deeper meaning of every human life. The whole natural-historical nexus functions according to God's "rules." It is open to his presence, his mystery, and his goodness. In the end, his way will endure, and all "who are called according to his purpose" (Rom. 8:28) will endure with him; and, along the way, nothing can separate them "from the love of God in Christ Jesus" (Rom. 8:39).

Fourth, for Calvin especially, as well as for Augustine and Luther, the doctrine of the providence of God possesses pragmatic urgency. It is meant to edify the church. Its purpose is to call men and women of faith to serve in the world in trust and joy, knowing that the ways of God endure and can transform society and the cities of mankind—even within the limits of a fallen humanity. This is where the emphasis ought to be— not on *how* or *why*. It is enough to know that God loves and provides for each of his children here and now and calls upon each person to act justly and with mercy toward his neighbor. On this side of the infinite—short of "our heavenly existence," as Calvin would have put it—the Scriptures tell us that we are part of a process that God loves and guides and will one day redeem and complete in accordance with his own good wishes.

Conclusions

We are now prepared to draw this project to a close. There are many facets which could be emphasized, but the following seem sufficient.

First, the sovereignty of God is simply indispensable to a doctrine of providence. This recognition is both biblically required and theologically defensible. As God says to Cyrus:

> I surname you, though you do not know me.
> I am the LORD, and there is no other,
>   besides me there is no God; . . .
> I form light and create darkness,
>   I make weal and create woe,
>   I am the LORD, who do all these things.
>
>   (Isa. 45:4–5, 7)

The Reformed tradition cherishes the concept of the sovereignty of God. It does so, not because it wishes to veil itself behind any misconceptions of divine power ("for my power is made perfect in weakness" [2 Cor. 12:9]), but because it knows that the God of the universe is without rival. Hence, whatever processes exist, whatever forms and laws there are, whatever powers and orders there may be, all are willed, allowed, anticipated, bestowed, and conferred by God himself.

At the same time, the doctrine of the sovereignty of God includes the concept of secondary causes and their efficient role in the universe. What Scripture makes clear, and what theological reflection attempts to fathom, is the realization that God chooses, for reasons purely of his own, to limit himself in the exercise of his power toward his creatures. Hence, although it is philosophically correct to argue that God alone is the total cause of all contingent occurrences and concurrently operates within their own operations and powers, nevertheless, every entity enjoys a reality apart from God, as well as a capacity for "partial self-determination." Thus every entity experiences its own existence, and does so within a context in which it functions as a cause and effect. As E. L. Mascall offers: "Thus God is not the only cause, though he is the only ultimate one. . . ."[7] Or as Calvin argues in his *Treatiste Against the Libertines,* God is not the unqualified cause of all causes.[8]

Furthermore, God has freely willed this order or process, and both preserves and works immediately within it. As Mascall states: "[God] maintains the order which is discernible in the universe not by annihilating the causal relationship of beings toward one another, but by preserving it."[9] Or in a more Calvinist tone, we are not to conceive of these conferred orders or powers as functioning in some abstract, mechanical, independent, or naturalistic sense.[10] Rather, God is always and everywhere present, "diligently" and "energetically" achieving his good pleasure in, with, through, and, when necessary, in spite of the intended efficiency of secondary causes ("as for you, you meant evil against me; but God meant it for good. . . ." [Gen. 50:20]).

Hence, we can concur with Gilkey, that though we may be partially self-determined we are never partially indebted to God. Every creature's "destiny" and "freedom" are given to it by God alone; yet, because God limits himself, every creature participates in and determines its own "destiny" and "freedom," as well as participates in and influences the "destiny" and "freedom" (or lack of it) for others.

God has freely willed this process. Its origins lie in him; its past, present, and future are possible only because of him; and he directs, participates in, and transcends it at every moment of its being.

Second, the Reformed tradition acknowledges that God's power, good-

---

7. Mascall, *He Who Is,* 123.
8. Calvin, *Treatises,* esp. chap. 14 of *Treatise Against the Libertines.*
9. Mascall, *He Who Is,* 123.
10. Calvin, *Institutes,* 1.16.3.

ness, and the reality of evil are real and indisputable. In a profound sense, the central concepts here are those Augustine expounded, that is, the immutability of God, the mutability of finitude, and the depth and mystery of God's wisdom, justice, and mercy. When these concepts are kept subservient to a biblical understanding of God, then they have the power to contribute to our understanding of God's relationship to the world.

More specifically, in the Augustinian tradition, where the divine is understood as immutable goodness, then the meaning of finitude becomes clear. At best, finitude can never be more—and never less—than a mutable good (Gen. 1:1–2:3). This insight has the power to guide us through all the conundrums of theodicy.

God alone is God. He alone is himself. He alone is immutably good and perfect. Had he created an immutable, perfect world, then God would have done nothing other than replicate himself, which would have been absurd. Thus God chose to create a mutably good world, not an immutably perfect one. As such, it would have the freedom to exist apart from him as well as possess the possibility to respond to him and be fulfilled in him, by virtue of his love for and his creative presence within it.

Hence, the universe, as we know it today, is a fitting "creation" of God's handiwork and will. Its very mutable form accounts for the possibility of natural "disharmony." Moreover, God's will to create a being for responsible and independent existence both accounts for and allows for the possibility of moral evil while not requiring its necessity. Hence the powers of death and hell are real, along with the bondage of the will. Yet, all the more thereby, owing to God's immutable goodness, does the need for redemption, incarnation, atonement, and eschatological action become apparent and—because of God's activity in history—each a reality in turn.

A Reformed theology does not have to argue that "this is the best of all possible worlds." God could have chosen to create some other world than he did. However, in his wisdom and goodness, he chose to create the one we know. Therefore, to long for a perfect and immutable world is to long for deification (a longing somewhat akin to that of the early church fathers). Certainly, this is a longing that would undermine our created mutability, which God found pleasing and "very good" (Gen. 1).

Hence God made us mutably good. He created us as creatures whom he loves, sustains, accompanies, and guides toward the highest possible fulfillment of our creatureliness in Jesus Christ. Why long for more? Why settle for less?

In the final analysis, is this not what the Reformed doctrine of the decrees is about? *The mystery of our human existence is a function of the gracious decree of God.* The true peace and wisdom of God is the grace and courage to accept the world as we find it (the courage to be) and to live boldly in it, in obedience to God's redemptive love in Christ Jesus.

Third, all God's purposes will be achieved. What God has willed to come to pass will be accomplished. From Genesis to Revelation, this is the unremitting note of Scripture. God will not, indeed cannot, be thwarted by any process he has created or allowed to come to pass. Every process and every event will yield to him the *telos* he has envisioned since eternity.

Creation itself will participate in the "glory" and "liberty" to be revealed to the children of God (Rom. 8:19–22). As for all who love God, "who are called according to his purpose" (Rom. 8:28), nothing "in all creation" can separate them from his love in Christ Jesus which will triumph in the end (Rom. 8:39).

Above all, central to the secret most counsels of God's will, is the role Christ plays in the *telos* God has planned for the world. Christ is "the plan for the fulness of time," in whom all things are to be united (Eph .1:10); he is the "eternal purpose" (Eph. 3:11); he is the secret power "in," "through," and "for" whom all things were created (Col. 1:16).

There is no doubt in the biblical writers' minds. All who are his will be with him. This is a high and holy mystery, and only the profoundest metaphors of eschatological longing can fathom the depth of the final satisfaction (John 14:1–3; Rev. 21:1–8, 22–27; 22:3–5). There in the end time, in the consummation, in his presence, we shall see him face-to-face (Matt. 5:8; 1 John 3:2); we shall know as we are known (1 Cor. 13:12); he who confronts the soul with his searching imperative—"Seek ye my face" (Ps. 27:8)—will finally be revealed in the splendor of his glory.

That glory will be experienced by the saints. Death will be swallowed up in victory. This is more than symbolic language. It points to a metaphysical reality, grounded in God, which gives our life both now and to come its ultimate sense of purpose. Therefore we can live in the present with vitality, hope, and courage, knowing that we belong to God and to each other, now and for all time.

"Therefore, my beloved brethren, be steadfast, immovable, always abounding in the work of the Lord, knowing that in the Lord your labor is not in vain" (1 Cor. 15:58).

References

Abernethy, George L., and T. A. Langford. *Introduction to Western Philosophy: Pre-Socratics to Mill.* Belmont, Calif.: Dickenson, 1970.

Ambrose. *Hexameron, Paradise, and Cain and Abel.* Translated by J. J. Savage. In The Fathers of the Church, vol. 42. New York: Fathers of the Church, 1961.

——— . *Seven Exegetical Works.* Translated by M. P. McHugh. In The Fathers of the Church, vol. 65. Washington, D.C.: Catholic University of America Press, 1972.

Amesius, Gulielmus. *Medulla Theologica,* vol. 1. Amsterdam, 1634.

Anselm of Canterbury. *Anselm of Canterbury.* 2 vols. Edited and translated by Jasper Hopkins and Herbert Richardson. Toronto and New York: Edwin Mellen, 1975. [See in particular *De Concordia Praescientiae et Praedestinationis et Gratiae Dei cum Libero Arbitrio, De Libertate Arbitrii, Monologion,* and *Proslogion.*]

——— . *Truth, Freedom, and Evil: Three Philosophical Dialogues.* Edited and translated by Jasper Hopkins and Herbert Richardson. New York: Harper Torchbooks, 1967.

Aristotle. *The Basic Works of Aristotle.* Edited by Richard McKeon. New York: Random House, 1941.

Augustine. *The City of God.* Translated by G. G. Walsh, D. B. Zema, G. Monahan, and D. J. Honan. Garden City: Image Books, 1958.

——— . *Confessions and Enchiridion.* Translated by A. C. Outler. Library of Christian Classics, vol. 7. Philadelphia: Westminster, 1955.

——— . *Earlier Writings.* Translated by J. H. S. Burleigh. Library of Christian Classics, vol. 6. Philadelphia: Westminster, 1953.

——— . *On the Gift of Perseverance* and *On the Predestination of the Saints.* In *Nicene and Post-Nicene Fathers of the Christian Church,* edited by Philip Schaff, vol. 5. Grand Rapids: Wm. B. Eerdmans, 1956.

Barth, Karl. *Church Dogmatics*. Vol. 3, *The Doctrine of Creation*. Translated by G. W. Bromiley and R. J. Ehrlich. Edinburgh: T & T Clark, 1976.

Beardslee, John W., III, ed. and trans. *Reformed Dogmatics: Seventeenth-Century Reformed Theology Through the Writings of Wollebius, Voetius, and Turretin*. Grand Rapids: Baker Book House, 1965.

Beardsley, M. C., ed. *The European Philosophers: From Descartes to Nietzsche*. New York: Modern Library, 1960.

Berkhof, Louis. *Systematic Theology*. Grand Rapids: Wm. B. Eerdmans, 1959.

Berkouwer, G. C. *Studies in Dogmatics: The Providence of God*. Translated by Lewis Smedes. Grand Rapids: Wm. B. Eerdmans, 1952.

Beza, Theodore. *La Confession De Foi Du Chrétien*. Introduction, préface, texte modernisé et notes de Michel Réveillaud. In *La Revue Reformée*, No. 23-1955/3, Tome 6.

————. *Questionum et responsionum christianarum libellus*. Ann Arbor, Mich.: University Microfilms International. Microfilm.

Boethius. *The Theological Tractates and the Consolation of Philosophy*. Translated by H. F. Steward, E. K. Rand, and S. J. Tester. Loeb Classical Library. Cambridge: Harvard University Press, 1973.

Booth, Edward. *Aristotelian Aporetic Ontology in Islamic and Christian Thinkers*. Cambridge: Cambridge University Press, 1983.

Bouwsma, William J. *John Calvin: A Sixteenth-Century Portrait*. New York: Oxford University Press, 1987.

Boyle, Robert. *The Theological Works of the Honourable Robert Boyle*. Edited by Richard Boulton. London, 1715.

Braunius, Johannes. *Doctrina Foederum sive Systema Theologiae didacticae et elencticae*, vol. 1. Amsterdam, 1668.

Brunner, Emil. *Dogmatics*. Vol. 2, *The Christian Doctrine of Creation and Redemption*, translated by Olive Wyon. Philadelphia: Westminster, 1952.

————. *Dogmatics*. Vol. 1, *The Christian Doctrine of God*. Translated by Olive Wyon. Philadelphia: Westminster, 1950.

Bullinger, Heinrich. *The Second Helvetic Formula*. In *Reformed Confessions of the 16th Century*, edited by Arthur C. Cochrane. Philadelphia: Westminster, 1966.

Bultmann, Rudolf. *Jesus Christ and Mythology*. New York: Charles Scribner's Sons, 1958.

Burkert, Walter. *Greek Religion*. Translated by John Raffan. Cambridge: Harvard University Press, 1985.

Burtt, E. A. *The Metaphysical Foundations of Modern Physical Science*. Rev. ed. New York: Humanities Press, 1951.

Butterfield, Herbert. *The Origins of Modern Science*. New York: Macmillan, 1953.

Calvin, John. *Institutes of the Christian Religion*. Edited by John T. McNeill. Translated by Ford Lewis Battles. Library of Christian Classics, vols. 20 and 21. Philadelphia: Westminster, 1960.

————. *Calvin's Treatises Against the Anabaptists and Against the Libertines*.

Translated and edited by Benjamin Wirt Farley. Grand Rapids: Baker Book House, 1982.

Camus, Albert. *The Plague.* Translated by Stuart Gilbert. New York: Alfred A. Knopf, 1948.

Castell, Alburey. *An Introduction to Modern Philosophy: Examining the Human Condition.* 4th ed. New York: Macmillan, 1983.

Cassirer, Ernst. *The Individual and the Cosmos in Renaissance Philosophy.* Philadelphia: University of Philadelphia Press, 1983.

————. *The Philosophy of the Enlightenment.* Princeton: Princeton University Press, 1951.

Chadwick, Henry. *Boethius: The Consolation of Music, Logic, Theology, and Philosophy.* Oxford: Clarendon, 1983.

Chrysippus. *On Providence.* In *The Stoics,* edited by F. H. Sanbach. New York: W. W. Norton, 1975.

Cicero, Marcus Tullius. *De Fato.* In *Cicero: De Oratore, Book III.* Translated by H. Rackham. Loeb Classical Library. Cambridge: Harvard University Press, 1982.

————. *De Natura Deorum.* Translated by H. Rackham. Loeb Classical Library. Cambridge: Harvard University Press, 1970.

Clement of Alexandria. *The Stromata.* In *The Ante-Nicene Fathers,* edited by Alexander Roberts and James Donaldson, vol. 2. Grand Rapids: Wm. B. Eerdmans, 1951.

Cobb, John B., Jr., and David Ray Griffin. *Process Theology: An Introductory Exposition.* Philadelphia: Westminster, 1976.

Cocceius, Johannes. *Summa Theologiae ex Scriptura repetita.* Amsterdam, 1665.

Cochrane, Arthur C. *Reformed Confessions of the 16th Century.* Philadelphia: Westminster, 1966.

Copernicus, Nicolaus. *On the Revolutions of the Heavenly Spheres.* In Great Books of the Western World, vol. 16. Chicago: Encyclopedia Britannica, 1952.

Copleston, Frederick. *A History of Philosophy.* 8 vols. New York: Image Books, 1962.

Cornford, F. M. *Plato's Cosmology.* New York: Humanities Press, 1952.

Crombie, Ian. *An Examination of Plato's Doctrines.* London: Routledge, 1930.

Davis, Stephen T. *Logic and the Nature of God.* Grand Rapids: Wm. B. Eerdmans, 1983.

Descartes, Rene. *Discourse on the Method of Rightly Conducting the Reason and Seeking for Truth in the Sciences.* In *The Philosophical Works of Descartes.* Cambridge: Cambridge University Press, 1911.

————. *Meditations on First Philosophy.* In *Descartes: Philosophical Writings.* New York: Modern Library, 1958.

Dihle, Albrecht. *The Theory of Will in Classical Antiquity.* Berkeley, Calif.: University of California Press, 1982.

Dillenberger, John. *Protestant Thought and Natural Science: A Historical Interpretation.* Garden City: Doubleday, 1960.

Dionysius the Areopagite. *On Divine Names.* In *The Works of Dionysius the Ar-*

eopagite, translated by John Parker. Merrick, N.Y.: Richmond, 1976. [In this same edition see also *On the Heavenly Hierarchy* and *Mystical Theology.*]

Ely, Stephen. *The Religious Availability of Whitehead's God: A Critical Analysis.* Madison: University of Wisconsin Press, 1942.

Erigena, John Scotus. *John the Scot, Periphyseon: On the Division of Nature.* Translated by Myra L. Uhlfelder. Summaries by Jean A. Potter. Indianapolis: Bobbs-Merrill, 1976.

Euripedes. *The Trojan Women.* Translated by G. Murray. In *The Complete Greek Drama,* edited by Whitney Oates and Eugene O'Neill, Jr. New York: Random House, 1938.

Farrer, Austin. *Faith and Speculation: An Essay in Philosophical Theology.* New York: New York University Press, 1967.

Geach, Peter Thomas. *Providence and Evil.* New York: Cambridge University Press, 1977.

Gersh, Stephen. *From Iamblichus to Eriugena.* Leiden: E. J. Brill, 1978.

Gilkey, Langdon. *Reaping the Whirlwind.* New York: Seabury, 1976.

Gill, Richard, and Ernest Sherman. *The Fabric of Existentialism.* Englewood Cliffs: Prentice-Hall, 1973.

Gilson, Etienne. *The Christian Philosophy of St. Thomas Aquinas.* Translated by L. K. Shook. London: Victor Gollancz, 1961.

————. *History of Christian Philosophy in the Middle Ages.* New York: Random House, 1955.

González, Justo L. *A History of Christian Thought.* Vol. 3, *From the Protestant Reformation to the Twentieth Century.* Nashville: Abingdon, 1975.

Griffin, David Ray. *God, Power, and Evil: A Process Theodicy.* Philadelphia: Westminster, 1976.

Griffith-Jones, E. *Providence, Divine and Human: A Study of the World Order in the Light of Modern Thought.* London: Hodder, 1925.

Grube, G. M. A. *Plato's Thought.* London: Methuen, 1935.

Grünbaum, Adolf. "Causality and the Science of Human Behavior." *American Scientist* 40 (1952): 665–76.

Harkness, Georgia. *The Providence of God.* New York: Abingdon, 1960.

Hart, Hendrik, and Johan Van Der Hoeven, eds. *Rationality in the Calvinian Tradition.* Lanham, Md.: University Press of America, 1983.

Hartshorne, Charles. *Anselm's Discovery: A Re-Examination of the Ontological Proof for God's Existence.* La Salle, Ill.: Open Court, 1965.

————. *Beyond Humanism.* Chicago: Willet, Clark & Co., 1937.

————. *Creative Synthesis and Philosophic Method.* La Salle, Ill.: Open Court, 1970.

————. *The Divine Relativity: A Social Conception of God.* New Haven: Yale University Press, 1948.

————. *The Logic of Perfection.* La Salle, Ill.: Open Court, 1962.

————. *Man's Vision of God and the Logic of Theism.* Hamden, Conn.: Archon Books, 1964.

————. *Omnipotence and Other Theological Mistakes*. Albany: State University of New York Press, 1984.

————. *Reality as Social Process: Studies in Metaphysics and Religion*. Boston: Beacon, 1953.

Hazelton, Roger. *God's Way with Man: Variations on the Theme of Providence*. New York: Abingdon, 1956.

Heppe, Heinrich. *Reformed Dogmatics*. Foreword by Karl Barth. Edited by E. Bizer. Translated by G. T. Thomson. Grand Rapids: Baker Book House, 1978.

Hesiod. *Works and Days*. Translated by H. G. Evelyn-White. Loeb Classical Library. Cambridge: Harvard University Press, 1926.

Hick, John H. *Philosophy of Religion*. 3d ed. Englewood Cliffs: Prentice-Hall, 1983.

Hodge, Charles. *Systematic Theology,* vol. 1. New York: Charles Scribner's Sons, 1899.

Holton, Gerald. "Johannes Kepler's Universe: Its Physics and Metaphysics." *American Journal of Physics* 24 (May 1956): 349–50.

Homer. *Iliad*. Translated by W. H. D. Rouse. In *The Story of Achilles*. New York: Nelson, 1938.

Hume, David. *An Enquiry Concerning Human Understanding and Dialogues Concerning Natural Religion*. In *The English Philosophers: From Bacon to Mill*, edited by E. A. Burtt. New York: Modern Library, 1939.

Irenaeus. *Against Heresies*. In *The Ante-Nicene Fathers,* edited by Alexander Roberts and James Donaldson, vol. 1. Grand Rapids: Wm. B. Eerdmans, 1950.

John of Damascus. *Orthodox Faith*. Translated by Frederic H. Chase, Jr. In The Fathers of the Church, vol. 37. New York: Fathers of the Church, 1958.

Johnson, Oliver A. *The Individual and the Universe: An Introduction to Philosophy*. New York: Holt, Rinehart & Winston, 1981.

Jones, W. T. *A History of Western Philosophy*. New York: Harcourt, Brace & Co., 1952.

Justin Martyr. *The First Apology of Justin*. In *The Ante-Nicene Fathers,* edited by Alexander Roberts and James Donaldson, vol. 1. Buffalo: Christian Literature Publishing Co., 1885.

Kant, Immanuel. *Idea for a Universal History with Cosmopolitan Intent* and *Prolegomena to Every Future Metaphysics That May Be Presented as a Science*. In *The Philosophy of Kant,* edited by Carl J. Friedrich. New York: Modern Library, 1949.

————. *Religion Within the Limits of Reason Alone*. Translated by T. M. Greene. New York: Harper, 1960.

Kaufman, Gordon. *God the Problem*. Cambridge: Harvard University Press, 1972.

Lactantius. *The Divine Institutes*. Translated by M. F. McDonald. In The Fathers of the Church, vol. 49. Washington, D.C.: Catholic University of America Press, 1964.

Leibniz, Gottfried Wilhelm von. *Theodicy*. Translated by E. M. Huggard. London: Routledge & Kegan Paul, 1951.

Leith, John H. "A Study of John Calvin's Doctrine of the Christian Life." Ph.D diss., Yale University, 1949.

————— . *An Introduction to the Reformed Tradition: A Way of Being the Christian Community.* Atlanta: John Knox, 1977.

Lightfoot, J. B. *Saint Paul's Epistles to the Colossians and to Philemon.* Grand Rapids: Zondervan, 1957.

Long, A. A. *Hellenistic Philosophy: Stoics, Epicureans, Sceptics.* London: Duckworth, 1974.

Luther, Martin. *Bondage of the Will.* In *Martin Luther: Selections from His Writings,* edited by John Dillenberger. Garden City: Anchor Books, 1961.

————— . *Lectures on Romans.* Translated and edited by Wilhelm Pauck. Library of Christian Classics, vol. 15. Philadelphia: Westminster, 1961.

————— . *Temporal Authority: To What Extent It Should Be Obeyed.* Vol. 45, *Luther's Works,* edited by W. T. Brandt and H. T. Lehmann. Philadelphia: Muhlenberg, 1962.

————— . *Whether Soldiers, Too, Can Be Saved.* Vol. 46, *Luther's Works,* edited by R. C. Schultz and H. T. Lehmann. Philadelphia: Fortress, 1967.

McNeill, John T. *The History and Character of Calvinism.* New York: Oxford University Press, 1954.

Madden, Edward H., and Peter H. Hare. *Evil and the Concept of God.* Springfield, Ill.: Charles C. Thomas, 1968.

Maimonides, Moses. *The Guide of the Perplexed.* Translated by Shlomo Pines. Chicago: University of Chicago Press, 1963.

Marenbon, John. *From the Circle of Alcuin to the School of Auxerre.* Cambridge: Cambridge University Press, 1981.

Mascall, E. L. *He Who Is.* London: Libra, 1943.

Meyer, Carl S., and Herbert T. Mayer. *The Caring God: Perspectives on Providence.* St. Louis: Concordia, 1973.

Muller, Richard A. *Dictionary of Latin and Greek Theological Terms: Drawn Principally from Protestant Scholastic Theology.* Grand Rapids: Baker Book House, 1985.

————— . "Giving Direction to Theology: The Scholastic Dimension." *Journal of the Evangelical Theological Society* (June 1985): 183–93.

Newton, Isaac. *Mathematical Principles of Natural Philosophy.* In Great Books of the Western World, vol. 34. Chicago: Encyclopedia Britannica, 1952.

Niesel, Wilhelm. *The Theology of Calvin.* Translated by Harold Knight. Grand Rapids: Baker Book House, 1980.

Nietzsche, Friedrich. *The Birth of Tragedy.* New York: Vintage Books, 1967.

Oakley, Francis. *Omnipotence, Covenant, & Order: An Excursion in the History of Ideas from Abelard to Leibniz.* Ithaca: Cornell University Press, 1984.

Oates, Whitney J., ed. *The Stoic and Epicurean Philosophers.* New York: Modern Library, 1940.

Ockham, William. *Philosophical Writings.* Edited by Philotheus Boehner. New York: Nelson, 1959.

————— . *Predestination, God's Foreknowledge, and Future Contingents.* Translated and introduced by M. M. Adams and N. Kretzmann. New York: Appleton-Century-Crofts, 1969.

Ogden, Schubert M. *The Reality of God and Other Essays.* London: SCM, 1967.

Origen. *De Principiis.* In *The Ante-Nicene Fathers,* edited by Alexander Pope and James Donaldson, vol. 4. Grand Rapids: Wm. B. Eerdmans, 1951.

Pannenberg, Wolfhart, ed. *Revelation as History.* New York: Macmillan, 1968.

Partee, Charles Brooks, Jr. *Calvin and Classical Philosophy.* Leiden: E. J. Brill, 1977.

Pascal, Blaise. *Pensées and the Provincial Letters.* Translated by W. F. Trotter and Thomas M'Crie. Modern Library. New York: Random House, 1941.

Philo Judaeus of Alexandria. *De Opifico Mundi* and *Legum Allegoria.* Vol. 1, *Philo,* translated by B. H. Colson and G. H. Whitaker. Loeb Classical Library. Cambridge: Harvard University Press, 1971.

─────── . *De Providentia.* Vol. 9, *Philo,* translated by F. H. Colson. Loeb Classical Library. Cambridge: Harvard University Press, 1968.

─────── . *Quod Deus Immutabilis Sit.* Vol. 3, *Philo,* translated by F. H. Colson. Loeb Classical Library. Cambridge: Harvard University Press, 1968.

Plato. *The Dialogues of Plato.* 2 vols. Translated by Benjamin Jowett. New York: Random House, 1937.

Plotinus. *Plotinus.* Translated by A. H. Armstrong. Loeb Classical Library, vol. 1. Cambridge: Harvard University Press, 1978.

─────── . *The Six Enneads.* Translated by S. MacKenna and P. S. Page. In Great Books of the Western World, vol. 17. Chicago: Encyclopedia Britannica, 1952.

Pollard, William G. *Chance and Providence: God's Action in a World Governed by Scientific Law.* New York: Charles Scribner's Sons, 1958.

Proclus Diadochus. *On the Subsistence of Evil* and *Ten Doubts Concerning Providence and a Solution of Those Doubts.* In *Proclus the Neoplatonic Philosopher,* translated by Thomas Taylor. Chicago: Ares, 1980 [1833].

Rahner, Karl, ed. *Encyclopedia of Theology: The Concise Sacramentum Mundi.* London: Burnes & Oates, 1975.

Ramm, Bernard. *The Christian View of Science and Scripture.* Grand Rapids: Wm. B. Eerdmans, 1955.

Rist, J. M. *Plotinus: The Road to Reality.* Cambridge: Cambridge University Press, 1967.

Rolston, Holmes, III. *Science and Religion: A Critical Survey.* New York: Random House, 1987.

Sandbach, F. H. *The Stoics.* New York: W. W. Norton, 1975.

Schaff, Philip. *The Creeds of Christendom.* Vol. 3, *The Evangelical Protestant Creeds, with Translations.* New York: Harper & Bros., 1877.

Scheffczyk, Leo. *Creation and Providence.* Translated by Richard Strachan. New York: Herder & Herder, 1970.

Schleiermacher, Friedrich. *The Christian Faith.* 2 vols. Edited by H. Mackintosh and J. Stewart. Introduction by Richard R. Niebuhr. New York: Harper Torchbooks, 1963.

Seneca, Lucius Annaeus. *De Providentia*. In *Seneca: Moral Essays*. Translated by John W. Basore. Loeb Classical Library, vol. 1. Cambridge: Harvard University Press, 1963.

Spinoza, Baruch. *Ethics Demonstrated in Geometrical Order*. In *The European Philosophers: From Descartes to Nietzsche*, edited by M. C. Beardsley. New York: Modern Library, 1960.

Stauffer, Richard. *Dieu, la création it la providence dans la prédication de Calvin*. Berne: Peter Lang, 1978.

Stumpf, Samuel E. *Socrates to Sartre: A History of Philosophy*. 2d ed. New York: McGraw-Hill, 1975.

Teilhard de Chardin, Pierre. *The Phenomenon of Man*. New York: Harper & Bros., 1959.

Tertullian. *Ad Nationes, Against Heretics* and *An Exhortation to Chastity*. In *The Ante-Nicene Fathers*, edited by Alexander Roberts and James Donaldson, vols. 3 and 4. Grand Rapids: Wm. B. Eerdmans, 1951.

Thomas Aquinas. *Summa Theologiae*. Vol. 14, *Divine Government*. Translated by T. C. O'Brien. London: Blackfriars, 1975.

————. *Summa Theologiae*. Vol. 5, *God's Will and Providence*. Translated by Thomas Gilby. London: Blackfriars, 1967.

————. *Summa Theologiae*. Vol. 4, *Knowledge of God*. Translated by Thomas Gornall. London: Blackfriars, 1964.

Thomas, George F. *Religious Philosophies of the West*. New York: Charles Scribner's Sons, 1965.

Thomas, Owen C. *God's Activity in the World: The Contemporary Problem*. Chico, Calif.: Scholars Press, 1983.

Tillich, Paul. *A Complete History of Christian Thought*. Edited by Carl E. Braaten. New York: Harper & Row, 1968.

————. *Perspectives on 19th and 20th Century Protestant Theology*. Edited by Carl E. Braaten. New York: Harper & Row, 1967.

————. *Systematic Theology*, vol. 1. Chicago: University of Chicago Press, 1951.

————. "Two Types of Philosophy of Religion." *Union Seminary Quarterly Review* (May 1946): 3–13.

Trinkaus, Charles. *The Scope of Renaissance Humanism*. Ann Arbor: University of Michigan Press, 1983.

Turrettino, Francisco. *Institutio Theologiae Elencticae*, vol. 1. Edinburgh: John D. Lowe, 1847.

————. "*The Theological Institutes* of Francis Turretin." Translated by G. M. Giger. Unpublished manuscript. Princeton Theological Seminary Library.

Ursinus, Zacharias. *The Commentary of Dr. Zacharias Ursinus on the Heidelberg Catechism*. Translated by G. W. Williard. Columbus: Scott & Bascom, 1851.

Victorinus, Marius. *Theological Treatises on the Trinity*. Translated by M. T. Clark. In The Fathers of the Church vol. 69. Washington, D.C.: Catholic University of America Press, 1981.

Walker, Williston, et al. *The History of the Christian Church.* 4th ed. New York: Charles Scribner's Sons, 1985.

Wendel, Francois. *Calvin: The Origins and Development of His Religious Thought.* Translated by Philip Mairet. New York: Harper & Row, 1950.

Whitehead, Alfred North. *Adventures of Ideas.* New York: Macmillan, 1937.

———. *Process & Reality: An Essay in Cosmology.* New York: Macmillan, 1957 [1929].

Whittaker, Thomas. *The Neo-Platonists: A Study in the History of Hellenism.* 2d ed. Freeport, N.Y.: Books for Libraries Press, 1970.

Wollebius, Johannes. *Compendium Theologiae Christianae.* In *Reformed Dogmatics: Seventeenth-Century Reformed Theology Through the Writings of Wollebius, Voetius, and Turretin,* edited and translated by John W. Beardslee, III. Grand Rapids: Baker Book House, 1969.

Wright, George E. *God Who Acts: Biblical Theology as Recital.* London: SCM, 1952.

———. *The Book of the Acts of God: Contemporary Scholarship Interprets the Bible.* Co-authored with Reginald H. Fuller. Garden City: Anchor Books, 1960.

Zanchius, Jerome. *The Doctrine of Absolute Predestination Stated and Asserted.* Translated by Augustus Montague Toplady. London: Sovereign Grace Union, 1930.

Zwingli, Ulrich. *On Providence and Other Essays.* Edited by William John Hinke. Durham, N.C.: Labyrinth, 1983.

Subject Index

Scripture Index